S-99

AF505899

WITNESS TO VIET NAM

The Author discussing world problems with the Prime Minister of Korea

WITNESS

TO

VIET NAM

The Containment of Communism
in
South East Asia

DR. ALAN GLYN

JOHNSON
—
LONDON

© DR. ALAN GLYN 1968

First Published 1968

PRINTED IN THE REPUBLIC OF IRELAND
BY CAHILL AND COMPANY LIMITED
PARKGATE STREET, DUBLIN 8
FOR JOHNSON PUBLICATIONS LIMITED
11/14 STANHOPE MEWS WEST, LONDON, S.W.7.

INTRODUCTION

The balance of power between nations has always been delicate and capable of altering one way or the other as a result of incidents which in some cases were unpredictable.

Japan's precipitate entry into the Second World War by her attack on Pearl Harbour altered the course of the war by increasing the strength of the Axis Powers, extending the area of conflict to the Far East and bringing the United States into the struggle. When the Axis Powers were defeated the Great Powers—Great Britain, the United States, Russia and China—had already divided the world into spheres of influence. Roosevelt never appreciated the possibility of the spread of Communism in Europe which would result from allowing Russia to occupy the satellite countries. Churchill, who did, was unable to prevent it. France played practically no part in the shaping of these policies, with the result that she tried to re-establish her authority and position as a major power—first by her return to Indo-China and later by endeavouring to play the dominant role in Europe.

The balance of power shifted again, for no sooner was the ink dry on the peace treaty than Russia's expansionist programme in the satellite countries placed her in a position of great strength and hostility towards the Western powers. In the years that followed, Russia's grip on Eastern Europe strengthened and the aggressiveness of her policy was demonstrated by the Berlin crisis and her infamous behaviour in Hungary.

In the first battle of Budapest the Russians suffered a major military defeat, largely as a result of their having employed too high a proportion of armour in the Budapest garrison and insufficient infantry support. They never thought it possible that such an impressive show of tanks could be destroyed by an outraged Hungarian people using improvised weapons. It was in these circumstances that the Russians were compelled to make a truce with Hungary and undertook to withdraw all their forces from the country. Personally I had no faith in the truce and decided to prove Russian duplicity myself by visiting that country. Fifty miles east of Budapest I met the Soviet divisions on their route from Russia, moving towards Budapest on a prearranged mission—the annihilation of all resistance and the reimposition of Soviet Communist control over Hungary. I thought then, and said later in my maiden speech in the House of Commons, "there was nothing in Europe at that time in the way of conventional forces which could possibly have stopped those armies proceeding westwards through Austria and right through Europe."*

It was not the conventional NATO forces which held Russia in check, but the possession by the United States and Great Britain of the nuclear deterrent. The Cold War continued and Russia gradually built up her own atomic weapons; but it was still the fear that America had superiority in this field which prevented further Russian expansion and was probably responsible for the Russians heeding the American warning not to invade Austria in 1956 after the Hungarian Revolution had been crushed.

The outbreak of the Korean war made the Americans realise there was a grave danger that Communism would spread throughout South East Asia but they were not prepared to risk a major confrontation with the Chinese by pursuing the war across the Yalu River, either with conventional or atomic weapons. If they had attacked China at that time they would probably have arrested Chinese expansionist policy for half a century, would certainly have prevented loss of life in the Korean campaign but would undoubtedly have risked the possibility of a third world war. It is this same fear of widening the conflict that has prevented the full-scale bombing of North Viet Nam by the Americans.

South Korean Independence is by no means assured. Each side still faces the other under an armed truce; a peace treaty

*Hansard, Feb. 10, 1960, col. 535.

has never been signed. Actual invasion of South Korea by Communist forces is inhibited by the presence of the United Nations Military Armistice Commission but this does not prevent large scale Communist infiltration into South Korea which could be as serious as actual invasion.

After the Korean Armistice in 1953 the balance of world power remained substantially the same, but in the meantime the Russians, by helping Mao Tse-tung to beat Chiang Kai-shek's army on the mainland of China and forcing Chiang to retreat to the Island of Formosa in 1949, had laid the foundation for a major change in the balance of power.

Communist China, with its population of between five and six hundred million people, until recently represented no threat to Russia, although the Russian High Command remembered that Napoleon and Hitler had each paid a heavy price for attempting to fight on two fronts, and the Russian generals had no wish, in any future wars, to be forced to fight a war in Europe and Asia at the same time. The buffer state of Outer Mongolia which she created gave Russia some protection along her thousand-mile frontier with China but it must be remembered that Mongolian neutrality might not be respected by China in view of Mongolia's association with Russia and the fact that China still regards it as a part of China. This was the state of affairs until Communist China began a serious attempt to develop her nuclear weapons in the province of Sinkiang. From that time on, Mao Tse-tung's China represented a grave threat to Russian security. Who can say that this might not result in Russia being drawn closer towards Europe and the United States as a means of self-preservation against possible future Chinese aggression?

The axis of power has now moved to South East Asia. It is here that the West must decide at what point it is prepared to halt Communist expansion before the whole area is engulfed. This could happen in the next quarter of a century, by which time Australia and New Zealand would be wide open to attack and could not survive unaided.

Viet Nam is the location for the actual armed conflict between two ideologies, but it is only part of the picture. It is

INTRODUCTION

sometimes forgotten that the Viet Cong are dedicated Communists of the Mao Tse-tung variety, and that, in fighting the Viet Cong, the South Vietnam Government, backed by the Americans, are fighting Communism in their country. Prime Minister Ky, and other leading non-Communist politicians in South East Asia, with whom I had discussions, realise that Viet Cong and Communism are synonymous in South Viet Nam. It is for this reason that the South Viet Nam Government was only too willing to enlist United States help in its fight against the Viet Cong.

If the Free World wins its struggle in Viet Nam it will be the first stage in halting the rising tide of Communism and preventing its spread to other countries of South East Asia. Those immediately threatened are Laos, Cambodia and Thailand. If a halt is not called in Viet Nam it will not be long before Burma and India follow the same path.

Assuming that the war in Viet Nam is won, this will still only be the first round; the struggle against Communism in South East Asia will continue. The only real guarantee of peace in that area would be the formation of a multi-lateral defence pact embracing Great Britain, the United States and all the uncommitted nations in South East Asia. But this must be combined with American civilian aid to the countries of South East Asia to help raise their standards of living as a practical demonstration that life is better in a non-Communist society. All this ultimately depends on the willingness of the American taxpayer to continue to make the necessary financial sacrifice.

Without America's help the struggle cannot be won.

CONTENTS

CONTENTS

ILLUSTRATIONS

The Author discussing world problems with the Prime Minister of Korea   *frontispiece*

An album of illustrations from photographs taken by the author on his visit to Viet Nam is placed between pages 128 and 129.

ACKNOWLEDGEMENTS

The Author would like to express his appreciation to the following people who were kind enough to give him personal interviews which have been a great help:

Prime Minister of the Republic of Viet Nam (Nguyen Cao Ky)

Prime Minister of the Republic of Korea

American Ambassador to Viet Nam, Henry Cabot Lodge

General William C. Westmoreland, Commanding General U.S. Army, Viet Nam.

The Vietnamese Minister of Defence, General Cao Van Vien.

Lt. General Chae Myung Shin, Commander-in-Chief of R.O.K. forces in Viet Nam.

Nguyen Ngoc-Linh, Director of the Viet Nam Press

M.A.C.V. Headquarters, Viet Nam

Vice President and Premier C. K. Yen, Republic of China

Minister of Defence, Republic of China, Chiang Ching-Kuo.

Director, Government Information Office, Republic of China, James Wei

Brigadier D. R. J. Bancroft, O.B.E., British Embassy, Seoul, Korea.

Among many others he would like to thank the Ambassadors accredited to London of those countries which he visited and Mr. Charles Wang of the Free Chinese Centre. Official British documents are reproduced by kind permission of H.M. Stationery Office.

To my wife

I
BACKCLOTH TO VIET NAM

THE CONQUERORS

16th PARALLEL AND 17th PARALLEL

SPARRING FOR ACTION

THE GENEVA CONFERENCE

AMERICA PADDLES IN THE SOUTH CHINA SEA

VIETNAM
& HER NEIGHBOURS
COMMUNIST CHINA
Yunnan
Hengyang
25°N
Canton
Macao
(Portuguese)
Hong Kong
BURMA
Dien Bien Phu
Hanoi
Haiphong
Gulf of Tonkin
20°N
HAI NAM
LAOS
Vientian
17th Parallel
Da-Nang
15°N
THAILAND
Bangkok
CAMBODIA
S. VIETNAM
Phonm Penh
Gulf of Siam
Saigon
10°N
THAILAND
SOUTH CHINA
MALAYA
SUMATRA
MALAYSIA
Kuala Lumpur
SEA
5°N
Singapore
100°E
105°E
110°E
0 100 200
Miles
N. VIETNAM
S. VIETNAM
CAMBODIA
LAOS
David L. Fryer & Co., Henley-on-Thames, Oxon

The Conquerors

A GLANCE at the map shows that Viet Nam's northern frontier is contiguous with that of China and it is not surprising that for centuries Viet Nam was dominated, except for short periods, by her powerful neighbour. Chinese influence over Viet Nam waxed and waned in direct proportion to Vietnamese resistance and to the power which individual Chinese Emperors exerted over their satellite dominions. Even in the short periods of freedom which they enjoyed, the Vietnamese people were always in the position of having this powerful neighbour lurking in the background and capable of re-conquering them.

Against this background of Chinese suzerainty the Vietnamese acquired a sense of individual independence and continued to cultivate their land, to go about their day-to-day business and to develop, like their Chinese masters, a strong familial system in which the family represented the basic unit and was really more important and dominant than any form of local or central Government control which was imposed upon them. It is this strength of family within the community which has been responsible for preserving Viet Nam as a nation with its own language and customs. It has enabled it to face the vicissitudes of fortune and subjection to government by other nations and, in spite of it all, to remain a nation.

Politically, the greatest change which took place in the country occurred at the end of the nineteenth century when the great European powers were acquiring a thirst for colonial expansion, and, as a matter of prestige, made a determined effort to acquire colonial possessions, in many cases without any consideration of their value to the mother country's economy.

France was no exception to her European neighbours, and in 1845 the French descended on Viet Nam under the pretext of making that nation tolerate the practice of the Christian faith. In a naval engagement in 1847 between French and Vietnamese warships the antique Vietnamese Navy proved to be no match for modern French naval vessels. In 1858 Tourane was captured, but in the eyes of the French was of little value compared with Saigon which, although undeveloped, presented excellent prospects as a deep water port. A year later, in 1859, Saigon was taken. Viet Nam's ability to resist the French attack was weakened by a rebellion against the Emperor which had started in North Viet Nam, but the French forces in Saigon had not had it all their own way—they had been subject to attack by small well-organised bands which had harassed the invaders. The capitulation by the Vietnamese Emperor was the first stage in the conquest of Indo-China by the French.

Metropolitan France was going through a series of crises. Napoleon III had embarked on a disastrous adventure in Mexico which had cost the French taxpayer millions of golden francs. The Franco-Prussian war resulted in a major military defeat inflicted by Prussia on the French armies at Sedan in 1870. These events caused a temporary halt in French territorial aggrandisement. The reparations demanded by the Prussians were not, however, as great a burden on France's economy as the Prussians had anticipated and, in fact, the French discharged their liability within a year. France was determined to efface her defeat in Europe by exhibiting her military strength in the Far East. History was to repeat itself nearly a century later; after her defeat in Europe in the Second World War she returned to Indo-China.

Having obtained a foothold in 1847 France gradually extended her influence not only into Viet Nam but also into Laos and Cambodia. French Indo-China had become a reality and was composed of Viet Nam, Laos and Cambodia which were grouped together under a French Governor General in a Federal type of state, each component having a different relationship through the Governor General with the Department in the French Government responsible for Colonial administration. Viet Nam was composed of the Provinces of Tonkin, Annam and Cochin China. Tonkin and Annam were Protectorates, each of which was under a Resident Superior, whereas Cochin China was a French Colony under a Governor. The towns of Hanoi, Haiphong and Tourane, which had been ceded to France in 1884, had the status of Colonies.

French Colonial Ministers regarded their responsibilities as a domestic affair within their own Ministry and were jealous of their powers. The nearest comparison in British Colonial administration would be the East India Company.

One of the great disadvantages of the system was that French Governments at home changed almost with the season; such changes were nearly always accompanied by the appointment of a new Governor General of Indo-China. These continual changes rendered any form of continuity quite impossible. The second great disadvantage was that there was really no definite legal framework within which the various Ministries' powers of administration were defined. Administration of the Colonies was based on a decree of Napoleon III which enacted that they were to be governed by decree of the Emperor of France until such time as the Senatus Consulate had re-defined the responsibility. This re-definition never took place. Napoleon III's debacle in 1871 was followed by France's creation of the Third Republic whose statutes were singularly silent on the question of France's relations with her Colonies.

Throughout Indo-China the pattern of French rule had a similarity, as indeed it had in France's North African possessions. It was that pattern that was to a large extent responsible for the vacuum which occurred when the French left their Colonial possession. Practically the whole of the Administration from postman to Governor was in the hands of Frenchmen, although, at each stage of Government level, there were French and Vietnamese working side by side. Even though these officials were doing exactly the same job, French officials received a very much higher scale of remuneration than their local Vietnamese counterparts. No real facilities, apart from education and, in particular, military academies, were accorded to the Vietnamese, nor was any measure of real responsibility given to them in the Government of their own country. As Diem found when he was appointed Minister of the Interior by the Emperor Bao Dai in 1933, his powers to carry out essential reforms were practically negligible. Vietnamese students and undergraduates went to France to take university degrees and technical qualifications. In France they were accepted as equals, but on their return they were unable to find jobs commensurate with their educational qualifications and were moreover treated as second-class citizens, being addressed by their French masters as *tu*, a form of address which to them was reserved for children and inferiors.

For those with assured incomes who had no political ambitions this period in France moulded them in the traditions of French civilisation and bound many of them intellectually to the mother country. But those Vietnamese who had political ambitions and had perhaps been fired by the enthusiasm of left-wing French students felt that their return to Viet Nam was an anti-climax and that there was no outlet for their talents and ambitions. The practical result of French policy in Indo-China was that there were insufficient numbers of people trained in administrative jobs, so that when the French evacuated the country there was a vacuum, which in the case of Viet Nam is still unfilled.

This situation was not rectified under Diem's administration. His whole concept of Government by a few top Vietnamese administrators did not allow for the creation of a strong civil service structure covering all aspects of administration. He simply ignored or failed to recognise the necessity and importance of this infra-structure. As we shall see, it was left to Premier Ky to rectify a situation which he inherited.

Britain, with all her faults, made a point in her colonial policy of filling all the lower positions from the indigenous populations, retaining only the senior posts such as District Commissioners and Magistrates. When India had a population of over three hundred million there were under five thousand British civil servants, in contrast to Indo-China where nearly the same number of French civil servants were employed to administer a tenth of the population of India. Towards the end of her colonial rule Britain made an effort to begin the process of replacing even the senior British civil servants by recruits from the country. Nevertheless when the British handed over their responsibilities there was still a considerable gap in the senior grades of the civil service. In many of Britain's former colonies this gap has still not been filled.

Throughout France's eighty years of rule in Indo-China hostility towards the French never ceased. Although France was able to recruit large numbers of loyal troops from her South East Asian possessions, the snob value of being a colonial power in this area did at the same time represent a heavy burden to the French taxpayer. It was the cost to the French Exchequer which was the principal factor that influenced Mendes France's decision to withdraw from Indo-China in 1954.

France spent vast sums of money on building administrative offices, on paying a civil service to run the country, and maintaining a large army in Indo-China. At the same time individual Frenchmen and some Vietnamese amassed great personal fortunes, either from land ownership or from the natural resources of the country, such as rubber. Frenchmen lived like princes at the French taxpayer's expense because the adventurers, entrepreneurs and investors were paying very little in the way of taxation towards the cost of maintaining the army, the civil service and other administrative costs necessary for the running of the country.

Active unrest in Indo-China was reduced to a low level as the French retained large military forces and a counter-espionage service which together were capable of controlling subversion. This state of affairs continued until Japan entered the Second World War. French Indo-China threw in her lot with the Vichy Government.

In the spring of 1940 France was obliged to sign an armistice with Germany, and from that time onwards Indo-China could no longer count on any help whatsoever from the homeland.

The United States' declared policy was non-involvement in this area. Recent research shows that both Sumner Welles and Cordell Hull believed, on the information available to them from the State Department, that it was unlikely that Japan would launch an attack in the Far East. To some extent this appreciation was based on the belief that Japan's involvement in Manchuria necessitated the use by her of all the armed forces at her disposal.

While France's Government was lying prostrate in 1940, Japan took the opportunity to address an ultimatum to General Catroux, the substance of which was that Japan and Indo-China should be responsible for the control of the Tonkin border. It was through this border that Nationalist China was receiving aid, and it could therefore be regarded as the vital link which was enabling Chiang Kai-shek to receive supplies and to continue his struggle against the Japanese in China.

Catroux had virtually no alternative but to accede to the request, and France's Third Republic, quite out of touch with reality and already the lackey of Nazi Germany, immediately relieved him of his command.

Catroux, in fact, had done everything that was possible to resist the demands, even to the extent of sending a mission to the United States asking for fighter aircraft to be allocated to him from the orders which France, as a nation, had not only placed but, in fact, paid for. The United States Government would not permit the despatch of these essential military supplies; under these circumstances it was not surprising that Catroux felt obliged to accept the ultimatum.

His successor, Admiral Jean Decoux, found himself faced with exactly the same problem; without supplies and aircraft, and with the United States still refusing to give any assistance, his position was impossible. He tried to play for time, only to be rewarded by a direct Japanese attack on border forts and the bombing of the port of Haiphong.

Abandoned by everybody, Decoux signed an agreement with the Japanese, who were to be allowed the use of three airfields in Tonkin, limited occupation by Japanese forces and transit facilities for a stated number of Japanese troops through Indo-China to fight General Chiang Kai-shek's forces. The Japanese were not satisfied with this agreement and virtually appealed to the Germans to force Vichy to extend these privileges. Decoux was once again put in the position whereby if he failed to sign, every one of his soldiers in the garrisons would have been taken prisoner and spent the rest of the war in prisons or concentration camps.

Too late in the day the United States realised that the appreciation which had been made by the State Department was incorrect. By now it was clear that the Japanese were going to launch a full-scale invasion of the Far East. Almost on the eve of Pearl Harbour, Hull delivered a note to Japan suggesting that Indo-China should be neutralised.

Decoux's rule of Viet Nam resulted not only in an improvement of the administration of the country but included large numbers of Vietnamese in that administration. The country was cut off from supplies, and many of the acts which Decoux carried out helped the Vietnamese to develop their home industry. Decoux even gave the Indo-Chinese members a majority on the Grand Council.

Some sides of Decoux's rule could very easily be criticised, but his hands were tied by Japanese occupation. In fairness it should be said that the virtually dictatorial powers which he wielded in the country were used to withstand Japanese interference in the Government, and at the same time to build up an administration which, for the first time, included a large number of Indo-Chinese.

Decoux had two choices: to fight the Japanese to the last man, or to let them tear down the Tricolour and impose a cruel domination over the country. As in other occupied countries, the Japanese were carrying out this role with a very small number of troops. Decoux preferred the second alternative, which was to co-operate to the minimum possible degree, save the lives of Frenchmen and Indo-Chinese, prevent chaos and minimise Japanese cruelty in the country.

Who could blame a man who had not only been abandoned by the mother country, but had had aircraft and supplies refused him by the United States and was virtually left isolated in a situation where he alone would be judged by posterity for the action which he took?

During Decoux's rule Frenchmen were not idle, and plans were being made in conjunction with the Allies to prevent the Japanese from annihilating the French garrisons. The leading figure in this underground movement was General Mordant, who was working in close co-operation with British Intelligence units and the American O.S.S. The Japanese intelligence were fully aware of the movement and on 9th March 1945 surrounded the French garrisons and arrested their leaders. Mordant's operation was probably launched too early; it was badly planned and ineffective. The Japanese took their revenge and carried out brutal reprisals.

During this period American policy appeared to be divided. Local American O.S.S. troops were co-operating, but at a national level the Free French military mission found it difficult to believe that failure to give more support had been decided by none other than the President of the United States.

Those who took part in the resistance endeavoured to escape to China, but suffered appalling casualties on the way. Japanese reprisals were in keeping with their behaviour in other occupied countries. The concentration camp which was set up was worse than the Germans', and loyal Vietnamese were put in monkey cages.

The sequence of events which led to this tragic situation is worth relating in detail as it reveals the origin of the fundamental distrust which de Gaulle has shown towards the United States. The United States had maintained a full-scale Embassy accredited to the Vichy Government, a fact which in itself could have been no source of pleasure to de Gaulle; but the main factor which contributed towards this discord was France's belief that she had been badly let down, not only during the war but particularly in the aftermath.

France was liberated in 1944 but was obviously incapable of reinforcing her troops in Viet Nam immediately. The problem of re-grouping her forces was considerable, but nothing like as great as finding sufficient transport to move those forces almost half way round the globe. It was clear to Frenchmen in Indo-China that Japan was incapable of withstanding the combined strength of the Allies after Germany and Italy had been defeated, and the Allies could turn their full attention to Japan, which was the last of the Axis powers to continue fighting. Under the brilliant generalship of General Bill Slim, it was now only a matter of time before the Japanese army was flushed out of Burma. France's generals in Indo-China—Mordant, Sabattier and Alessandria—made plans for an uprising in Indo-China against the Japanese. They had hoped that their efforts would be co-ordinated with help from the British in Burma and the Americans and Nationalist Chinese; presumably the latter were to mount an attack by driving South from the Chinese Province of Yunnan.

Already teams of American O.S.S. were operating in Indo-China alongside their British counterparts from South East Asia Command. It was not unreasonable for the French Generals to believe that the local resistance to the Japanese which they had planned would receive active help from the Allies and, in particular, from the Americans.

The plans made by the French Generals failed for two reasons: bad security and failure of American aid to materialise. Unfortunately these improvised plans were hastily prepared and were compromised before they were ever put into operation. The Japanese security informed the Military Authorities of Mordant's activities, and a mass of arrests took place. These arrests were followed by ruthless reprisals by the Japanese, not only against the armed forces but also against civilians and, in particular, those who were known to be pro-French.

Sabattier and Alessandria received early warning that their plans had been compromised, and new orders were issued so that they managed to extricate themselves and some of their troops, which they re-grouped in the area around the airfields at Dien Bien Phu. Their appeal for Allied support went unanswered; only South East Asia Command had responded by sending what little it could by air from a distance of 1,500 miles. The local American Commander, General Chennault, in Yunnan, had made a rapid appreciation of the relative positions of French and Japanese forces in Indo-China. His immediate reaction was to dispatch liaison teams to Sabattier's headquarters to ascertain the urgent strategic supplies of arms, ammunition and food required by that force. Sabattier had to wait until the end of the War to discover why those urgent appeals went unanswered. It was not the failure of communications between the American and French Commanders in the field, but the intervention by a direct command from General Wedemeyer that on no account were the French to be given any arms or ammunition; Wedemeyer had received orders from the American War Department—instructions which had come direct from President Roosevelt, who was still determined not to assist the French in their attempt to re-colonise Indo-China. In arriving at this decision he had become blind to the duty which he owed to his French allies to save them from being massacred at the hands of the Japanese. France was one of the Big Five Allied Nations and, like the United States, was still at war with Japan.

To put all the blame on the shoulders of the Americans would be unfair. The French Generals ought never to have put their troops and loyal members of the civil population at risk until they had co-ordinated their plans, both with South East Asia Command and General Wedemeyer. To give Sabattier his due, it may well have been that by virtue of his good intelligence service he had information in his possession which showed that in spite of the apparently calm situation the Japanese had secret plans to liquidate the French garrison; certainly he was the first to know of the Japanese plan to mount their attack on March 9th 1945. The decision of the French Generals might also have been influenced by General de Gaulle, who has since admitted that he was determined that French troops should have been seen by the Allies to have been actively engaged in fighting the Japanese in Indo-China. By so doing, the French would have strengthened their position in any post-war negotiations for France's return to Indo-China.

The end result was that the remnants of the French Union forces fought a rear-guard action back to Yunnan and suffered appalling casualties on their retreat. The French Army and its colonial troops put up stiff resistance to the Japanese but without allied help their fate was sealed from the moment the Japanese mounted their attack on March 9th. Those soldiers and civilians who were not murdered in cold blood, like the French garrison at Fort Briere de l'Isle, spent the rest of the war in prison or in concentration camps. The more unlucky were put in the infamous monkey cages.

Following the Japanese liquidation of the French in Viet Nam, the Emperor Bao Dai was informed by the Japanese that his country was now free. He repudiated the French treaty of 1885 and replaced it by an agreement which brought Viet Nam into the Greater East Asian Co-Prosperity Sphere. In theory Viet Nam was united and had cut herself loose from French control.

The French Government were in almost constant contact with their military missions in America and were at a loss to understand why America did not take immediate action to help her hardpressed Allies. Neither the French Government in Paris nor their military mission in America appear to have been aware of President Roosevelt's decision not to assist France's attempts to re-colonise Indo-China. The mounting pressure finally succeeded in breaking the deadlock, but, unfortunately, help did not arrive until the French Union forces had been captured, murdered or the remnants had fled to China or Laos.

The Americans had let the French down on the deliberate orders of the President of the United States—a fact which was not likely to be forgotten or forgiven by General de Gaulle in his subsequent dealings with the United States.

The last vestige of independence disappeared when the Emperor Bao Dai was compelled by the Japanese to collaborate with them and to repudiate the 1885 treaty with France. The Japanese had agreed, on the 8th August, to the incorporation of Cochin China with Annam and Tonkin to form a united Viet Nam. It appeared on the face of it that Viet Nam had been unified, but the country was in a complete state of chaos and Bao Dai, although he had achieved unification, had done so at the expense of collaboration with the Japanese and could have been said to have replaced French colonialism by Japanese domination.

Ho Chi Minh had been waiting for an opportunity like this. He had been in exile with his Party, the I.C.P., and had not been back to Viet Nam (except when he came in for a very short period as part of a Chinese Communist Mission) for 30 years. Although his Party had been subjected to mass arrests its main leaders had managed to escape, and had taken refuge with the Chinese Nationalist forces. The Chinese Nationalist generals had hoped to unite these extremists with the other Vietnamese patriots whom they had been sheltering in order to create a force capable of putting up resistance to the Japanese. The Chinese Nationalists had jailed Ho Chi Minh, for they considered that his I.C.P. was too communist-inspired and would be a disruptive influence on the national Vietnamese front which they were trying to form. Ho Chi Minh and the I.C.P. had appreciated that their chances of success would rest upon the help and co-operation they received from non-Communist groups. This, combined with a dose of Chinese jails, caused Ho Chi Minh to dissolve the I.C.P., and the Viet Minh was born as a result. The wisest decision made by the Viet Minh was not to remain in exile but to return to Viet Nam and spread their propaganda. They were thus able to create a nucleus of Communist cells throughout Japanese-occupied Viet Nam.

By being the only organised (though small) force operating against Japanese occupation they sowed the seeds whereby later on they could claim to be the party associated with liberation of their country from the Japanese. Ho Chi Minh could claim that the I.C.P. and the Viet Minh together had been the only party of Vietnamese to resist both French and Japanese imperialism.

The Allies played into their hands. At Tehran and Potsdam, it had been agreed that the area up to the 16th Parallel should be occupied by the Chinese Nationalists, and the area south of this line, by the British and Commonwealth forces. The British had few troops to carry out this task (about 1,500 men). The Chinese, however, had three armies totalling 150,000 men. Their march south with its locust-like advance reactivated the traditional hatred for Chinese occupation. In order to carry out this march the Chinese Nationalists were of course obliged to live off the country. This last factor did little to endear them to the Vietnamese population. The Viet Minh and I.C.P.

leaders swarmed into South Viet Nam and announced the formation of the Democratic Republic of Viet Nam, thus filling the natural vacuum created by the Emperor Bao Dai's administration which had disintegrated.

16th Parallel and 17th Parallel

Up to 1942 Indo-China had been regarded as a theatre of operations within the command of Chiang Kai-shek's Nationalist China, but at Potsdam in 1945 it was agreed that the Chinese writ should only run as far as latitude 16; this division meant that the northern part of Laos and the northern part of Viet Nam came under the Chinese. The same agreement provided that south of the 16th Parallel should be a British and Commonwealth responsibility exercised through South East Asia Command under the command of Admiral Lord Louis Mountbatten (later to become Earl Mountbatten of Burma).

Thus the foundations for a divided Viet Nam were laid at Potsdam. Chiang Kai-shek's Nationalist forces controlled the north, and the south was under command of Commonwealth and, later, French Forces. A French military mission had been established at South East Asia Command but there were no French forces immediately available, though the French government was anxious to restore its position in Indo-China at the earliest opportunity. They had appointed General Leclerc Commander-in-Chief of French Forces in South East Asia and Vice Admiral d'Argenlieu High Commissioner and Governor General Designate of Indo-China.

On August 13th the Supreme Allied Commander, South East Asia Command, had received instructions to despatch a Commonwealth force to Saigon. That force was to be replaced at a later date by French troops as and when they should become available for this task. Acting under these instructions Major General Gracey was appointed by Mountbatten as

Commander Allied Land Forces and Head of the Control Commission in Indo-China.

At the request of Mountbatten the British task had been defined in a Civil Affairs Agreement made at a high level in Europe between the British and the French. French interests were safeguarded, and the agreement specifically confined British responsibility in Indo-China to the surrender and disarmament of the Japanese forces and the liberation of prisoners of war together with those civilians who had been interned or imprisoned. The occupation by the British forces was to be limited to those areas south of the 16th Parallel that were essential for the satisfactory performance of this task. Although these areas were to be occupied by British forces, administrative control was not to be assumed except in so far as such control was necessary to carry out the role which had been defined in the Franco-British Agreement.

When the British forces arrived in Saigon on the 12th September 1945 they were limited in their range of action by the small number of troops available under the command of General Gracey. He had been allotted a mixed force which consisted largely of British and Indian troops, but the total number was approximately 1,500—a minute force to undertake an immense task. It was clear that the authorities had not appreciated the explosive nature of the political situation in this theatre of war. The only solution if anarchy was to be avoided was to leave the Japanese troops and administrative machinery in control for the time being.

During this period the Emperor Bao Dai's attempt to set up a government with Kim as prime minister failed completely.

In the northern part of Viet Nam events had moved rapidly, the Viet Minh having taken control of the main towns in the north. The emperor had been forced by Ho Chi Minh on August 23rd to abdicate, and six days later a Provisional Government had been proclaimed with Bao Dai appointed by Ho Chi Minh as Supreme Political Adviser to this Provisional Government. The Provisional Government claimed to have authority throughout Viet Nam but, in fact, the Communist Provisional Executive Committee which had been set up for

South Viet Nam carried no weight or authority in the south where there was in fact no government at all, and anarchy prevailed throughout the country.

It was these circumstances which compelled General Gracey to make the wise decision to extend his mandate to cover the security of Indo-China south of the 16th Parallel. He appreciated the seriousness of the Communist threat presented by the Provisional Executive Committee for the South and issued arms to both civilian and military prisoners of war who had been released, and allowed them to take over the building which had been occupied by the Communist Provisional Executive Committee.

General Gracey's courageous and imaginative decision led to protests by North Viet Nam but the military Chiefs of Staff realised that this action was fully justified.

By January 1946 General Leclerc had 30,000 troops assembled under his command in Indo-China, so that except for residual obligations in connection with Japanese prisoners the British force had completed the task allotted to them and left the country.

The tragedy was that Leclerc had insufficient troops, and although he was able to take the towns with his armour he was unable to control the countryside except for a channel on each side of the roads. If he had had a force of perhaps 200,000 men he would have been able to sweep the country and clear out the Viet Minh. Instead, old-fashioned tactics, limited to occupying key areas and towns and controlling the main roads, combined with insufficient forces to enable the Viet Minh to build up their own forces quickly in areas not subject to French control. The Viet Minh waited until their forces were sufficiently strong to enable them to have a guerrilla army which, even to this day, has never been defeated and provides the Americans with exactly the same problem. A much smaller Task Force than that employed today would have achieved victory in 1946 and altered the course of history in South Viet Nam.

It was not until 1954 that the French Union forces reached 200,000, but by this time the Viet Minh's strength had increased considerably so that the relative size of the French and Viet Minh forces made victory by the French impossible. It has become an accepted principle of guerrilla warfare that a ratio of between 10 and 12:1 is required to beat guerrilla forces operating under such conditions.

A force of perhaps a quarter of a million at this time could probably have defeated the Viet Minh in both North and South Viet Nam, whereas today it will probably require a combined strength of nearly two million to defeat an enlarged Viet Cong force in the South.

It was to the credit of this almost unknown British General that, on his own initiative, he disobeyed the instructions given to him. In so doing he had given the Viet Minh short measure and scotched in its embryonic stage a deliberate bid by the Communists to take over Viet Nam south of the 16th Parallel. Without this action there might never have been a democratic South Viet Nam. What would probably have happened would have been that, backed up by the Viet Minh, the Provisional Executive Committee would have been able to establish themselves in a sufficiently strong position, just as they had done in the North, so that by the time General Leclerc arrived in South Viet Nam with his force of 30,000 it would have been too late and the structure of Communist Government sufficiently established to have made it a difficult, if not impossible, task for Leclerc to have defeated them.

The new French High Commissioner continued where Gracey had left off. He also saw the dangers which lay ahead, and whilst Ho Chi Minh set off to France to negotiate in May 1946 the South was not idle. On 1st June 1946 d'Argenlieu, acting in his capacity as High Commissioner of Indo-China, readily agreed to recognise the Republic of Cochin China as a free state within the French Union.

North of the 16th Parallel the Communists succeeded in out-manoeuvring Chiang Kai-shek's Chinese Nationalists. Ho Chi Minh had dissolved the I.C.P. and had promised the Kuomintang Generals that they would give non-Communist parties more seats (than they would get as a result of the ballot box) in the Parliament which was to be elected in January 1946, provided that the non-Communists would not compete in the elections. The non-Communists made a fatal tactical error by agreeing to this course and not standing. It gave rise to the impression among the electorate that, there being no other candidates put forward at the election, the Viet Minh was the only political party in Viet Nam. Many of the non-Communist Deputies included in this Parliament became Viet Minh casualties and, despite their so-called Parliamentary immunity, disappeared without trace. By sheer trickery the Communists had succeeded in getting a Communist Government elected in a country which was still divided and occupied by foreign armies. In addition to this, under the eyes of the Chinese Nationalists, the Viet Minh forced the people to give up their private gold holdings,* which Ho Chi Minh proceeded to use for the purchase of arms and munitions from the Chinese Nationalists. This supply was augmented by the Viet Minh getting control of weapons made available from Japanese prisoners of war north of the 16th Parallel.

France had agreed with Chiang Kai-shek's Government (just as Great Britain did, except for Hong Kong) that she should give up her special privileges and rights acquired in China as a result of concessions and treaties.

France gave Nationalist China rights of access to the Port of Haiphong and the use of the Yunnan railway. These rights were vital to Chiang Kai-shek to keep his supply routes open (for the Communists had gradually got control of the mainland ports). In exchange for these concessions, which some authorities at the time described as "capitulations", the Chinese army agreed to evacuate Viet Nam. This was on 28th February 1946 and within a short time the Chinese had departed, but not before there had been an exhibition of Chinese fireworks in the form of an exchange of shots between the French and Chinese at Haiphong.

The Chinese withdrawal was to be completed by the 31st March, but by this time the Viet Minh had secured control of

---

*As in all eastern countries, gold was regarded as the only security (other than property) against inflation; this was particularly the case in a country which had been subjected to occupation and civil war.

North Viet Nam. Even before the Chinese troops had moved out, the first session of the Vietnamese National Assembly took place, on the 2nd March, and on the following day it elected a Government with Ho Chi Minh as President. Four days later, on 6th March, an Agreement was signed by General Sainteny representing France and Ho Chi Minh on behalf of the Democratic Republic of Viet Nam. The Democratic Republic of Viet Nam was now recognised as an independent state within the French Union. Under this agreement French troops were allowed to return unopposed and France recognised the Democratic Republic of Viet Nam as a free state with its own Government, legislature and finances, "forming part of the Indo-Chinese Federation and the French Union". A referendum was to be held to decide whether Cochin China should be united with Annam and Tonkin to form a single state.

An annexe to the Agreement signed by the same parties stated that 15,000 French troops were to be stationed in Viet Nam and that over a period of five years they were to be replaced by Vietnamese. Details were to form the subject of discussions.

This French Vietnamese Agreement of 6th March is interesting in its designation of the high contracting parties: on the one part the Government of the French Republic, represented by General Sainteny; a delegate from the High Commissioner for France, properly authorised by Admiral d'Argenlieu in whom resided the sovereign power of the French Republic; on the other part, the Government of Viet Nam, represented by its President, Ho Chi Minh and the special delegate of the Council of Ministers.

Having got this far, Ho Chi Minh as President of the Democratic Republic appealed to Attlee's Socialist Government on the 18th March 1946 for the recognition of Viet Nam as a Free State. The British Government very wisely did not accede to the request and took the view that the constitutional position of Viet Nam was still undecided and undefined.

On 31st May 1946 Ho Chi Minh and some of the other members of the newly constituted Government left Viet Nam by French warship to continue their discussions with the French Government in Paris. After protracted negotiations between Ho Chi Minh and the French Colonial Minister a *modus vivendi* between the two countries was signed, on 14th September. Article 9 made an oblique reference to Cochin China and the southern part of Annam but did not specify how union was to be effected. This was not in fact necessary since the details had already been inserted in Clause 1 of the Agreement of 6th March. On the same day that the Agreement was signed a joint declaration was made in which January 1947 was suggested as a date on which final negotiations between the two countries should take place and a firm treaty be signed between the two high contracting parties.

In the south of Viet Nam the moderate members of the Colonial Council were worried by events in the northern part of the country. They remembered what had happened in October 1945 when a large number of French and Franco-Vietnamese women and children had been murdered by the Communists. Admiral d'Argenlieu responded to these feelings, and with Ho Chi Minh thousands of miles away in Paris it was a golden opportunity for action. That action took the form of the recognition by d'Argenlieu of the Republic of Cochin China as a Free State. The terms of recognition, made on 1st June 1946, were similar to those of the Agreement between Ho Chi Minh and France, except of course that they had the effect of pulling Cochin China out from the Communist net. The authority by which d'Argenlieu acted has never been made clear.

Under the Potsdam Agreement the Chinese were responsible north of 16 degrees, and the British south of that latitude. On the 18th February 1946 an Agreement recognising France's administration south of the 16th Parallel was signed between Great Britain and France. Ten days later, on the 28th February, French authority over Viet Nam north of the 16th Parallel was recognised by China. France's legal authority over the whole country had been re-established. From that moment onwards, the practical significance of the 16th Parallel disappeared.

There was a period therefore from 1946 when the significance of the 16th Parallel had vanished, and till 17th Parallel was set up by the Geneva Agreement in 1954. France had recognised the Democratic Republic of Viet Nam in the North, and the Republic of Cochin China had been recognised by d'Argenlieu. It was this recognition of the Free Republic of Cochin China which formed a nucleus around which, at a later date, the Government of South Viet Nam was built, though it was not until the ex-Emperor Bao Dai returned to Viet Nam that France, by signing the Elysée Agreement in 1949, recognised a Southern Government. Once it is appreciated that Viet Nam gradually developed a Government in the South alongside a Government in the North it is easy to see how two sets of negotiations, one for the North and one for the South, took place with France. Both South and North Viet Nam were represented at the Geneva Conference (though South Viet Nam never signed the Agreement) and from the date of signature of the Geneva Agreement South and North Viet Nam became effectively divided at the 17th Parallel—a division which has remained effective ever since. Ho Chi Minh's Democratic Republic of Viet Nam rules north of the 17th Parallel, and the Government of South Viet Nam south of this line.

Sparring for Action

On the face of it, it would appear to an outside observer that the stage had been set for a lasting solution between France and Viet Nam. On 28th February 1946 the Chinese had agreed with the French to withdraw their forces and had left Viet Nam in accordance with that agreement. At the first session of the National Assembly, Ho had been elected as President. On 6th March the Franco-Vietnamese Agreement had recognised the independence of the Republic of Viet Nam; and the annexe to the agreement, signed by the same parties, had given legal authority to France for her troops to return to Viet Nam. The exact number of French troops was laid down, and a period of five years agreed for their phased withdrawal from the country. These agreements were solemnly signed between France and the Democratic Republic of Viet Nam. Locally the two military Commanders, Giap and Salan (who attained international fame and final disgrace for his role in Algeria), had signed an agreement on 3rd April for the detailed disposition of the respective forces.

French troops in their clean uniforms and accompanied by a formidable show of shining armoured vehicles bristling with guns entered Hanoi on 18th March, much to the relief of the French Colons but, somewhat naturally, arousing certain misgivings on the part of the Vietnamese.

On both sides the terms had been reasonable; the essential points of agreement were the recognition of Viet Nam's independence, France's forces to replace the Chinese army and, most important of all, the phased withdrawal within five years of the French forces.

On paper Ho Chi Minh had achieved a great deal, and on the 31st May 1946 he left for Paris for further negotiations with the French and to work out the details of a permanent solution. The Agreements on 6th March were basic and the necessity for detailed agreement on the many administrative problems such as customs, foreign relations, monetary matters, the disposition and future ownership of French property all required to be embodied in a formal document so that relations between the two countries could be put on a legal footing. Ho Chi Minh found conditions in Paris very difficult, for France had no proper Government; in spite of this, however, negotiations continued and on 14th September 1946 France and Viet Nam signed an agreement—a *modus vivendi* incorporating the points mentioned.

Two events of importance occurred which soured the relationship between the Democratic Republic of Viet Nam and France: it was bad enough that the Constitution of the Third Republic made no provision for fully independent states within the French Union, but even worse was the recognition of Cochin China as an independent state by d'Argenlieu (31st May—1st June). The recognition of Cochin China could be said, with justification, to be contrary to the spirit of Clause 1 of the Franco-Vietnamese Agreement of 6th March.

Looked at in perspective these two events would not necessarily have formed an obstacle to a permanent Franco-Vietnamese solution. Ho Chi Minh had obtained recognition of the independence of his Government, and had he had any democratic leanings he would have readily accepted that if Cochin China wished to opt out of membership of the Democratic Republic of Viet Nam she should be allowed to do so. The truth is that there was nothing democratic about Ho Chi Minh; nor had he any intention of reaching a compromise with France.

The two parties approached the problem from diametrically opposed and irreconcilable positions. Ho Chi Minh was bent on converting Viet Nam into a single Communist State of the Mao Tse-tung variety. The French were determined to retrieve the position which they had lost and to re-establish their influence in their former colony.

Ho Chi Minh by this time found himself with a force of nearly 50,000 Viet Minh at his disposal. This force consisted of men trained to a reasonable standard and equipped with modern weapons, acquired either from Japanese P.O.W.'s or purchased from Chiang Kai-shek's army. It has always been alleged that some of the arms came from America; this may have been true, but probably only to a small extent and confined to the period when the American O.S.S. teams were working in conjunction with the Viet Minh. Ho Chi Minh was convinced that he could defeat the French in a short campaign before they had time to consolidate their position. Subsequent events proved that although it took longer than he had anticipated, Ho Chi Minh's appreciation was correct.

The French, whose forces had been re-equipped, believed that the only solution in Indo-China would be through military action. As so often occurred throughout the campaign in Indo-China, the French not only overestimated their own military prowess but hopelessly underestimated both the military capacity of the Viet Minh and the political power which they exerted over the people.

BACKCLOTH TO VIET NAM

The fuel was ready to be ignited, and Ho Chi Minh only waited for an excuse to light the explosive mixture of sentiment which lay in the heart of every Viet Minh supporter—to whom the return of the French military presence represented a repetition of pre-war French dominance in Viet Nam.

On November 20th 1946 a French ship was escorting a Chinese vessel, loaded with contraband goods, into the harbour of Haiphong. Unfortunately a trigger-happy band of Viet Minh irregulars fired on the French ship, and as a result of these shots a state of panic prevailed in the city, in the course of which several French soldiers were killed or wounded. On this occasion French behaviour was above reproach and a Franco-Vietnamese liaison team (which had been set up under the Agreement) dealt with the incident and the French took no reprisals against the Vietnamese. But this was not the end; two days later a French burial team was attacked by the Viet Minh, an affair resulting in the death of six French soldiers. So far the French had acted with dignity and common-sense, realising that even one step taken in the wrong direction could have disastrous consequences. The death of the six soldiers, however, was regarded by the military Commanders as an incident which French pride would not allow them to ignore and the Commander of Haiphong was instructed to give the Viet Minh a dose of their own medicine. He issued an order for the Viet Minh to clear out of the Chinese quarter of Haiphong. The Viet Minh refused to obey. Once having issued these orders, the French military Commander had either to acquiesce in the flaunting of his instructions or to enforce the order. He chose the latter course. French troops moved into the area and a scene of near panic prevailed among the civilian population, who simply left their houses and took to the country. Unfortunately, this mass exodus was on the route towards the airport and was once again misinterpreted by the French Authorities. The French cruiser *Saffren* discharged the contents of its guns into the mob advancing towards the airport . . 6,000 people, the majority of whom were innocent civilians, were either killed or trampled to death in the pandemonium.

December 19th 1946 was one of the most tragic days in the history of post-war Viet Nam. Ho Chi Minh revealed himself in his true colours. He wrote a letter to General Sainteny purporting to offer a solution to the fighting which had been occurring between the French and Vietnamese during the previous month. Whilst he was writing this he was secretly organising a dastardly attack on the French forces and civilian population. The order issued by the French Commander, on the request of Ho Chi Minh, that the French troops should continue with their leave programme, was cancelled by the French Commander as soon as he discovered that Ho Chi Minh had planned a mass murder. But the armed attack on the French had begun and took place simultaneously all over the country. The French could not possibly have foreseen this treacherous attack; otherwise they would never have allowed their troops to be so isolated and unprepared, nor would they have permitted their civilian population to be completely unprotected. As a result of this action France became involved in a full scale war with her former Indo-Chinese colonies.

The French army had concentrated on holding the towns and the main routes which ran between those towns. They left the villages and countryside to fend for themselves, and at every stage in the campaign they consistently underestimated the Viet Minh's strength. This strength was considerably increased after May 1949, when the Chinese Communists secured the provinces adjoining the North Vietnamese frontier. From that time on the French had lost the war in North Viet Nam. Arms and ammunition could pass from Communist China to the Viet Minh and at the same time Viet Minh forces could seek sanctuary in Chinese Communist territory. The French protective screen along the border with China was totally inadequate and was no deterrent to the constant flow of men and materials into North Viet Nam. French High Command had appreciated the implications of the Chinese Communists securing the border area, and had sent their Chief of Army Staff General Revers to make an on-the-spot investigation and report. The Revers Report recommended that the border areas should be abandoned and that the

French should concentrate on holding what he described as "the useful part of the country", represented by the fertile rice deltas without which the Viet Minh could not hope to supply their forces with food. Unfortunately, the Revers Report was never adopted and the inevitable happened. Little by little, General Giap's forces attacked French positions so that by the end of October 1950 almost the whole of the Northern half of North Viet Nam was controlled by Viet Minh forces. But this was not the end of the story. France lost, in addition to her soldiers who were killed and wounded, sufficient stocks of arms and materials of war to equip practically a whole division of Viet Minh. The Viet Minh were by no means a rabble of guerrillas but a well organised force commanded by officers, many of whom had been trained either at Chiang Kai-shek's academy at Whaneoa or in Red China. The officer cadre was a strange but efficient assortment of military graduates.

By this time the Americans had realised the dangers which Communism would bring in Indo-China. And they appreciated that the Korean war could not be looked at in isolation but must be linked to the Indo-Chinese theatre of operations. It subsequently transpired that the only difference between these two wars was that in Korea the Red Chinese had actually become involved in fighting the Americans, whereas in Indo-China their help was confined to the supplying of arms and equipment, and to the training of Viet Minh soldiers. Even to this day no Red Chinese Communists have actually fought in Indo-China. American aid started in June 1950 and it is probable that agreement was reached between France and the United States whereby the French could continue their struggle against Communism and be provided with American aid. The exact nature of the agreement, if one ever existed, will probably not be known until the secret files are released to historians of the next generation.

When the Red Chinese poured over the Yalu river in October 1950 they inflicted a severe defeat on the American forces in Korea. After the armistice in Korea much of the equipment captured from the Americans found its way to the Viet Minh forces fighting in Indo-China. Some of it was reported to have arrived in Viet Nam even before the cease-fire agreement on Korea had been signed in July of 1953. Eisenhower had promised, as an election bait, a cease-fire in Korea, and the French may well have thought it implicit in their secret agreement with the Americans that, as soon as a cease-fire operated in Korea, American war efforts should be transferred immediately to Viet Nam. France, in fact, was called upon to bear the full weight of Communist aggression as soon as Korea had ceased to be an active theatre of operations. The French simply refused to realise that without massive American intervention the war in the North was virtually lost. In the military actions of 1951 it appeared that the French were on top of the military situation. Unfortunately the successes were not maintained, and the military situation as far as the French were concerned continued to deteriorate.

On the political front the French needed a sort of figure-head who was capable of attracting non-Communist Nationalists and they selected the ex-Emperor Bao Dai, who was then living in Hong Kong. Whatever faults the ex-Emperor may have had, he was basically a patriot and consistently refused to co-operate unless the whole of Viet Nam was united and included Cochin China. On 8th March 1949 the basis of agreement was contained in an exchange of letters between President Auriol of France and Bao Dai. These letters have subsequently been referred to as the Elysée Agreement. On 23rd April Cochin China voted to rejoin Viet Nam and their decision was ratified on 22nd May 1949 by the French Assembly.

The ex-Emperor Bao Dai became the head of an associated state within the French Union. Viet Nam's foreign relations were to be controlled by France, and French troops were permitted to remain and given the right of free movement within the country. French citizens were accorded special privileges under the judicial code. The Elysée Agreement was ratified by the French Assembly on the 29th January 1950, along with similar agreements for Laos and Cambodia. Britain and America both recognised these associated states, thus giving them what amounted to international recognition.

But all this was too late. Bao Dai failed to rally popular

support in the country and was not helped by his record of co-operation with the Japanese. The major factor, however, was the conduct of the war. Year by year the Viet Minh strength was growing, mainly as a result of the aid which they were receiving from Red China, so that as time went on the French task became harder and harder.

The final blow did not fall until 1954, when the French suffered a major military defeat at Dien Bien Phu. The French army in North Viet Nam had got itself into a position where it was completely surrounded by enemy forces, but the details of this battle are so well known that no detailed account is necessary here.

French military intelligence was so poor that it was not realised that the Viet Minh surrounding this small area was steadily equipping itself with artillery and mortars. The French military leaders could not believe that the enemy was capable of bringing up artillery and mortars, as in their view the nature of the terrain made such an operation impossible. In fact, the Viet Minh brought up artillery piece by piece and assembled it so that it overlooked the French defences at Dien Bien Phu.

The French garrison was dependent on air supplies and it suddenly became apparent that the enemy artillery was mounted in positions overlooking the French escarpment. From this position enemy artillery was able to destroy aircraft and helicopters, and also to deliver heavy attacks on the garrison itself. The French army at Dien Bien Phu required over 250 tons of supplies a day, and in order to carry out this task of provisioning, which had to be undertaken by air, they would have required a vast number of transport aircraft and fighter cover which could only have been produced by the Americans. Starved of supplies, and subjected to a murderous fire, the garrison held out as long as was humanly possible but on 8th May 1954 the city fell to the Communists.

To blame the whole of this sorry affair on the French army would be a miscarriage of justice. The French tax-payer was beginning to feel the strain of the war, and the Home Government in Paris refused to send the necessary reinforcements. In fact, quite the reverse: they reduced the number of troops by some 70,000. It could be argued that if the French Government had been prepared to employ more troops the disaster at Dien Bien Phu could have been avoided. But if the military position into which the French had got themselves at Dien Bien Phu is examined more carefully it will seem unlikely that reinforcements at this late stage would have been able to get the French army out of the trap.

Years later, when I was attached to the Foreign Legion, I met many Legionnaires who had fought in the Indo-Chinese campaign and some of them had actually participated in the battle of Dien Bien Phu and had been among the lucky survivors. Their quality as soldiers could not be disputed; they certainly could be counted amongst the finest fighting troops in the world. Their view, as soldiers, was that the French Government had let them down by refusing essential reinforcements and vital air power. "Indo-China was a political war and we lost it by the blunders of double-faced politicians ... we shall do the same in Algeria. It is always the same story. But the greatest tragedy of all is that we leave behind us not only our dead comrades in arms but many of those loyal people who have supported France, believing such support to be in the interests of their country. . . . Ours is a soldier's fate, but for them it is a fate worse than death at the hands of former insurgents."

The French army must take its responsibility for this disaster. The French military High Command was badly briefed by its Intelligence Service, for whom it was responsible as military commanders. The second grave error which the military command made was its belief that by committing a large Force against the Viet Minh main army it could beat them in open battle. Finally, it chose an unsuitable geographic area for the battle.

When the blow came, Western Europe was still unprepared for the defeat, and the Americans were of the opinion that the French forces could have carried on supplying Dien Bien Phu by air, although it has been alleged that General Ely had already warned American High Command, during his visit to

Washington of March 1954, that there was every likelihood of the French army being defeated at Dien Bien Phu.

Foster Dulles had thought out, and the Pentagon had been working on, a separate type of military operation which was modelled on the combined German and Italian attack on the Spanish town of Guernica (1937). This attack had been a once-and-for-all attack to destroy the town and to save the Spanish army. Dulles had considered the strategic position of America and come to the conclusion that with two U.S. carriers in the area, together with those stationed in the Philippines and Okinawa, it would be possible to mount a similar type of operation and so destroy by American airborne strikes Viet Minh forces surrounding Dien Bien Phu.

Apart from the political and international repercussions which an attack of this nature would give rise to there were serious doubts in the High Command and the United States as to the exact value which would result if it was carried out. The army was of the impression that, short of sending in ground troops, there was no hope of saving the French army. Some of the top Naval and Air Commanders, on the other hand, believed that this would be an effective method of dealing with the position. Eisenhower's attitude to all this was interesting. At the back of his mind he probably thought this operation would achieve some success, but he considered that the political consequences which would flow from it would be very serious. America could not really afford to stand alone, and he came to the conclusion that the plan could be carried out with success and with a minimum amount of opposition from other countries in the world provided he could string along every nation in Asia and, in particular, gain the sympathy of Great Britain. By April, a debate in the Senate had crystallized the opinion of the American people: America could not go it alone in the face of world opinion.

It is very unlikely that this plan would have succeeded, for similar types of attack carried out by the Americans in the present war have shown that aerial and artillery bombardment would have been insufficient to dislodge the Viet Minh and that the only way of beating the guerrilla type enemy is to fight him with ground forces. The American army Chief of Staff, General Ridgway, had in fact sent an observation team to Viet Nam. This team supported the view that only ground troops (supported by air and artillery) would be effective in saving the French army.

The British Government had also made up its mind that it would not be prepared to back military intervention. The whole position prior to the Geneva Conference was complicated. Probably one of the strongest cards of all was played by France's Prime Minister, Mendes-France. In addition to sending troops to Indo-China on an air-lift, he let it be known that he had given instructions that further French troops should be inoculated with the necessary injections so as to make them immediately available for dispatch to Indo-China, thus strengthening France's bargaining position at Geneva.

The Geneva Conference sat under the co-chairmanship of Britain and the Soviet Union. The chief participants were Eden, Mendes-France, Chou En Lai and the United States Under Secretary of State, Walter Bedell Smith. The fact that Dulles was not present in person throughout the whole Conference strengthened Chou En Lai's hand. It was only Molotov who managed to persuade Chou En Lai to accept a special and separate declaration by the United States which saved the situation. America, therefore, was never a party to the Geneva Agreement, nor were the South Vietnamese. In fact it turned out to be extremely fortunate that neither America nor South Vietnam signed the Geneva Agreement, otherwise they would have been compelled to see that elections were carried out before July 1956. Had these elections been carried out there is no doubt that Ho Chi Minh would have gained control of the country. The Communist organisation combined with the use of terror would have assured their victory.

Many criticisms have been made of the American policy during the Geneva Conference. Could better terms have been obtained? If so, which? Had the country remained united, it would almost certainly have gone Communist. Once it had been established that the French were not going to stay in the country, there was really very little that the Americans could do short of full-scale military action and committing ground troops, as well as air support. It could be argued that this is exactly what they did some years later, but against this it must be remembered that the South Vietnamese were probably far more ready to accept direct American military intervention when they had seen and experienced the attempts made by the North Vietnamese Communists to disrupt their political system and peaceful existence, and had seen the Viet Cong in their true colours.

Again, had the Americans given the French full co-operation earlier the same problems would probably have arisen. The Vietnamese were basically anti-French, and if the Americans had come in earlier the fact might well have brought about a situation in which great hostility arose, for they would have been supporting the French colonial system.

Even if the Americans had only acted as peace makers this would still have smacked of colonialism. The only useful alternative would have been that if the Americans had intervened and given help from 1940 onwards and prevented Japanese invasion, their whole history would probably have been different.

If the French had not suffered a major military defeat they might have been able to negotiate better terms and organised a more dignified withdrawal over a period of years. This would have left North and South Viet Nam as a united country willing to accept some form of French aid in return for some economic advantages for France. But the very nature of this assumption is destroyed if one looks into the intentions of Ho Chi Minh. United or divided, Ho Chi Minh would have fought any attempt at the formation of a democratic government in Viet Nam. In the long term it was probably better for the country to be divided so as to prevent Ho Chi Minh from imposing his Communist government on the whole country. As a result of the Geneva Agreement Viet Nam was once again divided, this time at the 17th Parallel. Tonkin and part of Annam became incorporated in North Viet Nam. The remainder of Annam together with Cochin China became

South Viet Nam. It was an artificial line, since the Vietnamese are essentially one people though in the Mekong Delta there is a traditional hostility against Northerners; it is for this reason that the Communists have deemed it unwise to have North Viet Nam soldiers fighting with the Viet Cong there. Many of today's leaders in South Viet Nam are Northerners, and some of them could be counted among the 750,000 refugees who poured across the frontier to get out of the hands of Communist-controlled North Viet Nam. Seen side by side in prison camps in South Viet Nam it was impossible for a stranger to see the difference between a North Vietnamese soldier and a young man of the same age from the South. The essential difference between the two is that the North Vietnamese has been indoctrinated with Communism, whereas the South Vietnamese is beginning to become sceptical of the benefits which that form of government could bring to the people of South Viet Nam and in particular to himself. During the French occupation and the Japanese invasion, and later during the re-occupation by the French after the Second World War, there was a resistance movement of patriots in the country whose sole desire was to see their country free from foreign tutelage. Many of these had no sympathy with Communism, but the Communists played on their nationalistic feelings and persuaded them to co-operate with the Communists against their common enemy whether that enemy was France or Japan. In the North, Ho Chi Minh had used that cloak of non-Communist nationalist feelings behind which he could hide his Communist aspirations. Ho Chi Minh has been on the international scene for a long time, whereas the present South Vietnamese leaders such as Premier Ky have had to start from rock bottom in order to build up an international reputation.

France's decision to return to Indo-China has been bitterly criticised. After complete destruction in 1940 by a superior German army France perhaps saw herself regaining self respect and exhibiting a revitalised military role. It seemed an easy target, a country which had been conquered by Japan and possessed practically no army. Had she not returned she might have been able to have reached an agreement, but this is very doubtful. Ho Chi Minh would never have rested until he had communised all Viet Nam. It is possible therefore that France's great sacrifice in men, material and money has resulted in the end in sparing half of the country from Communist domination. But the price paid by France was perhaps out of proportion even for this benefit.

When France pulled out she left a legacy of French civilisation, a first class system of education, a railway system, and roads. Many Vietnamese had had the benefit of education in French institutions, and some of South Viet Nam's best military leaders received their instruction in French military academies. The result is a queer sort of love-hate relationship between the French and the Vietnamese. One fallacy ought to be exploded, and that is that the French milked the country dry. In fact, the French tax-payer could be criticised for being over-tolerant in the demands which this part of France's colonial empire cost her in French francs. The real tragedy of Viet Nam was that the outbreak of the Second World War stopped any possibility of a gradual development within the framework of French Union into a self-governing country tied to France only by language and traditions.

The Geneva Conference

Between 25th January and 18th February 1954 the Foreign Ministers of France, the United Kingdom, Soviet Russia and the U.S.A. were debating at a meeting in Berlin the problems which at that time were threatening the peace in the Far East. On the last day of the Conference the Ministers proposed that representatives of the United States, Soviet Communist China, the Republic of Korea and the People's Democratic Republic of Korea, should meet on 26th April to discuss the Korean question. It was also agreed that at this Conference the problem of Indo-China should be discussed between the representatives of the United States, France, the United Kingdom, the Soviet

Union, Communist China and other interested States, but at the same time it was made clear that membership of, or invitation to, the Conference did not amount to the diplomatic recognition of a Government, except where such recognition had already been accorded.

The situation in Indo-China was becoming more serious every day, with the French Union forces surrounded at Dien Bien Phu. Great Britain was not prepared to back the Americans in their proposed operation to give military assistance in the form of air strike to the French forces at Dien Bien Phu. The United Kingdom maintained that any interference by force at this juncture would destroy the possibility of a settlement at the Conference table.

What is not always appreciated is that there were two conferences held at Geneva, but that the first, on Korea, achieved little of value.

The second, on Indo-China, ran into immediate difficulties over the important question of who should occupy the Chair. It was finally agreed that the United Kingdom and the Soviet Union should occupy it for alternate sessions. This was a logical decision as these two countries had been instrumental in setting up the Conference. All through the Conference it was these two who managed to keep it together and prevent it from fragmenting. These two great powers became the leaders whose task was virtually to reason with their own blocs to achieve agreement through compromise at the Conference table.

The first hurdle was the demand by North Viet Nam that the resistance movements in Laos and Cambodia should be included in the delegation on the grounds that they had fought in the struggle for the liberation of their countries. Once again private talks between Eden and Molotov resolved the difficulty, and admission of these two groups was refused. Their inclusion would have meant the end of the Conference so far as Laos and Cambodia were concerned, neither of whom was prepared to sit down with Communist organisations which were endeavouring to disrupt, by force, the Governments of these countries.

BACKCLOTH TO VIET NAM

Events had moved fast, and on the day that the first plenary session of the Conference took place (8th May) French Union forces at Dien Bien Phu were defeated and the city fell to the Viet Minh. It was clear by now even to the French that the battle in North Viet Nam was lost. On 8th May M. Bidault made proposals to the Geneva Conference for a settlement the substance of which was the withdrawal of Viet Minh forces from Laos and Cambodia, and in Viet Nam the re-groupment of opposing forces in prescribed areas, supervision to be carried out by international commissions working in each of the three states. On the other side, the Democratic Government of Viet Nam demanded the withdrawal of all French troops from Laos, Cambodia and Viet Nam, the recognition by France of the independence of these three countries, and the holding of elections in all three countries. The delegation from non-Communist Viet Nam demanded the recognition of the state of Viet Nam under H.M. Bao Dai as Head of State, and that a General Election should be held under United Nations supervision. These and other suggestions were considered in private informal talks and in the sessions of the Conference.

During the sessions of the Conference not only had Dien Bien Phu fallen (on the first day of the Conference), but on 12th July the French Government under Laniel collapsed. Three days later Diem had become Prime Minister of Viet Nam. Then, on 18th June, came the stunning news that the new Prime Minister of France, Mendes-France, had stated that he would make an honourable peace by 20th July. The war was going from bad to worse as far as the French were concerned, and French Union forces had been compelled to evacuate the Red River Delta by 29th June. On 4th July the Commander of the French Union force began talks with the Viet Minh at Truggia on the question of an armistice, and provision for the exchange of prisoners. Ten days later the exchange began.

It was not until 21st July that the final agreements for the cessation of hostilities were signed. In the Cambodian cease fire agreement the Commander-in-Chief of the Cambodian

Army signed for Cambodia and the Vice Minister of Defence of the Democratic Republic signed on behalf of the Viet Minh units in Cambodia and the Khmer Resistance forces. The Laos cease fire agreement was signed by the Commander-in-Chief of the French Union forces in Indo-China on the one part and on the other by the Vice Minister of National Defence for the Democratic Republic of Viet Nam who signed on behalf of the Pathet Lao units and the People's Army of Viet Nam.

The really important agreement on Viet Nam was signed on behalf of the Commanders-in-Chief of the French Union forces and the Commander-in-Chief of the People's Army of Viet Nam.

"The Agreement on the Cessation of Hostilities in Cambodia was signed on behalf of the Commander-in-Chief of the Cambodian Army and by the Vice-Minister of National Defence of the Democratic Republic of Viet-Nam who signed on behalf of the Khmer Resistance forces and the Viet-Namese Military Units in Cambodia. The agreement provided for the complete cessation of hostilities throughout the country. French and other foreign troops and all foreign persons working with the Viet Minh forces were to withdraw from the country within ninety days. The Khmer Resistance forces were to be immediately demobilised, but the Cambodian Government undertook not to engage in reprisals against them or to discriminate against them in any way. Control and supervision of the execution of the Agreement were to be exercised by an International Commission composed of representatives of India (Chairman), Canada and Poland, with power to set up fixed and mobile inspection teams. The belligerent parties were to form a Joint Commission to facilitate the operation of the military clauses of the Agreement. The International Commission was to report to the members of the Geneva Conference any obstruction of its work. It was to work in close co-operation with the parallel Commissions in Laos and Viet-Nam, and might, after consulting those Commissions and with due regard to the situation in those two countries, progressively reduce its activities.

On 21 July, the Royal Government of Cambodia made a

Declaration (Document No. 25), promising to integrate all citizens into the national community and to allow all Cambodian citizens freedom of voting in general elections. A further Declaration of the same date (Document No. 26) affirmed that the Government of Cambodia would not engage in any aggressive policy or enter into any military alliance not in conformity with the principles of the United Nations Charter (6) or allow the establishment of any foreign bases in the country unless Cambodia's security were threatened, or seek, except for purposes of defence, any foreign military aid during the period between the cessation of hostilities in Viet-Nam and the final settlement of that country's political problems.

In the Agreement on the Cessation of Hostilities in Laos, signed on behalf of the Commander-in-Chief of the French Union forces in Indo-China and by the Democratic Republic's Vice-Minister of National Defence on behalf of the Pathet Lao fighting units and the People's Army of Viet-Nam, it was provided that after the proclamation of the cease-fire no foreign troops should enter the country, though the French High Command might provide a training-mission for the Laotian National Army to a limit of 1,500 men; no new military bases were to be established, but the French forces might maintain bases at Seno and in the Vientiane area with a total maximum strength of 3,500 men. Except for such supplies as might be needed for defence, the introduction into Laos of military equipment was prohibited. Both French and Viet Minh forces were to leave the country within 120 days. Pending a political settlement, the Pathet Lao forces were to move into the provinces of Phong Saly and Sam Neua, and should be allowed freedom of movement along a corridor connecting these provinces. Neither party was to engage in reprisals or discrimination against those who had opposed it during the period of hostilities. As in Cambodia, control and supervision of the execution of the Agreement were entrusted to an International Commission of India (chairman), Canada and Poland, with powers and obligations of a parallel character (Document No. 27).

The Laotian Government, like that of Cambodia, issued on

21 July two Declarations. One (Document No. 28) undertook to integrate all citizens into the national community and promised special representation in the Royal Administration of Phong Saly and Sam Neua of Laotian nationals who had not supported the Royal forces during the hostilities, this special representation to apply in the interval between the cessation of hostilities and the holding of general elections. The other Declaration (Document No. 29) was couched in terms similar to the second Declaration by the Cambodian Government.

The Agreement on Viet-Nam was signed on behalf of the Commanders-in-Chief of the French Union forces and the People's Army of Viet-Nam. It provided that a demarcation line should be drawn, roughly at the 17th parallel of North latitude, with a 5-km. demilitarised zone on either side; the Viet Minh forces were to regroup north of the line and the French Union forces south of it. These movements were to be completed within 300 days. Pending general elections which were to bring about the reunification of the country, civil administration in each zone was to be in the hands of the party whose forces were regrouped there. Each party undertook to refrain from reprisals and discrimination, and to allow democratic freedom. During the period allowed for the movement of troops, civilians wishing to transfer their residence from one zone to another might do so. Troop reinforcements were not to be introduced into the country, though the rotation of units would be allowed. No military equipment or supplies were to be imported except for purposes of replacement, and the arrival of any war material was to be reported to the International Commission. As in Cambodia and Laos, the Commission was to be provided by Canada, India and Poland, and was to exercise the same powers and incur the same obligations as the parallel Commissions in those States (Document No. 30)."

All of these agreements must be regarded more in the light of a truce or armistice signed by Military Commanders. In the casc of Indo-China these agreements vents were not signed as they normally would be in the Field (as in the Second World War between the British and German Commanders-in-Chief) but were signed in Geneva. Annexed to these documents were two declarations by the French Government (as distinct from the Commander-in-Chief Union Forces). The first of these documents declared that France was willing to withdraw her troops from all three countries, and the second undertook to respect their independence, sovereignty and territorial integrity.

The agreements on the cease fire, together with the above two declarations by the French Government were placed before the Conference on 21st July 1954 and were taken note of in the final declaration of the Conference (which was its eighth and last plenary session).

Eden was Chairman for this session and he first listed the agreements of which the Conference was to take note. First there were the three agreements regarding the cease fire in Laos, Cambodia and Viet Nam. Included in these agreements were the texts concerning the supervision of the Armistice in the three countries by the International Commissions and the Joint Committees.

The Chairman (Eden) then listed the declarations made by the Governments of Laos and Cambodia. The last point noted (eighth) was the declaration by the French Government on the withdrawal of troops from the countries of Indo-China.

Eden then drew the attention of the delegates to the draft declaration by the Conference which took note of all the documents. Eden, as Chairman, then called upon the representatives of each nation to express themselves on the draft declaration:

"The representative of France:—

M. Mendes-France (France): Mr. Chairman, the French delegations approve the terms of this declaration.

The Chairman: The representative of Laos, Mr. Phoui Sananikone (Laos): The delegation of Laos has no observations to make on this text.

The Chairman: The representative of the People's Republic of China: Mr. Chou En Lai (People's Republic of China): We agree.

The Chairman: On behalf of Her Majesty's Government

of the United Kingdom, I associate myself with the final declaration of this Conference.

The Union of Soviet Socialist Republics: Mr. Molotov (U.S.S.R.): The Soviet Delegation agrees."

So far all the nations had agreed without any reservations whatsoever, although each of them used their own form of words in their approval of the draft declaration.

The Chairman then called the representative of Cambodia, Mr. Tep Phan, who made a declaration on the part of his country requesting the Conference to take note of the fact that there were certain territorial adjustments which ought to be made between his State and Viet Nam, and in particular the Franco-Khmer Treaty of 8th November 1949.

Communist Viet Nam also agreed but made reservations about Cambodia's claims to Vietnamese territory (which, incidentally, had only just been handed to the Chairman).

When it came to the United States turn on the roll call they took note and made a declaration to the effect that the United States would not seek to disturb the agreement by the use of force.

Bao Dai's Government expressed their disapproval of the whole basis of the settlement. The agreement had been signed by the French, and not by Viet Nam whose sovereignty the French had already recognised. But worst of all, as far as they were concerned, it meant the partition of their country. They did not agree to the draft declaration.

Thus South Viet Nam is *not*, and never has been a party to the Geneva agreement; nor has the United States.

An important, but often forgotten part of the Conference, was the setting up of three international Commissions for supervision and control of the agreements. These teams were provided by India, Canada and Poland. But in setting up these Commissions the Conference did not terminate its liability, for it expressly provided that members of the Conference should consult together on matters raised by the Commissions. The great loophole of course was that the Conference did not devise any means whereby the member states could discharge this residual liability of putting into effect those recommendations which it considered ought to be implemented. It is, of course, doubtful if it would have been possible to get the Conference to agree to the establishment of the required machinery. Eden had had a tough job in getting as far as he had, especially when the United States and South Viet Nam had not been able to agree to the final declaration.

The Commission in Viet Nam is very much in the position of the younger son sent abroad to earn his living. Housed in inferior quarters in Saigon it comes at the end of the diplomatic list, yet day after day, week after week, this valiant little team makes reports on the infringements of the Armistice terms. Some of the more important breaches are quoted. The abduction, torture and murder of their Vietnamese liaison officer is a highlight of Communist practice, an endeavour to intimidate the Commission. Its members represent the only official link between North and South Viet Nam. In any future negotiations they could be of value. But in the meantime they investigate incidents which are reported to them by North and South. It is for them to investigate the incidents and see if they have any foundation. Here the Commission cannot be said to be really independent; it has become biased.

The Polish and Indian members are absorbed in the acts of the United States directed against targets in North Viet Nam and have spent time on recording matters which are common knowledge. Thus, on 13th February 1965 the Indian representative and the acting Polish representative sent a special report to the Co-Chairmen. The substance of the report was bombing of North Viet Nam, as reported by the North Viet Nam Government. But it did add as an annexure the announcement on 7th February 1965 by the American Ambassador.*

The Americans and South Vietnamese have made no secret of the attacks on military bases and installations in North Viet Nam.

The above report was incorporated in a British Government

*H.M.S.O. Cmnd., 2604, p. 6.

White Paper, Cmnd. 2609, presented to Parliament in March 1965.

It contained a minority report by the Canadian representative which stated that the matter should be seen in perspective. The North Viet Nam Government was actively assisting the Communists in the South.

This report admitted that attacks had been made on North Viet Nam military targets which were well known to be supplying the Viet Cong with materials of war.

America Paddles in the South China Sea

In the early part of the Second World War America was firmly convinced that the Japanese would not become involved in a war in South East Asia. This view had been based on the assumption that Japan required all the forces which were at her disposal in order to carry on her war with China. When it proved to be incorrect, and Japan had launched a major offensive in South East Asia, the Americans still did not envisage the possibility that when the Japanese had been defeated there would be a threat of a Communist take-over in that region. Their attitude is understandable, for Chiang Kai-shek still had control of large areas of China and it was not until after the War that his defeat on the mainland by the Communists took place.

Franklin D. Roosevelt's whole attitude towards French Indo-China had been that on no account should France be allowed the opportunity of recolonising her former Indo-Chinese possessions. He was reputed to have said that France's eighty years of occupation had left the country worse off than it was before France took over: a statement which was not strictly accurate nor one that was calculated to please General de Gaulle.

In the early part of the Second World War France had placed orders in the United States for arms and although she had actually paid for them they were never delivered. After the fall of France, Catroux, acting in his capacity as Governor General of Indo-China, endeavoured to get some of these arms and supplies released so that he could use them against the Japanese in Indo-China. General de Gaulle was not concerned with the finer points of law as to whether or not they could be released on instructions from Catroux; to him it was simply one more indication that America was not prepared to assist France in her struggle in Indo-China.

When the Japanese were defeated the United States made no effort to help French troops re-enter Indo-China. On the contrary, they put considerable obstacles in their way. They had even refused help when the French forces were hard-pressed by the Japanese and General Sainteny was fighting a rear-guard action in an endeavour to get the remnants of his army into Nationalist China. Roosevelt's personal orders prevented the local military Commanders from giving any help to Sainteny.

It frequently happens that international relations can be tarnished or improved by individual experiences, and many Frenchmen who were involved in the Indo-Chinese campaign were later to become important personalities in France. General Sainteny, who returned again to Indo-China between 1954 and 1957, later held the position of Minister of Veterans' Affairs. In 1945 it was Hoppenot who pleaded for United States air support—and in the 1950s he was a French delegate to the United Nations. At the end of the War Lieutenant Ramadier together with a number of his brother French officers were in a prison camp which was guarded by a mixed unit of Japanese and Viet Minh soldiers. He pleaded with American officers to be released from prison. An American officer replied, "If you are there, there must be some reason for it". Little did that short-sighted American officer realise that two years later that same prisoner's father would be the Prime Minister of France.

Then there was General Massu, that legendary figure who attained international fame by his command of the paratroops in the Algerian War and played a considerable part in the restoration of de Gaulle to power and who, unlike some of his friends, subsequently imprisoned, did not participate at a later date in the rebellion against de Gaulle and has still remained in favour with the President. He commanded the first regimental combat team that landed in Viet Nam in October 1945 and had first hand knowledge of American policy. The personal experience of these men did not help to smooth relations between France and the United States for they knew full well that their experiences could not be attributed to the action of individual American officers. The officers were in fact acting under strict orders which had originated from President Roosevelt.

In 1941 Roosevelt regarded the Japanese invasion of the Far East as a direct threat to American interests, and when the Japanese Government made demands on Indo-China America decided to freeze Japanese assets in the United States. Some authorities have maintained that this action precipitated the Japanese attack on Pearl Harbour. Natural rubber at this period in the War represented a vital product and it was the possibility of the loss of Indo-Chinese rubber which represented one of the main reasons for Roosevelt's anxiety over South East Asia.

In 1943 the American President proposed to Anthony Eden that after the war Indo-China should not be restored to the French but placed under an International Trusteeship which was to be the first stage towards complete independence for those countries. At Yalta Roosevelt canvassed this idea of Trusteeship and whilst the proposal was favoured both by Chiang Kai-shek and Stalin, the British were not receptive to the suggestion.

Two events which occurred in quick succession suddenly jolted the Americans out of their apathy and alerted them to the Communist danger: the loss of the Chinese mainland in 1949 by Chiang Kai-shek, and the invasion of South Korea by the North Korean Communists in 1950. American Aid to Viet Nam began in June 1950, and from this date America started to become actively involved there. By this time war-time dependence on natural rubber had ended, as indeed had the American necessity for obtaining rubber from Asia. This was not the motive behind their support of the French; it was the realisation that Communism would spread throughout South East Asia if it were not nipped in the bud.

By 1954 nearly 80 per cent of the cost of the French war in Indo-China was being met by the United States Treasury, although the French were contributing 136 billion old francs a year towards its cost. In the eyes of the French the Americans had given them insufficient support. They felt that as soon as the Korean War was over America ought immediately to have stepped up the help which France required in order to fight Communism in Indo-China.

At the time of Dien Bien Phu Eisenhower had compared that situation with the one that had prevailed during the Hitler/Mussolini era. Consultations took place with Eden and Churchill, and the possibility of military assistance to the French in Indo-China was discussed. So far America had not become involved militarily in Indo-China. Churchill took the view that he was being asked by the Americans to use his immense international prestige to mislead Congress into approving a military operation which, apart from being ineffectual, could bring the world to the edge of a major war.

One of the proposals for military intervention was put forward by Foster Dulles, its object being an American air strike on Viet Minh forces surrounding the French Army at Dien Bien Phu (described on page 45). General Ridgeway, who occupied the position of Chief of Staff, put it as follows: "In Korea we had learnt that air and naval power alone cannot win a war and that inadequate ground forces cannot win one either. It was incredible to me that we had forgotten that bitter lesson so soon—that we were on the verge of making that same tragic error."

John Kennedy had paid a visit to Indo-China in 1951 and had been convinced that the War would never be won by de Lattre de Tassigny's military legions. The War could only be won by the active co-operation of the South Vietnamese people in establishing a non-Communist régime . . . an appreciation which still holds good in 1967.

The policy of committing troops to South Viet Nam came under sharp criticism from Lyndon B. Johnson, the Democratic leader in the Senate. In retrospect it is impossible to judge what would have been the effect of American intervention by ground troops at that stage of the War. A pitched battle between the Viet Minh and the Americans would almost certainly have resulted in an American victory—but would the Viet Minh have ever allowed themselves to be committed to a major battle against the Americans? Even today the Viet Cong avoid such major confrontations. They might allow battalions, and even divisions, but certainly not whole armies. American intervention at this stage would have stiffened Communist and other resistance and the Viet Minh would have lost no opportunity in pointing out that the American presence was to support French Colonial policy.

The final decision was made by Eisenhower. The United States would not intervene in a military capacity: a solution was to be sought under Foster Dulles's direction at the Geneva Conference of 1954. Two months after the Geneva Conference Foster Dulles set about organising the South East Asia Treaty Organisation and a special Protocol was added to this Treaty so that South Viet Nam, Laos and Cambodia were to be protected (under the Treaty).

As soon as the SEATO Treaty had been signed Eisenhower acceded to a request made by the South Viet Nam Prime Minister (Ngo Dinh Diem) for economic assistance from the United States. Eisenhower pledged American support to assist the South Viet Nam Government in developing a strong viable state capable of resisting subversion or military aggression. The SEATO Treaty and the letter from Eisenhower to Diem appear to be the only legal basis for direct involvement of American forces in Viet Nam. The provisions of the SEATO Treaty do not appear to cover American military intervention, the authority for which must rest upon the letter from Eisenhower to Diem. SEATO, unlike NATO, does not have a provision in its articles whereby an attack on one member nation calls for military action by the other members without further consideration.

BACKCLOTH TO VIET NAM

By 1960, Viet Cong guerrilla activity had increased considerably and took the form of daily attacks on villages with resulting murder and torture of all who opposed the Viet Cong authority. At the same time Diem was becoming increasingly unpopular. Upper class, French speaking and Catholic, he paid little respect to the aspirations of the ordinary people and refused steadfastly to allow any real form of democracy to develop.

In November 1960 popular feeling against Diem's Government was reflected in a revolt which was put down by Diem. The Americans found themselves in exactly the same position as they were in in Batista's Cuba; that of bolstering up a thoroughly unpopular and corrupt régime.

After a visit to Saigon in 1961, Vice-President Lyndon Johnson told Kennedy that the Americans had either to give "all out" aid or throw in the sponge. Johnson was right in his estimate that the involvement of American troops would antagonise national feeling in South Viet Nam. In his view American combat troops were not only not required but not desirable. But what Lyndon Johnson failed to appreciate, at this stage, was that bombing and airstrikes alone could never win the War. The Americans have still not realised that no guerrilla force can be beaten by air strikes alone. The only way of defeating them is either by fighting them with troops on the ground and killing them or by cutting off their reinforcements of men and denying them essential food supplies.

Kennedy sent General Maxwell Taylor and Walter Rostow on a mission to Saigon, but unfortunately he rejected their recommendations both as regards the necessity for bombing the North and for the use of American combat soldiers. The drift began. Kennedy had made the classic mistake of committing too little too late. He increased the number of advisers and got America wading up to her knees in the struggle, but without committing sufficient forces for a decisive victory. Even by 1963 the American Secretary of State was implying that Vietnamese Government forces had the initiative in most areas. This estimate was made on the faulty and inaccurate information which Diem's provincial administration were sending him. Rather than lose their positions they were giving a series of false reports to the Prime Minister.

Following the unnecessarily brutal handling of the Buddhist riots the Vietnamese army managed to get rid of both Diem and the corrupt and inefficient politicians who surrounded him.

In the Presidential elections of 1964 Viet Nam played a certain part, and from the speeches made by President Johnson it was clear that he was still against military intervention there. What a politician says in his campaign and what he does when he is elected are often quite different. Once elected Johnson stepped up the number of troops in Viet Nam so that by August 1965 there were 125,000 men there. So far the Americans had employed at each stage what they deemed to be the size of force strictly necessary for a military victory—but once again their estimation of the strength of the Viet Cong was incorrect.

By February 1967 there were nearly half a million American soldiers committed in Viet Nam, but to this figure must be added some of the troops maintaining bases in South East Asia and also the additional number of men back in the United States required for the logistic support of the Field Army fighting in Viet Nam.

Yet still the War goes on, and General Westmoreland has asked for and been given further troops. But again not enough. The accepted ratio of 10 to 12 regular troops to counter one guerrilla would mean that the Americans would have to commit a third of their standing army estimated at three million before victory could be envisaged. If the present ratio of teeth to tail in the American expeditionary force in Viet Nam is not increased in favour of the teeth and at the expense of the tail then a million would still be insufficient. America must have many more of its expeditionary force actively employed in combat units even if this means a substantial reduction in the comforts to which her soldiers have become accustomed.

American participation in the Viet Nam anti-Communist war must not be measured only in terms of her fighting capacity. The tremendous work which is being carried out under

American Aid programmes is as vital if not more vital than her military effort. It cannot be repeated or stressed too often that the raising of the standard of living and the winning of the Vietnamese people over to the anti-Communist camp is the most vital task in this strange war against Communism.

II

VIET NAM TODAY

THE KEY FIGURES: HO CHI MINH—THE EMPEROR BAO DAI—NGO DINH DIEM—PREMIER NGUYEN CAO KY—GENERAL NGUYEN VAN THIEU

WHO ARE THE LIBERATORS ?

Ho Chi Minh (*alias* Nguyen Ali Quoc)

UNDOUBTEDLY Ho Chi Minh is better known as a world figure than any of the other Viet Nam politicians because he has been associated with Viet Nam's politics for nearly a quarter of a century, first as the architect of the Viet Minh and its predecessor, the Indo-Chinese Communist Party (I.C.P.) and then as the absolute ruler of the North.

This ascetic-looking old man, by virtue of the help he is giving to the Viet Cong, is responsible for the continuation of the war in Viet Nam against the Communists and the tying up of over half a million United States troops in South Viet Nam. In spite of all this he has never been the subject of a complete and accurate biography. May 19th is celebrated in North Viet Nam as his birthday but there is uncertainty over the exact year, which has been variously put at 1890, 1891 or 1892. There is no definite information about his name at birth, but most authorities believe it to have been Nguyen Ali Quoc. It is assumed that he is unmarried, has no children, and that his brother and sister are dead. His family background could be described as rich peasant but his father was obviously a highly educated man, who was employed by the Vietnamese Imperial Government. It has been inferred that it was his father's anti-French attitude and nationalistic leanings that were responsible for the termination of his employment by the Imperial Government, after which he earned his living as a practitioner of oriental medicine.

Probably the factor which moulded Ho's life more than anything else was his period at the *lycée* in Hué. This school had been set up with the object of providing the type of education given in French schools, but without Western and, particularly, French influence. The Hué *lycée* can count among its pupils (some of whom were expelled before the completion of their course) such personalities as Giap, Pham Van Dong and Diem, all of whom have left their mark on Viet Nam's history. It is doubtful if Ho completed his course at the *lycée*, and he appears to have taken a teaching job at the private school Phan Thiet and then to have taken a course in catering which enabled him in 1911 to become a cook's apprentice. The following year he signed on as a galley boy on a French ship. It was as a member of a ship's crew that he got his first impressions of life in the ports of Europe, America and Africa.

Ho is known to have worked as a pastry cook under Escoffier at the Carlton Hotel in London at the beginning of the First World War; thereafter, he probably travelled to France via America. After the war he went to Versailles, and his meeting with the Chief Intelligence Officer responsible for Vietnamese affairs was said to have been cordial. But Louis Arnaux, who was accustomed to sizing up characters, recognised Ho as a potential danger, and, during Arnaux's long period of responsibility for security in Indo-China, Ho never returned to his homeland. The National Congress of the French Socialist Party, held in Tours, in 1920, was attended by Ho in the capacity of a delegate from a colonial area. During this Conference he became a founder member of the French Communist Party and had the advantage of having such men as Vailant Couturier as his mentors and helpers. In the immediate aftermath of the First World War the French appear to have allowed him to travel throughout France stirring up trouble among Vietnamese troops and civilian war time workers who were waiting to return home. 1922 found him in Moscow at the Communist Conference, and in the following year he was sent there by the French Communist Party. His studentship at the University of the Toilers of the East in Moscow put him on the Communist map.

About this time Chiang Kai-shek was going through a period of honeymoon with the Communists, and Ho Chi Minh assisted in training Vietnamese agitators. But as soon as the honeymoon ended, in 1927, Ho beat a hasty retreat back to Russia. He seems to have left active agitation to his braver friends, like Giap and Pham Van Dong (later to become respectively Minister of Defence and Prime Minister of North Viet Nam). Whilst they were serving sentences in French prisons Ho Chi Minh watched from the safety of Hong Kong and confined his activities to renaming the Party, calling it the Indo-Chinese Communist Party. British records show that he was arrested with all his documents in Hong Kong in 1931 and given a prison sentence for his subversive activities. The French were hoping to get their fingers on him, but British law, ably pleaded before the Privy Council by the late Sir Stafford Cripps, frustrated the French Government's request for his extradition. Once again he returned, via Moscow, to China, where the Japanese Army were making considerable inroads into Chinese territory, and once again Chiang was only too glad to receive help from Moscow. Ho had a mild dabble in military activities in 1940, but only as a member of a Chinese Communist Military Mission. Chiang Kai-shek was still training troops for the Vietnamese liberation movement in an attempt to hold down more Japanese Forces in Viet Nam. But Ho's form of Communism appears to have been too much for Chiang Kai-shek, who imprisoned him. A year inside Chinese jails cooled off Ho's enthusiasm and made him realise that he would have to toe the line and submerge his Communism for the time being. As a result, the Indo-Chinese Communist Party was buried and the Viet Minh born in its place. It was at about this time that Ho changed his name to Ho Chi Minh.

Even a brief look at Ho Chi Minh's background shows him to be first and foremost a Communist of the Mao Tse-tung variety, who just happened to be born Vietnamese. In his thirty years of exile he did scarcely anything to help the Vietnamese in their struggle to overthrow the great colonial power of France, leaving the dangerous work of active insurgency to those who had been endowed with more courage and physical bravery. Yet, in spite of all these failings, he managed to control the I.C.P. and later the Viet Minh, and was able to come out of his hiding to lead that Party to absolute power in North Viet Nam. From the time of his return to Viet Nam in 1945 he became North Viet Nam's undisputed political master. From that time on, the history of North Viet Nam is virtually a biography of Ho Chi Minh. The day to day military operations were conducted by Giap, who proved to be the outstanding Vietnamese Communist General. His administrative skill was responsible for the building up of the Viet Minh strength, and his tactics out-manoeuvred those of all France's experienced Generals including that great soldier, Marshal de Lattre de Tassigny. Admittedly, de Lattre died before he was able to re-organise the French Union Forces. The military successes in North Viet Nam under the combined plan of Ho Chi Minh and Giap succeeded in bleeding the French Union Forces to such an extent that they eventually capitulated at Dien Bien Phu in 1954. However, Ho's diplomatic successes with the French were nothing like as successful as the Emperor Bao Dai's negotiations, although, of course, the steady bargaining between Bao Dai and France was helped along its path by Giap's military successes against the French Union Forces in the North.

The Emperor Bao Dai

The Emperor Bao Dai has often been portrayed in the unflattering term "the night-club Emperor", but his contribution to Viet Nam's independence must not be underestimated. Bao Dai had been educated in France and had acquired a realistic approach towards his country's relations to the Colonial Power. Perhaps the only mistake in his education was that in the ten years after 1922 he had only returned to his country once. As soon as he was established on the throne he did his best to modernise the Court and to introduce essential reforms in Viet Nam.

Under the French Colonial system the powers vested in the Emperor were restricted and Bao Dai soon discovered that there were limitations to the reforms which he could carry out. His most popular move as far as his countrymen were concerned was his marriage to a Vietnamese village girl. Like many love matches, it won the hearts of his subjects.

During the Japanese occupation of his country Bao Dai remained Emperor and earned severe criticism from many quarters for his collaboration with the conquerors, but he, like Catroux, realised that resistance would only result in his country being torn to pieces by Japanese brutality. France's authority over his country was set out in the Treaty of 1885, and when on March 10th 1945 he was forced by the Japanese to repudiate this Treaty he achieved what proved to be only a paper victory in securing independence for a united Viet Nam.

The Emperor had very little choice of men from among whom he could pick a leader of sufficient calibre to face the immense problems which confronted Viet Nam. On April 17th he nominated Tran Trong Kim as his Prime Minister, but the appointment of a man who was known to have collaborated with the Japanese was not likely to appeal to a country which had suffered so much at Japanese hands. Tran Trong Kim's Cabinet was composed of men of adequate though not outstanding ability. It lacked one essential element —a leader capable of rising to the situation and tackling the immense economic and social problems that face a country about to suffer famine and civil unrest. Tran Trong Kim's Government was dwarfed by the magnitude of the task and only lasted until August 7th of that same year.

Bao Dai's appreciation of the situation in Viet Nam was set out in a letter addressed to the Heads of State of the Big Five Allied nations (Great Britain, U.S.A., Nationalist China, France and Russia). The Emperor was addressing his plea on behalf of a theoretically united Viet Nam. The former French Free Towns had been handed back to Viet Nam and Cochin China had joined the rest of Viet Nam, thereby completing the process of re-unification.

Bao Dai's letter to de Gaulle contained a plea for independence, but proved to be a masterly prognosis of the course of events which would result from an attempt by the French at re-colonisation.

WITNESS TO VIET NAM

Letter from the Emperor Bao Dai to General de Gaulle; August 18th 1945.

"I address myself to the people of France, to the country of my youth. I address myself as well to the nation's Leader and Liberator and I wish to speak as a friend rather than as a head of State. You have suffered too much during four deadly years not to understand that the Vietnamese people, who have a history of 20 centuries and an often glorious past, no longer wish, can no longer support, any foreign domination or foreign administration.

You could understand even better if you were able to see what is happening here, if you were able to sense this desire for independence has been smouldering in the bottom of all hearts and which no human force can any longer hold back. Even if you were to arrive to re-establish a French administration here, it would no longer be obeyed; each village would be a nest of resistance, every former friend an enemy, and your officials and colonists themselves would ask to depart from this unbreathable atmosphere. I beg you to understand that the only way to safeguard French interests and the spiritual influence of France in Indo-China is to recognise frankly the independence of Viet Nam and to renounce any idea of re-establishing French sovereignty or administration here in whatever form it may be.

You would be able to listen to us so easily and become our friend if you would (only) stop aspiring to become our masters again. Making this appeal to the well-recognised idealism of the French people and the great wisdom of their leader, we hope that peace and the joy which has rung for all the people in the world will be guaranteed equally to all people who live in Indo-China, native, as well as foreign.

Bao Dai
18th August 1945"

It did not take the Emperor long to realise that the cause was lost; he had been deserted by his own Government even before the Viet Minh guerrillas had descended on the country. It was not surprising that the Emperor, deserted by his Cabinet and with no established Government, cut very little ice, either in the North or the South of the country or indeed on the international political scene. Ho Chi Minh's Viet Minh units entered both Saigon and Hanoi. Bao Dai's instrument of abdication, forced on him by Ho Chi Minh, was dated the 24th August and became effective the following day. Ho Chi Minh was wise enough to see the value of the Emperor as a front behind which his Communist Government could hide. He appointed him Citizen Adviser to the newly formed Republican Government. The very fact that the Emperor had agreed to become associated with Ho Chi Minh's Government gave the impression to the Americans and the Allies that the new Government was not Communist-dominated. From then on Bao Dai's influence within the Government was virtually nil, but neither his own person nor any of his family was ever threatened by Ho Chi Minh. Under the pretext of seeking military supplies from Chiang Kai-shek he was given an American aircraft on 18th March 1946. The plane never landed in Chungking, but flew direct to Hong Kong. (Presumably the Americans knew of its intended destination.) It was during this period in Hong Kong that Bao Dai acquired the name of "the night-club Emperor". He had done all in his limited power, had been deserted by his Government and betrayed by Ho Chi Minh. There was little he could do for his country by remaining, nor was his estimate of the position inaccurate. In December 1947 a local court stripped him of his Vietnamese citizenship and sentenced him to death. To his credit the Emperor stuck to the instrument of his abdication and refused to be persuaded to say that he had signed at pistol point. Ho Chi Minh, with his usual double-faced approach, never upset the court's decision of December 1947 (depriving Bao Dai of his Vietnamese citizenship and condemning him to death) and continued to say that the "Citizen Adviser" enjoyed his full confidence. The criticism made by François Mitterand in the French Chamber of Deputies on 19th January 1950 was hardly fair. The substance of his speech was that France paid Bao Dai from the time of his ascent to the Throne in 1932 until he decided to collaborate with the Japanese and received his tribute in Japanese yen. When it appeared (said Mitterand) that Ho Chi Minh was in command of the situation Bao Dai abdicated; and hoped for payment from Ho Chi Minh. When nothing materialised from this source he returned to his money lenders and the Bank of Indo-China: and repaired to the comforts of Hong Kong.

Whatever his conduct in Hong Kong, Bao Dai remained adamant in his determination not to return to Viet Nam unless the French granted his country complete independence. He left Hong Kong later and moved to Switzerland. Within the confines of this neutral nation Bao Dai settled down to negotiate with the French. He had already received feelers through the French High Commissioner, Bollaert, and it was not until Bao Dai had received adequate assurances in writing concerning Viet Nam's independence that he consented to return to Viet Nam.

On 5th June 1948 the Agreement recognising Viet Nam's independence was signed on board a French cruiser lying off the coast of Viet Nam at Along Bay. Tagged on to the end of the Agreement was a qualification defining Viet Nam's membership as an associate state within the French Union. Bao Dai protected his future interests by initialling, not signing, the document. This was a precaution on his part in case the French should go back on their undertaking or place a different interpretation on the "independence" of Viet Nam. In 1948 Viet Nam was still under French Administration, so France was within her legal rights in recognising Bao Dai as a representative of his people.

After the initialling ceremony on the French cruiser Bao Dai went straight to Paris. The Viet Minh were embarrassed by the Agreement and tried to pass it off as a plot between France and Bao Dai in which the ex-Emperor had been fooled. The immediate result of the Agreement had been a wave of desertions from the Viet Minh on the part of those moderates who had little sympathy with the Communist aspirations of the Viet Minh. Within Viet Nam the new Agreements were boycotted by the French colons, and as far as the Vietnamese were concerned, those members of the National Congress whose task it was to ratify the Agreement were torn by internal political division to such an extent that some of the delegates refused to sit down at the same conference table with each other. Some met in Saigon in November 1948, and others in Hanoi in December.

On the 8th March 1949 President Auriol set out a new Agreement with Bao Dai known as the Elysée Agreement. The only stumbling block left was the position of Cochin China. This was resolved by holding an election in Cochin China on the issue of whether or not that State wished to be incorporated in a united Viet Nam. The affirmative result was ratified by the French National Assembly of 21st May 1949.

From the time of Bao Dai's flight from Viet Nam in 1946 there had been a constant stream of official and unofficial emissaries to Hong Kong, but Bao Dai had remained adamant and refused either to sign any Agreement or to return to his country until France had recognised Viet Nam's independence. Bao Dai obtained more concessions from the French by these protracted negotiations than Ho Chi Minh had gained as a result of years of fighting between the Viet Minh and the French Union Forces. Bao Dai's contribution towards Viet Nam's history was substantial.

The ex-Emperor's return to Viet Nam on 24th April 1949 was an anti-climax. Although Cochin China had voted for a return to a united Viet Nam the Agreement had not yet been ratified by France. For constitutional reasons Bao Dai could not return direct to Saigon, but proceeded to Dalat. The reception he received there was cool and to some extent his own fault. He did not put himself out in any way to express thanks or gratitude to those Vietnamese notables who had taken the trouble to assemble at the airport to greet the return of their ex-Emperor. Two months later he went to Saigon, where he found an almost deserted city whose population expressed no enthusiasm for his return. He had no alternative but to assume the Premiership and to promulgate a Constitution, under which the Chief of State virtually ruled by decree and left a considerable amount of the detailed administration to Provincial Governors. This Constitution survived until

Diem created a new Constitution in October 1956. Bao Dai remained Chief of State until his overthrow by a so-called Referendum, instituted by Diem in July 1955.

Viet Nam's independence necessitated a change in the fiscal arrangement which had prevailed in Indo-China. As in most federal states the budget was pooled between the component states. The essential division was between Cochin China, Annam and Tonkin, which now formed a united Viet Nam, and the other two states, Laos and Cambodia. Long and complicated negotiations took place. Viet Nam got the lion's share of federal property and also had physical possession of a high proportion of bank deposits. In addition, she was allocated the greater part (71 per cent) of customs dues collected through the Port of Saigon.

Viet Nam made a great mistake both in refusing to pay even the small amount of customs duties due to Laos and Cambodia and in her high-handed appropriation of Federal funds located in Viet Nam banks. This attitude, which was in direct breach of the Agreements, sowed the seeds for discord between Cambodia and Viet Nam which have continued to spoil relations between these two countries. These conventions were concluded by Bao Dai and he cannot escape responsibility for failing to see that they were implemented in a just manner. This illustrates not only the ex-Emperor's personal weakness but also the difficulties which he was experiencing with Viet Nam's political groups. During this period of his rule there was a gradual reduction in the number of French civil servants and a corresponding number of Vietnamese replacements. Unfortunately, the transfer of Vietnamese from French Union Forces to the Vietnamese National Army, which had been started by de Lattre in 1951, did not proceed at a corresponding pace.

Internationally, Bao Dai's Government achieved a great deal. The French had persuaded the United States and Great Britain to recognise this Government in 1950, and Viet Nam's application, sponsored by France, for admittance to the United Nations was only blocked by the Soviet Veto. Nevertheless, Viet Nam did become a member of six of the United Nations' Agencies.

France struck a blow at Bao Dai's Government against which Bao Dai had no weapons with which he could fight back. For a long time the French Government had been embarrassed by the rate of exchange between the two countries, which had proved to be a paradise for currency speculators and represented a burden on the French Exchequer. Without warning, in 1953 France devalued the piastre. This was an easy manoeuvre as the international price of the piastre was only sustained by virtue of its link with the French franc. In Viet Nam's opinion (which was probably correct) this was tantamount to a violation of the Agreements. Bao Dai now felt that he needed the backing of other political figures, and he summoned a National Congress to be held in October 1953. The Congress was a failure, and succeeded in alarming the French by its demand for complete freedom from French authority. Bao Dai's Prime Minister resigned in December and was succeeded by a stopgap, Prince Buu Loc, who opened negotiations with France. Although an Agreement was signed on 4th June 1954 it was completely eclipsed by France's military defeat at Dien Bien Phu and the subsequent Geneva Agreements.

The Geneva Conference was now in session. Bao Dai followed the proceedings from his château near Cannes, and during the Conference he replaced Buu Loc as Prime Minister by Diem. Fortunately, he still had the services of Tran Van Do, who was South Viet Nam's representative at the Geneva Conference. The latter decided not to sign the Agreement (along with America), a decision which, though criticised at the time, proved to have been a wise one. Bao Dai then found himself in a difficult position. The American State Department were convinced that he ought to be discouraged from returning. What really sealed his fate was his decision to allow his own Imperial Guard to be used by Diem for internal security against the religious sects. Had he retained it under his personal command he could have flown direct to Dalat, to an area which would have been protected by loyal troops.

The attitudes of both France and America appear to have been directed against Bao Dai and in favour of Diem. Diem was instrumental in creating a revolutionary committee and a so-called General Assembly which divested Bao Dai of his authority. On 7th July 1955 the Vietnamese Government announced that a National Referendum would be held. This was preceded by a nationwide pressure campaign so that the results of the Referendum, held on 23rd October 1955, were a foregone conclusion: a mere 1 per cent voting against the abolition of the Monarchy and, as a direct result, Bao Dai's dismissal.

Why Diem turned against Bao Dai has never been made clear. The ex-Emperor had appointed him Minister of Internal Affairs as far back as 1932 and Diem had repeatedly professed his loyalty to the Monarchy. The most likely explanation is that Diem saw in Bao Dai an obstacle standing in the way of the fulfilment of his own ambition to be South Viet Nam's absolute ruler. Throughout his various periods of rule Bao Dai never had a united country or a strong political body he could rely upon to carry out the essential reforms which Viet Nam so earnestly required. Had he been more forceful in pushing through a stronger and effective measure to tackle land reform he would certainly have had a popular backing which would have made it difficult for Diem to dismiss him from the scene with so little ceremony.

Bao Dai's abdication in 1945 did not affect the position of the Monarchy, but only his personal position as Emperor. Even when he returned he never actually went back on his instrument of abdication and was in fact styled Chief of State. The position of Monarch was, therefore, technically vacant, though many Vietnamese probably still regarded him as their Emperor. The General Assembly which demanded the dismissal of Bao Dai had an interesting composition. It consisted of Communists and former Communists and other members who had been bribed by Diem to support Bao Dai's dismissal. The Referendum of 23rd October 1955 abolished the monarchy and so precluded any descendant, including the Crown Prince, from becoming Emperor. This cloak and dagger operation by Diem was followed by the rapid dismissal of the revolutionary Committee, most of whose members went into exile, and an attempt to reveal the machinations of the operation was bought off by Diem in hard cash. A chapter of Vietnamese history was closed and gave place to the autocratic rule of Diem.

Bao Dai never returned to Viet Nam. He remained an exile and is at present living in the South of France. Who can say what the result would have been if he had behaved courageously, had landed at Dalat and taken up the reins of Government? The answer, of course, is that in all probability a man who had not the courage to return to his native land, would not have been sufficiently strong to have survived for any length of time as Chief of State in opposition to a forceful and unscrupulous character like Diem.

Ngo Dinh Diem

We come now to the man who controlled the destiny of 14 million South Vietnamese from July 1954 until he met a violent end in November 1963.

There was nothing ordinary about Diem's background—no romantic story of a village boy rising from the paddy fields to the palace of autocratic authority. Diem belonged to the Mandarin class, whose philosophy was that they were the sect born to rule and that there should be an established code between the people and the rulers. He was born in 1901, when his father occupied the position of Minister of Rites and Grand Chamberlain to the Emperor. When his master, the Emperor Thanh-Thai, was deposed by the French, Diem's father resigned his position in protest against France's interference with the Vietnamese Monarchy. From early youth Diem was in favour of reforms carried out through negotiation by Viet Nam's upper classes rather than of those obtained through the efforts of mob violence and proletarian revolution. Diem's ancestors had been early converts from Confucianism to Catholicism and had been members of the Catholic Church for three centuries. His brother, Monseigneur Ngo Dinh Thuc, was a Roman Catholic Bishop.

The formative years of his life were spent at that celebrated *lycée* in Hué in which Ho Chi Minh had been a pupil some ten years earlier. In 1921 Diem passed out top of his class at the School of Law and Administration, an academic achievement which was rewarded by his appointment as a District Chief. Seven years later he became Governor of Phan Thieq in which capacity he was regarded as a steady and honest administrator who was unenthusiastic towards those attempting to bring about changes through revolutionary action. The position which he held was under French administration and some critics have suggested that by accepting such an appointment he was collaborating with the French. But this attitude fails to take into account Diem's background and mentality. By serving in such an appointment he was continuing the centuries' old tradition of rule exercised by an hereditary Monarchy through an élite corps of Mandarins, admittedly under French overall control.

Phan Thieq was a difficult province which included mountain tribes and minority sects and was essentially poor and backward. Diem's success in the administrative field came to the notice of the Emperor Bao Dai, who in 1933 appointed him to the post of Minister of the Interior. Prior to this appointment Bao Dai had put Diem in charge of any inquiry which was to be directed towards reform of the administration. This first job, by its nature, required only recommendations whereas the job of Minister of the Interior entailed putting essential reforms into practice. When Diem found that severe limitations were placed by the French on the range of his activities as Minister in the field of reform he resigned, barely two months after his appointment, and a period of voluntary political exile followed, during which he retained his links with nationalist leaders in Viet Nam and other Asian countries.

There were those who looked towards Japan as a country whose help would be of use in the fulfilment of their revolutionary aspirations. Diem's views on the value of Japan's intervention in other countries is not clear, but what is certain is that when the Japanese took over in Viet Nam he steadfastly refused to occupy any position in their Government and was able to escape the stigma of collaboration, though he was not so independent as to refuse protection by the Japanese from arrest by the French.

Diem's type of revolution was very different from Ho Chi Minh's Communist-inspired Viet Minh, a fact which is illustrated by the execution of Diem's brother by the Viet Minh and Diem's own imprisonment by Ho Chi Minh in the period immediately following VJ Day. Ho Chi Minh appreciated his prisoner's value as an administrator and offered him a post in his Government, for it had not escaped his attention that the appointment of someone of Diem's background would help to allay suspicions in the minds of international politicians that his Government was Communist-dominated. Just as he had used Bao Dai's name and influence, so he hoped to use Diem.

When confronted by the offer, Diem refused and rounded on Ho Chi Minh telling him in no uncertain terms that he was responsible for the murder of Diem's brother, Ngo Dinh Khoi. Whether his actions were dictated by family loyalty or not is a matter for conjecture. Undoubtedly the nation needed the services of men like Diem, who might have been capable of steering Viet Nam's Government away from Communist domination. But, for all we know, Diem may have been convinced by this time that no forces in the country were sufficiently strong to deter Ho Chi Minh from his dedicated mission to create a fully Communist state in Viet Nam. Diem returned to prison but for some reason was released, along with many other political prisoners, after the Agreement signed between the French and the Viet Minh in March of 1946.

Diem's refusal in 1949 of the Premiership offered by Bao Dai was a continuation of his policy not to re-enter the political arena until such time as he was satisfied that Viet Nam's independence had become a reality and was not just a matter of words on paper. His visits to Japan and America in 1950 were not a resounding success; the Americans were worried about the outcome of France's position in Viet Nam and were unwilling to upset the status quo. Diem's brother, Monseigneur Thuc, had far more success once he had enlisted the support of Cardinal Spellman, whose influence in Catholic circles in America was considerable. It was largely due to Spellman's influence that Diem was able to lobby Congressmen and U.S. Government officials. Following a brief stay by Diem in Belgium in 1953, Bao Dai once again offered him the Premiership early in 1954, but he refused. Bao Dai's Prime Minister, Prince Buu Loc, had begun negotiations in Paris with the French, and on 4th June 1954 the Treaty of Independence was signed between representatives of France and Viet Nam. These negotiations and the Treaty which followed them were entirely separate from the Agreements reached at Geneva on 21st July and were never put to a legal test by either party because they were overtaken by events, particularly France's military defeat at Dien Bien Phu and the Geneva Agreement. Nevertheless, Diem considered that the Agreements signed by Buu Loc in June 1954 gave Viet Nam a sufficient degree of independence to warrant his participation in the Government of Viet Nam.

Diem's master stroke and the highlight of his political career came in June 1954, when he persuaded the Emperor to give him (Diem) absolute power. Up to this moment Bao Dai had never relinquished his power, and in doing so he threw away the throne of Viet Nam both for himself and his descendants. Bao Dai must have known that the Oath of Allegiance which he had insisted Diem should swear would be broken by Diem if and when it suited his convenience. Diem doubled back to Saigon and arrived there only a week after Bao Dai had given him these powers. Diem retained these absolute powers until the proclamation of a new Constitution in October 1956, but even after that time he clung on to them by invoking an article in the Constitution which permitted the President to use such powers in the interests of public security or national defence. After 1961 he had to go to the National Assembly for their renewal. An obsequious Assembly not only acceded to his request but continued to renew the powers on an annual basis. They were given further Constitutional authority as a result of the Referendum held on 23rd October 1955, when the Monarchy was abolished and Bao Dai became redundant.

Viet Nam was divided as a result of the Geneva Agreement,

so Diem became the undisputed, dictatorial ruler of South Viet Nam from the date of his appointment by Bao Dai in June 1954 until his murder by military Commanders on 1st November, 1963.

During the months of September and October 1963 all was not well with the administration. Colonel Tung was Head of the special forces in Saigon and was being financed, along with other units, by American dollars. He had formed himself into a private army and became one of the most hated men in the city, embodying all the corruption of the Diem régime. The force he commanded ought to have been fighting the Viet Cong instead of being used as the mailed fist controlling Saigon. The American administration realised this and had already given him an ultimatum, namely that he would get no more money until his forces were employed in fighting the Viet Cong instead of being located in the comfort of Saigon.

During these two fatal months the Communists were consolidating their position in the vital area of the Mekong Delta. The brothers Nhu and Diem became anxious. For some obscure reason Nhu even let it be known that he was entering into negotiations with Hanoi, and at the same time he poured abuse on the Americans who were in fact responsible for the finance necessary to keep Diem in the saddle. The whole atmosphere became complicated with plots and counterplots. Diem and Nhu were both aware of the young officers' plot, and decided to launch a counterplot to which the Americans were privy. It was an amateur affair which relied on the loyalty of Colonel Tung and General Dinh. The idea was that Diem and his family should escape to Cap St. Jacques. Saigon was to be treated to a dose of thuggery which was to be terminated by a combined operation by Tung and Dinh. Probably Dinh had it in mind to use the Americans as scapegoats for an attack and to try to steer Viet Nam into a neutralist course.

An attempt by senior and junior officers to mount a combined operation followed. Commands in the Viet Nam army were extremely complicated, and many of the senior Generals whose reliability was in question had been fobbed off with meaningless but well paid jobs so that they were no longer in command of military units. Thus General Don had been given the title of Chief of the Army, but no troops were under his command.

The three Generals who were to be finally responsible were Minh, Kim and Don, but they all realised that without the help of Diem's close associate, General Dinh, who was military Governor of Saigon, no coup would have any chance of success. They played their cards well and flattered him, suggesting that he should persuade Diem to put some of the military into the Cabinet and, further, that Dinh himself was worthy of a job as important as Minister of the Interior. Diem was furious at the suggestion and told Dinh to go off to Dalat for an (enforced) holiday.

Dinh at first was not privy to the real plans of the Generals, but he fell for the bait which they had laid. They presented to him a picture of himself as a great national hero who had been badly treated by Diem and Nhu. Having been fed with false information of the Viet Cong activities and of plots to overthrow Diem the brothers became alarmed and were only too willing when Dinh came forward with a plan for a counter coup against the Vietnamese said to be plotting Diem's overthrow. It worked like a charm. Dinh got permission to bring in armoured units to Saigon. Furthermore, he had been given authority to liaise with Colonel Khoi and Colonel Tung. The American political machine, through Cabot Lodge, was alerted by the plotters, who preferred to deal with him rather than with their military counterparts.

Cabot Lodge had accompanied Admiral Felt, who was Commander of the United Forces in the Pacific and was about to leave the country. A shrewd politician, Cabot Lodge was apparently very non-committal in discussing the rumour of a revolt. The commander of the Viet Nam Navy was given the opportunity of joining the rebels, and when he refused he was quietly disposed of.

General Don, the leader of the rebels, had been obliged to go to the airport outside Saigon (Tan Sanut) to bid farewell to Admiral Felt, who was paying a tribute to the nation's leadership before his departure. General Don's subordinates had done their work well and had moved two airborne battalions, whose loyalty they doubted, out of the Saigon area and replaced them by armoured units. Diem and his brother still thought this was part of their own troop movements, but when, just after lunch, the radio station and the main police station were taken over Diem began to wonder and got one of his aides to telephone General Dinh who, though present, made an excuse for not talking to him.

Earlier on, Dinh had deliberately leaked part of the plot to Diem and had got the latter's agreement for him to move troops into Saigon. It was not unreasonable therefore for Diem to believe that the troop movements into the area were part of his own instructions to Dinh. Dinh had specifically asked to be allowed to summon the Commander of the Presidential Guard and Colonel Tung. The following is exactly what happened. The head of the Presidential Guard together with Tung and his brother, the Garrison Commander of Saigon and the Airborne Commander, were invited by General Don to the routine luncheon held by the General's staff which was used as an occasion for a weekly conference. Having got them all assembled, Don quietly got up and informed them of what was about to take place, inviting his guests to lend their support to the coup. There were two dissenters, Colonel Tung and his brother. Tung was forced to telephone his officers and order them to surrender. The other Generals detested Tung, and as soon as he had performed this function they "liquidated" him. What really complicated the issue and kept some of the waverers from interfering was the fact that Diem and his brother, Nhu, believing that the movements were being carried out under Diem's instructions, had told some of the loyal troops that no action on their part was necessary.

The next stage was to cut off the Presidential Guard, whose barracks were separated from the palace, and leave Diem isolated in the palace. The master stroke on the part of the rebels was getting control of the radio station. From this position of vantage they were able to use the national broadcasting net. One after the other the Division and Corps Commanders could be heard so that the junior officers in the units could identify their Commanders. This was the most effective way of informing those in charge of the country that Diem's days were numbered.

When the palace finally fell, Diem and Nhu were not to be found. They had escaped through a special tunnel and taken refuge at a pre-arranged rendezvous. It was fortunate that they did not accept the offer of sanctuary given by the United States Embassy. Had this occurred Diem might have attempted a come-back, and although by that time his support was small it could have caused further bloodshed. As it turned out, somebody gave away his hiding place and on the final Saturday morning he and his brother were found in a Catholic church in a suburb of Saigon. They left the church alive, but by the end of their journey in an armoured car they were no longer so.

"Personality cult" would be the best description for Diem's Government during the ten years of its existence. His strong family loyalty concentrated power in the hands of his brothers and even went as far as to include a nephew, Tran Trung Dung. His brother's wife, Madame Nhu, was named first lady of the land and assumed the important role of Diem's official hostess. In a country used to corruption at a high level, Diem found no difficulty in disposing of nearly $12 million (supplied by the Americans) in order to win over certain important people. His policy of divide and rule separated the various factions and left the field clear for a period of unbridled rule by a small clique. This is not to say that Diem was without personal courage; he also possessed a shrewd political judgement. In November 1960 rebel troops had surrounded his palace and the situation took on an ugly look. Diem held the insurgents at bay by protracted talks until such time as he could bring up sufficient loyal troops to assure the safety of himself and his family.

The tragedy of Diem's rule was his misuse of his absolute power. He kept Parliament busy debating frivolous bills, one of which was introduced by Madame Nhu. He made no serious attempt to tackle Viet Nam's major problems, the most important of which was land reform. He allowed the country to drift and this gave the Viet Cong the opportunity of getting a grip on the villagers, who had become utterly disillusioned with the Government's continual procrastination and its failure either to improve their standard of living or to help the minority tribes inhabiting the mountain areas.

It was not until Diem's death that a true appreciation of the situation within the country could be arrived at. The lack of positive information was not entirely due to the strict censorship within the country, which prevented news from percolating from Saigon to the outside world. Nor was it the fault of the reporters, who did their best under difficult circumstances to try to find out the state of the Vietnamese nation. The fact was that Diem controlled everything. Diem was the United States' nominee, and the Americans felt they had to back him at all costs. Perhaps they feared that if the tensions within the country were allowed to build up the generals would quarrel among themselves and anarchy would result. The first attempt by the Army to overthrow Diem was unsuccessful, but the last attempt was planned by soldiers who had come to realise that the country could never beat the Communist menace so long as Diem was in control. It was an efficient coup, and even those who at first could not bring themselves to revolt were eventually pushed or persuaded into joining forces with those in charge of the revolt.

The reason for the lack of accurate information about the country's internal situation is not difficult to assess. It was the District and Provincial Governors, together with the Zone Commanders, who controlled the entire Government machine and of course were responsible for sending back situation reports to Diem. When Diem finally fell, many of the military commanders and province chiefs admitted that their security returns were inaccurate. An illustration of this would be the returns which they were required to submit of the number of villages or zones in their area which they regarded as pacified. Clearly a military commander or province chief who sent an accurate return would not last five minutes. Too often the province chiefs and military commanders might say that in their area they held 75 per cent of the villages. But after Diem's over-throw these same sources were prepared to admit that in fact the figure was more like 55 per cent, the rest being actively controlled by the Viet Cong. It was not surprising, therefore, that the figures given to the Americans through Diem had been entirely misleading, and even the observers in the field had been fed with inaccurate reports. The Americans had fallen for it, hook, line and sinker; and had genuinely believed that Diem was making progress in the country.

Far worse than this were the strategic hamlets which Diem had set up. Here, what happened all too frequently was that a hamlet was set up, and provided with its own defence, but as soon as Vietnamese troops were withdrawn from the area the hamlet fell to the Viet Cong, and a train of atrocities was set about. But according to reports the hamlet had been set up, and so far as the authorities were concerned it had been classified as a safe area.

On the military side it was just the same. Clearly, if the areas had been marked as safe, no one, especially Diem and the Americans, would expect that friendly casualties in the area should arise. The result was that even though military commanders knew where the Viet Cong hideouts were situated they were not prepared to commit their troops for fear of sustaining casualties. If there were casualties, Diem would turn round and say—But you have already reported these areas as friendly; how could you possibly have so many casualties?

The truth revealed itself in all its ugliness when commanders and provincial officials felt themselves, after the downfall of Diem, able to give a more accurate appraisal of the situation in their localities. It was a severe shock to the Americans.

Premier Nguyen Cao Ky

The power complex within South Viet Nam is complicated, not only inside the South Viet Nam Government itself but also between the South Vietnamese and the United States Authorities. After Diem's death many of his lieutenants disappeared, for one reason or another, from the political and military scene. The military junta which was responsible for the coup still wields considerable power, and even after elections have been held there will remain considerable residual powers which can be employed through the province chiefs and are outside Parliamentary control. In a country at war this is essential.

Perhaps one of the easiest ways to follow the history of Viet Nam, both North and South, is to study the biographies of Viet Nam's leading figures, who between them controlled the destiny of Viet Nam until the death of Diem and the end of his régime in November 1963. The time-lag between the murder of Diem and the appointment of Ky illustrates this, for during it there were no less than seven changes of government. At best, the country might be said to have drifted.

Against this mass of power groups in the background the figure of Premier Ky looms large. He was made Prime Minister by the military junta in June 1965, but since he has been Prime Minister he has virtually controlled all policy in South Viet Nam. Ky pictures himself as a military rather than a political figure. He certainly was an extremely good Air Force Commander but he is also developing a shrewd sense of politics, and has, besides, a very good command of the English language. His dealings with reporters are frank and courteous; he has acquired the ability to stand up to the representatives of the World Press, and he does not allow himself to be caught out. His answers are always straightforward, and he makes no attempt to evade the issues. Upper class by background, he was born in 1930 in North Viet Nam and, like many senior members of South Viet Nam's Administration, was educated in a French Military Academy (Namdinh Reserve Officers School) and followed this up with a period of training from 1952–1954 in France and North Africa.

The Americans sent him on an Air Staff course in the United States in 1958 and at the age of 34 he was the Commander of South Viet Nam's Air Force. At the age of 35 he found himself Prime Minister of a nation enmeshed in fratricide. One of his greatest difficulties has been to establish his position as a world figure in such a short time.

Prime Minister Ky is fortunate in having, as Minister of Foreign Affairs, the services of Dr. Tran Van Do, who had already become well known as head of the Vietnamese delegation at the time of the Geneva Conference in 1954. Tran Van Do was one of many who disapproved of Diem's policy and particularly of his dictatorial powers, a difference of opinion which in his case was rewarded by trial and imprisonment. It was not until Diem had been got rid of that Tran Van Do was set free, and in February 1965 he returned to the Government as Deputy Prime Minister to Phan Huy Quat. He retained his position of Minister of Foreign Affairs when Prime Minister Ky was appointed in June 1965. Tran Van Do has been invaluable to Prime Minister Ky, by reason both of his knowledge of world affairs and of his long association with Vietnamese politics. When Ky visited Australia and New Zealand, Tran Van Do accompanied him.

Premier Ky's independence was illustrated when he dismissed the Minister of Defence in 1967, appointing General Cao Van Vien as his successor.

General Nguyen Van Thieu

Vietnamese politics are no different from those of any other nation in essence; intrigue and backstage-operation feature in South Viet Nam in just the same way as they do in Paris, London, Washington or Peking. The men who pull the strings very often remain outside the public eye. General Nguyen Van Thieu is an example. Like many other upper class Vietnamese he was educated at Hué, in one of Viet Nam's national military academies. And after Dien Bien Phu, he concentrated his efforts in the field of military operations. His first Divisional command was the First Division itself, and then he commanded the Fifth Division. As Chief of the Joint Staff, in 1963, he moved quietly to the position of Secretary General of the Military Revolutionary Council but later reverted to his military career, as

Fourth Army Corps Commander. In the 1965 putsch he was second Deputy Prime Minister, and from the 16th February he combined that post with that of Minister of the Armed Forces. On 14th June of the same year he became Chairman of the National Leadership Committee and Chief of State, a position which gave him immense power but brought with it very little international publicity.

The importance of Thieu in Vietnamese politics should not be underestimated, and his nomination for the Presidency at the forthcoming election (1967) will bring him from the wings of the stage to face an international audience. In this way he will probably retain the invaluable services both of Ky and Tran Van Do. The stresses and strains inside the power machine of Viet Nam are already beginning to be felt. The Military Junta met on Wednesday, 28th June, 1967 and the final announcement, which included the all-important decision that Ky should run as Vice-President, was made public on the 1st July, 1967. It became obvious that there was a deep division of loyalties within the Army itself. For this reason, Premier Ky agreed to stand down and allow Nguyen Van Thieu to run for President with himself as Vice-President. This is a further illustration of Ky's absolute loyalty to his country and his ability to divorce himself completely from personal ambition. Whether the President would appoint him Prime Minister again remains to be seen.

In the end, the President will have tremendous reserve powers and even after the election of members to the House of Representatives and the Senate in democratic processes, those who pull the strings from behind will still be there exerting their influence.

The power struggle revealed itself even during the preliminary processes of election. The Assembly with its special Election Committee at first refused to recommend General Thieu and Marshal Ky. But the ruling military junta again resolved the problem by calling an emergency meeting, and Ky himself got in touch with a number of prominent members of the constituent Assembly.

The so-called challenge to the recommendation of Thieu

and Ky was based on the grounds that all military personnel and civil servants were expected to take leave of absence before presenting themselves for office, and although both General Thieu and Ky had taken leave of absence, they continued as Chief of State and Premier. The fact that they did this could not, however, be interpreted as unconstitutional; even in Great Britain during an election the Prime Minister and the Cabinet remain to carry out essential decisions until such time as the electorate have made their views clear and a new government has been formed.

An Assembly Member, Nguyen Ba Lung, had taken the view that the rule in question could not apply to the nation's leaders, and it was made clear by many Deputies in the Assembly itself during the Session that they had already agreed that Thieu and Ky would be permitted to remain in office during the campaign.

The principal line of complaint was that if Thieu and Ky remained in office they would have the Government machine of power in their hands, and it could be employed to influence the election. A vote was eventually taken in the constituent Assembly, by a show of hands. 56 out of the 75 Deputies backed the General. The voting of the Assembly was the final cachet required for the vetting of the candidates. Seven of the applicants in the presidential race had already been eliminated. The final list, therefore, contained eleven approved candidates, and the campaign was to open on August 2nd.

During the election debate the Security Chief, Brigadier-General Nguyen Ngoc Loan, appeared in the gallery accompanied by two of his own personal body guard. Many authorities had already said that Loan had made too thorough a job of paving the way for getting Ky elected as President, and that the military junta had decided that a better combination would be Nguyen Van Thieu for President and Ky as Vice-President.

VIET NAM TODAY

Who are the Liberators?

The answer to this rhetorical question depends on whether one's sympathy lies in the Communist camp or with the Free World. The South Vietnamese Government, backed up by the Americans and other allied nations, is fighting a fierce battle in South Viet Nam against Communism. There is no secret concerning the composition of the forces employed by the Free Nations in this struggle and even the details of the actual numbers have been the subject of reliable reports in the World Press. The aim, as far as the Free World is concerned, is to eliminate active Communism in South Viet Nam and to prevent it from spreading throughout South East Asia.

Much less is known about the so-called "Liberation Movement" of the Communists operating inside the country. Their object has been clearly defined on a number of occasions by Ho Chi Minh through various media and in particular on the Hanoi Radio.

Although a certain amount is known about the Communist organisation in South Viet Nam no accurate statistics have been compiled as to their numbers or location.

The South Vietnamese call the guerrilla forces which are operating in their country Viet Cong San, the literal translation of which is "Vietnamese Communist". This is a generic term used to cover all the enemy troops operating south of the 17th Parallel in opposition to the Government of South Viet Nam. It includes both individual soldiers and formed units of the North Vietnamese army as well as the South Vietnamese guerrilla forces. Under pressure from Chiang Kai-shek, Ho Chi Minh, the founder and leader of the Indo-Chinese Party, was compelled to change the name to Viet Minh in order to give an air of respectability to the Party which might attract non-Communist Vietnamese moderates. From Ho Chi Minh's biography it can be seen that the Viet Minh under his leadership became identified with the struggle against the Japanese

ORGANIZATION OF THE PEOPLE'S REVOLUTIONARY PARTY

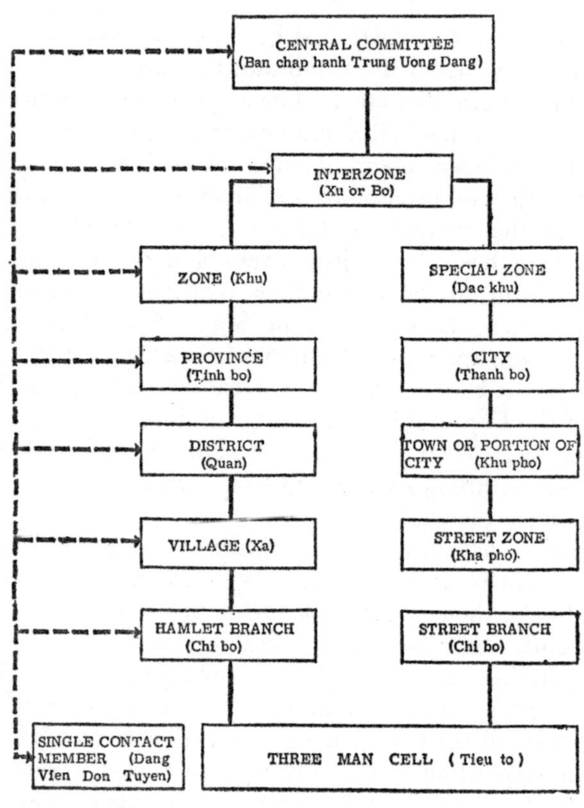

invaders and later against the colonial rule of the French. By the time the Chinese had evacuated their forces from their positions north of the 16th Parallel, Ho had become the President of the Democratic Republic of Viet Nam with a strong, well-organised Viet Minh army at his disposal. After the Hanoi incident, in true Communist style, he commenced negotiations with the French Army Commander and at the same time launched attacks on all the French garrisons and French civilians throughout Viet Nam. From then on he led the Viet Minh in the war against the French, 1946-1954. French Union casualties during this period were variously estimated. In all probability French Regular Forces, Indo-Chinese and Foreign Legion Regiments—that is to say, all French Union Forces fighting under the French Tricolour—probably suffered just under 90,000 casualties. Viet Minh losses are thought to have been two or three times this figure. It was Ho's Viet Minh under General Giap which was responsible for inflicting the defeats suffered by the French and which culminated in the major military disaster at Dien Bien Phu.

Following the Geneva Conference the country was once again divided, this time at the 17th Parallel. Under the terms of this Agreement free movement on each side of this Parallel was permitted. Just under a million people elected to move out of the Communist-dominated North, whereas only a tenth of this number moved from the South to the North. Many of those who decided to move North were probably unaware that North Viet Nam's Government was Communist-dominated and in some cases they were motivated by the desire to join their families in the North. It was not until a year later that the great massacres took place in that region. The figure of one million gives a false impression of the anti-Communist feeling which was already in existence there. In many instances the Government of North Viet Nam simply refused to allow the teams of the International Control Commission (which had been set up at the Geneva Conference for the purpose of supervising these movements) to enter whole areas under its control. It is estimated that, had the teams been given authority and access to all areas in the North, a further three or four hundred thousand would have moved to the South. As it was, whole villages in the North, often led by their local Catholic priest, moved down to the South leaving behind them their land and all their personal possessions other than those which they could carry with them.

The exact composition of those 100,000 who moved to the North is not known but undoubtedly some of them were members of the Viet Minh. The majority of the Viet Minh fighting south of the 17th Parallel crept out of their guerrilla hiding places and under the Agreement supervised by the International Control Commission were taken North, many of them in French and Polish ships. Although the majority of the Viet Minh migrated to North Viet Nam they left behind them their weapons, which were carefully treated and greased to protect them from rust before being buried or concealed. Left behind in South Viet Nam were the hard-core of Communist organisers who, under the general amnesty, were able to leave their hiding places and return to the villages, where they probably set about organising a nation-wide Communist network.

Ho Chi Minh realised, very soon after the signature of the Geneva Agreement, that since neither America nor South Viet Nam were signatories it was highly unlikely that elections would take place in the South. Ho was fully aware that had elections been held, his in-built majority in the North would have been sufficient to ensure a Communist majority over the whole country. That small majority could have been used to give a semblance of constitutional authority to the complete communisation of the whole country (exactly as had occurred in Czechoslovakia in 1947). Ho Chi Minh's plan to use the Geneva Agreement for a take-over bid of the whole country had been foiled. From then on he realised that the only hope lay in the organisation of a strong Communist guerrilla force capable of overthrowing the South Vietnamese Government. In July 1949 he wrote an article in the Belgian *Drapeau Rouge* in which he stated:—

"we are building Socialism in Viet Nam but only in one

part of the country, while in the other part we still have to direct and bring to a close the middle class democratic and anti-imperialist revolution".

After 1957 the comparative peace which South Viet Nam had enjoyed was disrupted and by 1960 Viet Cong acts of terrorism had increased so that the murder of village chiefs and police had reached a monthly average of six hundred. At this time the control Commission (the Polish delegation dissenting) confirmed that there was a regular flow of arms and men from North to South.

Those of the former Viet Minh who had been left behind and remained South of the 17th Parallel must have contained some northerners as well as southerners but, of course, there are no breakdown statistics of this hard-core which elected not to accept the offer to return North. What has become apparent recently is that in the Mekong Delta there is and always has been an inherent dislike and distrust of northerners, so that even today there are few, if any, northerners operating in Communist cells in this rice bowl of South Viet Nam.

Many reasons have been suggested for the sudden emergence of the guerrillas in 1957 after a period of inactivity which had seen the enjoyment of a peaceful existence in the villages of South Viet Nam. As a result of the Geneva Agreement and the mass movement of people southward and the comparatively few moving North, the whole position in the North and South had become confused.

The majority of the Viet Minh had left the South, and only a fraction of their original force now remained south of the 17th Parallel. It is more than likely that the years between 1954 and 1956 were used by the Communists for re-organising their forces and making plans for future insurgency. For the Communists who were left in the South it was really a question of starting again from the beginning, for not only did they have to dig up the arms which had been hidden but their whole system of supply of essential food had to be re-established together with a command network of communications.

This is only part of the story. The Communists in South

Viet Nam, who from now on will be referred to by their Vietnamese name, Viet Cong, had still to be convinced that they could not bring into being a Communist Government by means of the elections which were supposed to take place. By 1956 it was clear to Ho and his supporters that the possibility of imposing Communism through the ballot box had vanished; the only possibility left was through a more active campaign. In the years following 1954 the Communists began a relatively peaceful campaign of subversion. The Communists found an ideal medium for the growth of a resistance movement against the Government.

Immediately following 1954, contrary to all the estimates and expectations of the North, the economy of the South did not collapse. On the contrary, it made a slow but steady advance. North of the 17th Parallel the picture was different: the combined effects of transformation from a capitalist to a Communist controlled industry and the disruption of the agricultural system occasioned by the new land reforms instituted by Ho Chi Minh, had a disastrous effect on the country's economy. Ho Chi Minh had his hands full, and blood dripped from them as a result of the "liquidation" of over 100,000 people who had dared to oppose his Communist methods. Even as late as 1956 a mass rising by peasants and farmers took place in Ngag-An province. Having throttled all opposition to his methods in the North, Ho Chi Minh was in a position to turn his attention to that part of the country lying south of the 17th Parallel.

It was the medium provided by South Viet Nam which made possible the growth of Communism in the South. In 1954 the people in the South were not expecting miracles. Their country had been a battle ground for civil war for over a decade, and it took a long time for the natural patience inherent in the average Vietnamese to be exhausted. They were prepared to give Diem's Government a chance of putting things right.

Had Diem's Government taken the trouble to organise a proper and just system of Government and to make a genuine effort to carry out essential reforms—and in particular land reform—then the Viet Cong movement could have been strangled at birth. But Diem's corrupt Government aroused hatred among even the moderates in the country; it antagonised almost everyone. This was the negative role played by the Diem Administration, but superimposed upon this was his strong-man activity in the villages. Those mailed fist operations would have been tolerated if they had been confined to genuine Communists and not directed against all who had the audacity to query Diem's dictatorial powers or criticise his policies.

From December 1946 until the cease fire in 1954 the Viet Minh had concentrated their military efforts against the French in the northern part of Viet Nam. (Tonkin was divided into Interzones 1, 2 and 3; Annam, 4, 5 and 6, and Cochin China, 7, 8 and 9). Although most of the fighting took place in Interzone 1 the Viet Minh were also active in other zones such as Zone D in Interzone 7, the Plain of Reeds in Interzone 8 and the so-called liberation area of Camu in Interzone 9.

A high proportion of the estimated 100,000 who elected to go to the Communist-held North after the Geneva Agreement of 1954 in fact came from Interzone 5. The inhabitants of this area had given what little support they could to the Viet Minh in their struggle against the French. Although no generalisation can be made as to their reasons for electing to go to the Communist North it is significant that the land which they farmed in Interzone 5 was of poor quality and it is possible that the promise of better quality land and improved living conditions, as a reward for their loyalty to the Viet Minh, may have influenced their decision to move North and throw in their lot with the Communists.

The Viet Minh did not have it all their own way, and Bao Dai's Administration from 1949 to 1954 was not as bad as many authorities have claimed. He was not, it is true, able to modernise his Administration, and he had the reputation of being too pro-French, but in the main, those under him were honest. The whole machine lacked imagination, however, and the wheels of power ground slowly. Until 1954 the Viet Minh's success in the South was not spectacular, and they had made fundamental errors; the old Communist-trained Tran Van Giau dealt so harshly with the people, and the scorched earth policy which he entered upon antagonised the Southerners to such an extent, that Ho replaced him by Nguyen Binh. Viet Minh's success in the South was hampered by the natural antipathy of the South for their northern brethren. To complicate matters, the powerful sects of the Cao Dai and Hoa Hao had created small areas of self-government to the West and South of Saigon which the French deemed it wise to leave alone. In Saigon itself the police and many other activities were controlled by Binh Xuyen. The Administration in South Viet Nam suffered another setback after 1954 when many Frenchmen who held posts in the Government of the South saw the red light and disposed of their personal, and where possible their real, property to start a new life elsewhere. This exodus resulted in difficulties for the Diem Administration, which turned towards the new reservoir of manpower which had arrived in South Viet Nam in the form of a million northern refugees. Many of these were highly qualified, and Diem utilised them to fill the gap, but here again, his action in placing the Northerners in positions of power in the South regenerated the centuries old friction which existed.

Diem's policy was always the same. He allowed the murmurings in the cafés and at cocktail parties which were reported to him by his informers to continue unchecked. In his view they represented no real danger. It was not until dissentients formed themselves into groups that he regarded them as a threat and as a challenge to his own power. Diem never had any real popular support in the country, and his pro-French Mandarin approach was not likely to make him a popular figure. He relied to a great extent on the army backed up by a nationwide secret police and informer system. As soon as the army withdrew its support, as it did in 1963, Diem's whole Government collapsed. He never learnt, and was blind to the signs of discontent such as the publication of the Caravelle Manifesto which had been signed by eighteen respected professional politicians, and their abortive *coup d'état* in November 1960. These drove him to acts of repression, imprisonment, murder and torture, but never along the road to reform. To the outside world the land development reform, the institution of the strategic and New Life Hamlets all looked like major advances in social progress—but how could they really be successful in combating Communism when the whole fabric of Diem's Government was cruel, corrupt and inefficient? It was against this background that the Viet Cong's political strength grew, and in many areas was able completely to dominate the activities of the population. Gradually the acts of terrorism by the Viet Cong increased, and they were directed not only against those who represented the central Government of South Viet Nam but also against innocent people working on public projects such as irrigation. A typical instance occurred in Kien Long, where the district leader had his arms and legs broken before he and his children were killed. Public exhibitions such as disembowelling became a common occurrence. International opinion of the Viet Cong's activities had already been aroused; the Free World condemned, the Communists denied, but what they could not deny was the torture and murder of Colonel Hoang Thuy Nam, who was Chief Liaison Officer for the International Control Commission.

As time went on, it was clear that the reign of terror which prevailed in South Viet Nam could not possibly have been carried out by those of the Viet Minh who had remained in the country after the Geneva Agreement. What had happened was that the Viet Cong had attracted recruits from two different sources. Hostility in some South Vietnamese villages to Diem's régime, combined with persuasion by Viet Cong agents, had succeeded in recruiting disenchanted South Vietnamese to the ranks of the Viet Cong. In some of the districts held by the Viet Cong they had pursued a deliberate policy of giving assistance to the villagers, thereby attracting recruits to their cause. The second and more important source of recruits came from the North, and during the period 1959–1964, 39,000* specially trained guerrillas had left North Viet Nam and found

*These figures are based on the special report of the Control Commission of 1965.

their way to join forces with the Viet Cong. The accompanying map shows the infiltration route of one of the Viet Cong who later defected to the South Viet Nam Government. The importance of the infiltration route down the Ho Chi Minh trail cannot be overestimated; it is for this reason that a chapter in this book has been devoted to Laos and Cambodia, both of which play an important part in the Viet Nam War.

In 1961 the North Vietnamese Communist Central Committee passed a resolution calling for a front which would rally "all patriotic forces to overthrow the Diem Government". This was followed by the setting up in North Viet Nam of the National Front for the Liberation of South Viet Nam. The political objects of the N.F.L.S.V. were the withdrawal of all American forces and the holding of elections in South Viet Nam. From then on, Hanoi Radio set out to give the impression that the N.F.L.S.V. had support in South Viet Nam and even went on to say that a radical Socialist Party, a Democratic Party and a Trade Union Movement had joined the Front. Needless to say, they did not announce that none of the Parties existed in South Viet Nam.

In July 1962 the Communist nature of the N.F.L.S.V. was revealed when the Viet Nam People's Revolutionary Party was formed, to be the controlling Party in the Front. Captured documents have made it clear that the People's Revolutionary Party receives its instructions direct from Hanoi and is no more than a branch of its counterpart in the North. Further evidence that the Front was, and is, controlled by Hanoi is illustrated by the fact that all but 12 of the 52 members of the Central Committee have been named and that few of these are southerners. Those who have been identified as southerners are not men of any political standing. The President, Nguyen Huu Tho, is a lawyer while a former school master and journalist, Nguyen Van Thieu, is the Secretary General, whose only claim to be known by the West was his leadership of delegations to international conferences between 1962/63. It is clear that the real power rests in the hands of the North. Another indication that this is the truth was the statement made to Press correspondents by a North Vietnamese delegate to the Geneva

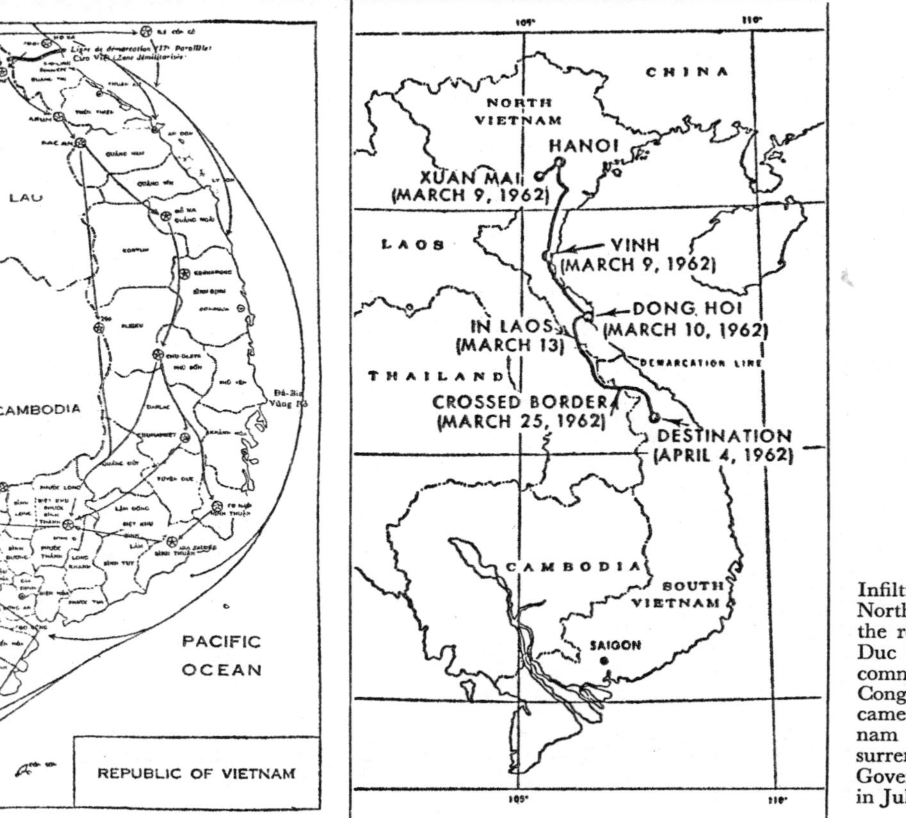

Infiltration from the North: Map shows the route of Huynh Duc Tha, deputy commander of Viet Cong company; he came to South Vietnam in 1962, surrendered to Government forces in July 1963.

INFILTRATION ROUTES INTO VIET NAM

Conference on Laos in 1962 "that several members of the Party Central Committee in the North were actively engaged in running the War in the South". The N.F.L.S.V. is always trying to get itself recognised by other Communist countries: to this end it has established missions in Moscow, Peking, Havana, East Berlin and Prague, and Agreements for opening up other missions are always in the course of negotiation. Where North Vietnamese missions are in existence the N.F.L.S.V. works through these, and members of the Front nearly always travel on North Vietnamese passports. The Front makes a great show in getting itself accepted in the international capitals of the Communist world, but it has little support in the country it purports to represent, South Viet Nam.

The Communist Party in South Viet Nam was called the People's Revolutionary Party, with the National Liberation Front Central Committee forming the apex of the pyramid from which the command structure radiates. The People's Revolutionary Party replaced the Lao Dong (Workers' Party) of South Viet Nam.

In 1962 a captured Lao Dong document was turned over to the International Control Commission, extracts from which are enlightening:

"In regard to the foundation of the People's Revolutionary Party of South Viet Nam, the creation of this Party is only a matter of strategy; it needs to be explained within the Party; and to deceive the enemy it is necessary that the new Party be given the outward appearance, corresponding to a division of the Party (Lao Dong) into two and the foundation of a new Party so that the enemy cannot use it in his propaganda."

"Within the Party, it is necessary to explain that the founding of the People's Revolutionary Party has the purpose of isolating the Americans and the Ngo Dinh Diem Régime, and to counter their accusation of an invasion of the South by the North. It is a means of supporting our sabotage of the Geneva Agreement, of advancing the plan of invasion of the South, and at the same time permitting the Front for liberation of the South to recruit new adherents, and to gain the sympathy of non-aligned countries of South East Asia."

"The People's Revolutionary Party has only the appearance of an independent existence; actually, our Party is nothing but the Lao Dong Party of Viet Nam (Viet Minh Communist Party), unified from North to South under the direction of the Central Executive Committee of the Party, the Chief of which is President Ho. . . . During these explanations, take care to keep this strictly secret, especially in South Viet Nam, so that the enemy does not perceive our purpose. . . . Do not put these explanations in Party Bulletins."

The headquarters of the People's Revolutionary Party was in Binh Duong. This headquarters was overrun by the Americans and a large number of very useful documents fell into their hands.

What the North has been trying to do is to give the Liberation Front the appearance of having different political parties within its organisation. The easiest way to link the military and political structure would be to say that the Viet Cong is the military set up and the N.F.L.S.V. the political machine, but this might be criticised as an over-simplification of what is in fact an extremely complicated inter-relationship. What is true is that most of the leading personalities in the Liberation Front People's Revolutionary Party and the Viet Cong remain hidden from the public, and certainly hidden from the West.

Ho Chi Minh is Chairman of the Communist Workers' Party Central Committee. This Committee is the overlord; policy decisions come through it and through a re-unification Commission. Military operations of the Viet Cong are believed to be directed by the Deputy Chief of North Viet Nam's Army General Staff (Major General Nguyen Van Vinh), and it is possible that he is also responsible for the co-ordination of all military and political activity in the South.

The P.R.P. Central Committee in the South commands five regions, with a separate command for the Saigon area. Every region is sub-divided into provinces, districts, villages and hamlets. Thus a skeleton organisation is run whose administrative machine is an exact parallel to the administration of the South Viet Nam Government. The Viet Cong's military administrative chain of command corresponds to its civil counterpart. It appears that command for the Viet Cong and other irregular units is different from that of formed regular units of the North Viet Nam Army. The top command for the North Vietnamese Army units probably rests ultimately in Hanoi with General Giap, whereas the Viet Cong orders appear to be transmitted through P.R.P. channels.

The military organisation of the Viet Cong has been broken down largely as a result of information obtained either from prisoners or from captured documents. The Australians have been particularly good at this and were able to show me not only a complete order of battle for those Viet Cong units operating in the area for which the Australians had been given responsibility; they had also been able to make a breakdown of the command structure from Division level down to sub-units.

III

THE WAR IN VIET NAM

WAR CORRESPONDENTS AT WORK

MILITARY OPERATIONS

ODE TO THE WHITE HORSEMEN

ARMY OF THE REPUBLIC OF VIET NAM (A.R.V.N.)

WE ARE ALL AMERICANS

War Correspondents at Work

SINCE the fall of the Diem régime correspondents in Viet Nam have been accorded very good facilities for observing all aspects of the struggle and there is virtually no censorship. Naturally the normal rules of Press etiquette apply in Viet Nam as they would anywhere else in the world, so information which is given on "background" should not be used for publication. In the same way a correspondent listening to a briefing on a plan for future operations must not release it until he has been given the go ahead. But from a practical point of view a correspondent in the field would not be able to use this information, for in the first place military lines of communication would not be available to him if he wished to pass information which was still of a classified nature. The Press, here as elsewhere, acts in a responsible way, for failure to do so would mean that no further special information would be given to the individual correspondent if he were to break the rules governing the conduct of war correspondents.

In the case of a field operation, the correspondent would be invited to attend the briefing conference which the Commander of the formation concerned always holds prior to the launching of that operation. After the conclusion of the operation correspondents are welcome to attend the Commander's summing up and criticisms, if any, of the operation which has just taken place. In South Viet Nam the operation may be reported upon, always provided that there is no special security involved, and the Press are permitted to take, develop and send back to their newspapers abroad photographs which they have taken of the operation. There can always be special circumstances where a high degree of security must be observed, particularly if it relates to future operations.

An instance of where the Americans did not clamp down on a correspondent took place when one of the broadcasting companies took some close-ups of the way in which a Viet Cong prisoner was handled by American troops. This particular incident was far from complimentary to the American soldiers involved, but nevertheless was allowed to be flown out of Viet Nam and as far as I know was displayed to the American public as a news item on the television screen.

Again, here as elsewhere, the most reliable and trustworthy correspondents are given the most information "on background". As in the case of the Lobby correspondents in the House of Commons, it enables them to have the basic information from which they are able to write about the subject concerned. As in all walks of life there are good and bad, and the United States Military Assistance Command Viet Nam Headquarters in Saigon (M.A.C.V.) is the centre from which correspondents from all over the world assemble—radio, television and newsmen.

Here in Saigon some of the great figures of the news world brush shoulders with representatives of small local newspapers, many of whose readers may understand little or nothing of the Viet Nam War. M.A.C.V. handles them all with ease, the polite and the aggressive, but M.A.C.V. knows in advance where the great battles are going to take place and is able to tip off trusted correspondents and newsmen so as to enable them to arrive in time to witness the battle.

How, it might be asked, can six hundred accredited correspondents all be able to get first hand information of the military campaign in Viet Nam? In the first place, the battles take place in many different parts of the country at the same time. In the second place, some of the Press concentrate on the military activities of certain nations and may well be running a serial in their home newspaper on the Koreans, the Australians, or perhaps on American naval operations.

Finally, there are those gifted with the ability to spend their evenings and days in the bars of Saigon and rely on the excellent press handouts which are released daily by M.A.C.V. A little bit of "tarting up" or embellishing can make the press release look like a first hand story. The reader can imagine the reporter lying behind a mound of earth, with small arms and mortar fire all around him. If the reader could in his mind replace the mound of earth by the wood of a Saigon bar, and the hum of bullets by the clink of glasses he would understand that it was perhaps as a result of the consumption of the contents of the glasses that the correspondent had been able to fill in the details of the battle from imagination.

The war correspondent going out on patrol or operating with troops in the field would not wish to be made conspicuous by the clothes he is wearing. It could endanger his life as well as those of the soldiers with whom he was fighting. Some correspondents bring with them their own uniform, but for those who have nothing of their own an arrangement has been made whereby they can buy the basic uniform and equipment required. Of these a tin helmet is probably the most essential, and if the fighting is likely to take place in paddy fields a pair of specially protected boots prevents injury from the sharp stakes placed in the fields. Dressed in an American combat uniform the correspondent blends in with the rest of the patrol and the only difference is that he has no rank or insignia on him but carries with him his national passport together with American and Vietnamese identity cards both of which include a signed passport photograph.

The correspondent may well elect to take with him such additional items as a water bottle and a haversack, or if he is planning to stay in a particular area for a long time he might even carry a holdall with a complete change of clothes, but in this case he would be well advised to leave it at base headquarters. The less the correspondent carries, the easier it is for him to climb in and out of helicopters and to accompany troops to the forward areas. British battle dress was the envy of many correspondents as it had no skirt to get in the way when crawling through the undergrowth and its deep thigh pocket was large enough to hold all essential items.

M.A.C.V. does not make provision to arm correspondents. This is a personal matter and it is up to the individual to make his own arrangements. Most units are willing to oblige and to lend the correspondent a weapon for his personal use during a particular operation. Those correspondents who have been in the country for a considerable time have usually managed to acquire "a weapon of their choice". The booking clerks and receptionists at the leading hotels in Saigon are so used to the spectacle of civilian correspondents carrying lethal weapons that they do not trouble to ask any questions or make a report to the civilian police. Saigon is relatively free from actual warfare, but after all it is the capital of a nation embroiled in an all out struggle to preserve its independence.

No one could fail to be impressed by the ability of the first class war correspondents to cross-question military commanders on questions of tactics. This is all the more surprising since many of them have had no military training or service experience. The military commanders in South Viet Nam are delighted when they come across a war correspondent who has been an ex-serviceman, no matter in which branch of the armed forces he has served. This is only natural, for it renders the process of briefing of military operations easier and more pleasant for the fighting commander. In the field this is even more important, as in the case of an ex-serviceman the fighting unit is not lumbered with a passenger; any war correspondent without military experience can represent a positive danger to the lives of the soldiers taking part in the operation. The ex-serviceman who puts on his tin hat, grabs a weapon (provided he holds it the right way round) and then falls in with the patrol is appreciated. He knows instinctively when to keep quiet and not attract the attention of the enemy and does not open his mouth and ask questions until there is a convenient lull in the battle. But what is far more important is that he knows instinctively what to do when the firing starts and regards himself as under the orders of the local military commander whatever rank that local military commander may hold. War correspondents maintain that they should rank as field officers, but on a small patrol it may well be that the sub unit commander is a top sergeant or even lower in rank. If the correspondent wishes to go out fighting with such a sub unit then he ought to regard himself as under the command of that top sergeant and in just the same position as any other soldier on the patrol.

The position of correspondents is laid down in international agreements. A study of these makes it clear that a correspondent should not participate in the fighting; but there is nothing to stop him carrying weapons for purposes of self defence. The object of these international agreements is to ensure that all correspondents who are captured are treated as non-combatants and in the case of local wars should be released as soon as any information which they have acquired as a result of being captured has ceased to be of any military value.

In Viet Nam the whole concept of international agreement has little or no significance. North Viet Nam is not a signatory of, nor a party to, the International Red Cross agreements on prisoners, whereas South Viet Nam most certainly is. Correspondents are fully aware of the atrocities committed by the North Viet Nam authorities on American and South Vietnamese prisoners and know that they can expect no mercy at the hands of their captors, so most of them would prefer to shoot it out if ever they got into a tight spot. Better to die fighting than to risk the terrible fate of capture.

There are always exceptions to the treatment received by captured correspondents and in one spectacular case in 1966, that of Michele Ray, the Viet Cong decided that they could make considerable international political capital, not only by treating their prisoner exceptionally well but also by releasing her in the shortest possible time; thus giving the impression that the treatment received was in accordance with humanitarian principles and that other prisoners received similar treatment.

The war in Viet Nam is essentially of a guerrilla type and it is the exception rather than the rule for major confrontations to take place. The country is like a patchwork quilt; comparatively few areas are completely under Government control, many are still Viet Cong dominated, and the remainder could be described as uncommitted, either to the Government or the Viet Cong. The question therefore arises as to how to get to the battlefield to witness the fight between units of the Free Nations and the Viet Cong. At first sight the simple and obvious way would appear to be to hire a taxi or a car with driver in Saigon and drive out to the area. This would not be possible, as in the first place one would be most unlikely to get a driver to undertake this task, and secondly one would be unlikely to get there without being ambushed by the Viet Cong. Even from Saigon to Dalat there is always the danger of being stopped by the Viet Cong. Their reactions are quite unpredictable and they are just as likely to stop the traveller and, after an exchange of words, allow him to proceed as, on the other hand, to drag him and his companions out of the car and make short work of them.

Even the main roads cannot be classified as entirely safe, although once inside a pacified province there is a high degree of security prevailing; but, even so, it is wise to take an escort vehicle or guard of some kind and to restrict travel to the hours of daylight.

Escort vehicles tend to give a false sense of security, because in the case of a major ambush the escort would be of little help if the Viet Cong had laid their ambush well and were firing from a vantage point at short range along a path of fire which had already been carefully checked. Almost as soon as the small party had got within fire they would probably find the leading vehicle blown up by a carefully laid mine, made out of captured American materials; and before the escort had any chance of returning the fire most of them would have been wiped out. Even in pacified villages or areas this can happen from time to time. What often happens is that the first party is immediately wiped out, but in most cases they have had an opportunity of sending a wireless message back notifying headquarters of the exact position of the ambush. The Viet Cong wait around until the main relief force arrives and treat them to a vicious dose of cross-fire. Frequently the Viet Cong remain in their positions just sufficiently long to do the maximum amount of damage and then retreat rapidly into the surrounding country, perhaps breaking up into small sub units and thereby making any form of pursuit difficult if not impossible. Their object has been achieved: maximum casualties inflicted on the Allies with the minimum amount of effort, and probably very few Viet Cong killed or wounded. Local villagers would be far too frightened to apprehend them; any attempt by unarmed villagers to do this would be suicidal.

The degree of security which exists in the pacified areas varies considerably; and personally I always felt most secure in those areas for which the Korean forces were responsible. The Vietnamese villager has acquired a healthy respect for his fellow Asiatics and whilst the Korean soldiers treat the villagers well and help them in their daily tasks in practical ways, such as giving assistance in the building of schools, roads, etc., yet, at the same time, the Koreans stand no nonsense with those Vietnamese who have sympathised with, or connived at, Viet Cong outrages.

The whole country is like a vast lake with hundreds of islands, the islands representing pacified areas, and the water communications between those areas. Thus, while the islands themselves may be relatively safe, the road communications between them can never be depended upon. Many convoys travel along these roads unmolested, but there are always occasions when successful ambushers wreak havoc, not only on the troops guarding the convoys, but also on the supply vehicles moving in convoy. The only relatively safe method of travel for the war correspondent and, indeed, in many cases for troops, casualties and supplies, is by aeroplane, and for short journeys helicopters, known in local language as "choppers".

All over the country supplies of men and materials are being flown throughout the hours of daylight to the operational areas and the drone of aircraft can be heard at all times. In many cases there are more or less regular runs between the various landing places known as helicopter pads. In addition to this, road convoys require considerable numbers of troops as escort.

Press representatives are given a very high degree of priority for travel by air; and as soon as they show their Press cards they are nearly always found a seat on an aircraft. These Press cards are issued by the Vietnamese and American authorities to all those members of the Press who have been properly accredited to M.A.C.V. as official war correspondents.

Although it may be a somewhat frivolous comparison, a typical day's visit to the battlefield is not unlike a day's hunting in the Shires. It probably means a very early start, leaving the luxury of the Caravelle Hotel as early as three o'clock in the morning, departing by a military station wagon which leaves M.A.C.V. headquarters for the airbase at Tan Sanut. It is here that the largest airport in the world has to deal with bombers delivering their lethal weapons to North Viet Nam, with planes on routine reconnaissance, and with the departure and arrival of helicopters. Even to find one's way about these miles of buildings and runways presents a major problem and one is obliged to travel in a military vehicle; taxis and civilian vehicles are not permitted to enter the airfield, so the correspondent who is not fortunate enough to get military transport to the airfield is compelled to leave his civilian vehicle at the gates and to thumb a lift by military transport to the air departure point. The helicopter into which you are strapped is already heavily loaded down as it is obliged to carry not only a pilot and co-pilot, but also two rear gunners armed with machine guns, mounted on the aircraft. This only leaves enough room for, possibly, half a dozen passengers, the exact number depending on the temperature. The hotter the weather, the lighter the air and the fewer the passengers that can be carried with safety.

The enemy have no aircraft, so the likelihood of the helicopter being brought down is comparatively slight, though in the course of a year a number of helicopters are brought down by small arms fire from the Viet Cong.

Having arrived at the helipad in safety, you usually find a public relations officer waiting to conduct you to the force commander, who may be in charge of anything from a division to a company. Some commanders are very reluctant to allow you to take part in action, but the co-operative commander who is anxious to see that you get your information at first hand will allow you to go forward and operate with a patrol or a fighting force. In one case General Knowles, after some persuasion, lent me his personal helicopter so that I could see one of his units in action. He had just left the area himself and knew that they were preparing for patrol action.

In many cases the choice as to whether you remain in the forward Tactical Headquarters or actually go out to some of the units is left to individual taste. If the battle finishes early and there happens to be transport available you can probably get back to Saigon the same night, though it may mean doing a number of short journeys from helipad to helipad in order to pick up a courier plane to Saigon. In one case a friend of mine was so anxious to get back that night that he was prepared to share a helicopter with the dead.

Thus if the battle is within helicopter range of Saigon it is possible, by making a very early start, to leave the comfort of a luxury hotel, witness a battle and, provided you don't mind travelling with the corpses or the casualties, return to Saigon in time for a bath, a whisky and soda and an excellent dinner. But it is equally possible that you might return as a corpse or casualty yourself.

This death and luxury combined in one single day tends to give the wrong impression of the fighting going on in Viet Nam; it is, in fact, a desperate business and the wounds suffered are appalling. Flame throwers and tumbler bullets make a nasty mess of the human torso and it is this type of war the Allied troops and the Viet Cong share as part of their daily lives in the forward areas.

But even in these islands of fighting the war knows no pattern, nor are the streets of Saigon free from their share of mortar fire and plastic bombs. Hotels are damaged, members even of the International Commission for Control have been attacked, and in one case a member abducted by the Viet Cong died from torture. Tan Sanut aerodrome has had its share of satchel charges, and desperate commando raids by members of the Viet Cong have been launched against strategic in-stallations in Saigon. The Viet Cong commandoes are just as brave as any of the Allied soldiers who fought behind the enemy lines in the Second World War.

But in war there are always the routine jobs which have to be carried out, not only at the base but also in the front line. Examples are the routine patrols by day and night on the rivers to check the contents of sanpans and barges; to stop, search, and if necessary arrest the crews. In the Mekong Delta there are thousands of miles of navigable waterways and it would not be possible to patrol every stretch. The main river can be navigated right through Viet Nam into Cambodia. It is regarded as an international waterway, and free navigation by international vessels must be allowed and may in no way be impeded or restricted under international law. Such vessels, however, while they may pass and repass along the course of the river and carry any cargo they choose, can only do this provided that they do not unload or try to tranship part or all of their cargo in Viet Nam. If they attempt to do this, the river patrol have certain powers of action. No shipping company of any standing would consider this risk worthwhile for contraband goods. And in any case, once they have sailed up the river to a point beyond the Cambodian border they are no longer within the jurisdiction of the patrols. They can then discharge their cargo in so-called neutral Cambodia, from whence it can be transported by land over the Cambodian border into Viet Nam at a convenient point.

A typical evening for a river patrol would start in the mess room, which in the case of the particular unit I have in mind was a two-storey brick building reputed to have been used as a house of pleasure for the French Foreign Legionnaires. It was now utilised as a mess room where American style food was dished out by the master cook and served by local Vietnamese girls. The very presence of these local girls, who probably understood more of the English language than they would admit, represented a breach in the security that might have attached to the routes to be taken by patrols. This was a combined mess for officers and other ranks, the only division being that the officers had a separate table reserved for their use. Five o'clock seemed very early for dinner, but the patrol commander to whom I had been introduced told me that the weather would be cold and that we were not expected back before sunrise on the following morning, so I would be well advised to eat some food while I had the opportunity. For the crew, it might be the last meal they would have in the land of the living.

The town itself had a sad air, the buildings standing up like ghosts; elegant French colonial buildings, parched for a coat of white paint, the plaster and stucco peeling from their walls. The patrol, which consisted of two boats, set out from a small wooden jetty and it was not until the boats had reached the centre of the river that the beauty of the small jetty became apparent. Stuck up on stilts in the river it had been an exclusive yacht club and one could well imagine luxury yachts, owned by French colons or rich Vietnamese merchants, lying there. The club house itself had been a place for gay parties to be attended by women dressed in the latest Paris fashions; now it is a building falling into decay from which patrol boats come and go whilst carrying out their duty.

No sooner had we got into the main stream than the size of our little craft became apparent; we were dwarfed by a vast international boat flying a South American flag. The skipper of our boat pointed out to me how annoying it was for these international vessels to remain immune from search, so long as they did not attempt to discharge their cargoes. He and his men were restricted to searching the small sanpans and were obliged to allow these international vessels to pass by unsearched. Yet all our crew knew these ships might be loaded with arms and ammunition.

The long hours of patrol were not unpleasant for the visitor, but for those members of the crew who were obliged to do it day after day, night after night, in eight hour shifts, it was one of the more monotonous tasks of modern warfare, requiring careful scrutiny both of the banks on each side and of any small vessels afloat. The patrol boat itself afforded no protection whatsoever against even small arms fire and it was essential that the point from which enemy fire came should be located immediately if retaliation was to be effective. The enemy Viet Cong had mastered the art of covering their fire points, and when we were fired on it was impossible to see where the fire was coming from. All that was possible was to fire in the general direction from which it appeared the attack was being launched. After the exchange of fire the patrol commander explained that recently the Viet Cong had started to fire through coconut matting, probably on pre-arranged lines of fire, and that use of coconut matting hid the muzzle flash. Fortunately neither of the boats nor any of the crew was hit on this occasion. Since the patrols had become regular, Viet Cong activity had declined. Previously the small sanpans had had unlimited scope for moving arms and ammunition from point to point along the river, but of course, if the patrols were ever to let up, Viet Cong activity would soon be increased. The imposition of a curfew at night made the work of the patrol much easier. Anything which moved at night, other than an international vessel, had to be regarded as suspect. Even if it contained no contraband goods when it was actually stopped its crew could be detained and handed over to the police. In all probability it had discharged its cargo, or might even have dropped it overboard as soon as it had sighted one of the patrol boats. All patrol boats are equipped with powerful searchlights capable of picking up any vessel, whether on the river or tied up to the bank. In spite of all this the river patrols, some of which are operated by the Vietnamese Navy, can only control a small proportion of the inland waterways.

Air Operations

The bombers which are allocated targets in North Viet Nam fly not only from Viet Nam, but also from bases in Thailand. Newsmen are not normally allowed to accompany these flights without the express permission of the U.S. Government, but any other air operations are open to members of the international Press.

One such operation consists of the routine air patrol over the Saigon area. The city and the surrounding area are not immune from Viet Cong attack, and throughout the day and night in shifts of eight hours' duration old-fashioned Dakotas fly over the city and the surrounding areas, keeping in constant radio touch with base. Should a target present itself, base passes the location of that target and the plane goes into the attack with its machine guns blazing, discharging something in the neighbourhood of six thousand rounds a minute. These

Dakotas fly at a very low speed, and during our night patrol the pilot allowed me to fly the plane for more than an hour. It was as steady as a large motor car on an open motorway and had about the same range of speed and was equally easy to drive.

As this particular flight was conducted at night it was essential that the targets should be illuminated. Two men standing on the edge of the open side of the plan threw out the flares and, as they left the aeroplane, pulled a string releasing the parachute, thus allowing the flares to glide gently in the wind and provide a perfect illumination of the ground target for a short period of time. The pilot then got on target and fired the guns, which discharged their lethal dose out of the side of the Dakota. The flares were passed down the Dakota in a chain-gang style from their storage space forward. Interpreters and passengers made up the chain-gang. Suddenly the whole sky was illuminated as though a giant firework had been set off or a miniature *aurora borealis* had appeared.

The news soon came over the radio and the pilot explained that a fire had taken place in the napalm dump situated just outside Saigon. It turned out that a satchel charge had destroyed nearly half the entire stock of napalm located in the Saigon area. Personally I can't say I was sorry, as I have always regarded flame throwers as one of the most loathsome forms of warfare—one which should have been outlawed at the same time as poison gas. The enemy had once again penetrated the perimeter of the defences which surrounded this important stock of napalm, showing that no place was exempt from attack by Viet Cong guerrillas. Only recently the Viet Cong had actually moved mortars up to within a short distance of Tan Sanut airport and had fired on, and damaged, American aircraft. These aerial patrols give a good view of any enemy activity, and at the same time ground forces in the Saigon area can call upon them to assist in their operations. Should an aircraft be called upon to perform a specific task which is calculated to take some time, a second aircraft is immediately put in the air so that the process of routine patrol can be continued without interruption. Assistance from aircraft suffers the same disadvantage as any other form of aerial support. If there is a battle between Allied forces and Viet Cong units fighting at close quarters there is always the danger that, if air support is called upon, it may cause casualties among Allied troops. This is a risk which has to be assessed by the military commander on the ground. It is particularly hard in close country where it is difficult to pinpoint areas accurately, and the Viet Cong have been known to listen in on their own radio nets to Allied messages and confuse the issue by setting off their own flares.

Enemy materials which have been captured show that the Viet Cong are in possession not only of modern weapons but are also, in some cases, equipped with modern radio communication. Some units, like the Koreans, make a point of having an exhibition stand of captured enemy equipment.

Military Operations

A glance at the accompanying map shows that South Viet Nam has been divided for the convenience of military organisation into four Corps Areas. This division corresponds very roughly with the four civil regions of administration. The Corps Areas are commanded by a Vietnamese Corps Commander, who is responsible for political control and military operations. He is subordinate to the Minister of Defence for Viet Nam.

In addition to this, there are certain autonomous cities such as Saigon, which has a Council of 30 members and a Mayor.

Within the Corps Areas, or the Regions, there is a civil administration which consists of the Province Chiefs, whose chain of command runs through district and village to hamlet level. The Province Chief has two duties. He is responsible for law and order within the province and is also the Commander of a military sector.

Within the Corps Areas the divisional areas of responsibility correspond geographically with the provinces so that

VIET NAM:
WAR ZONES

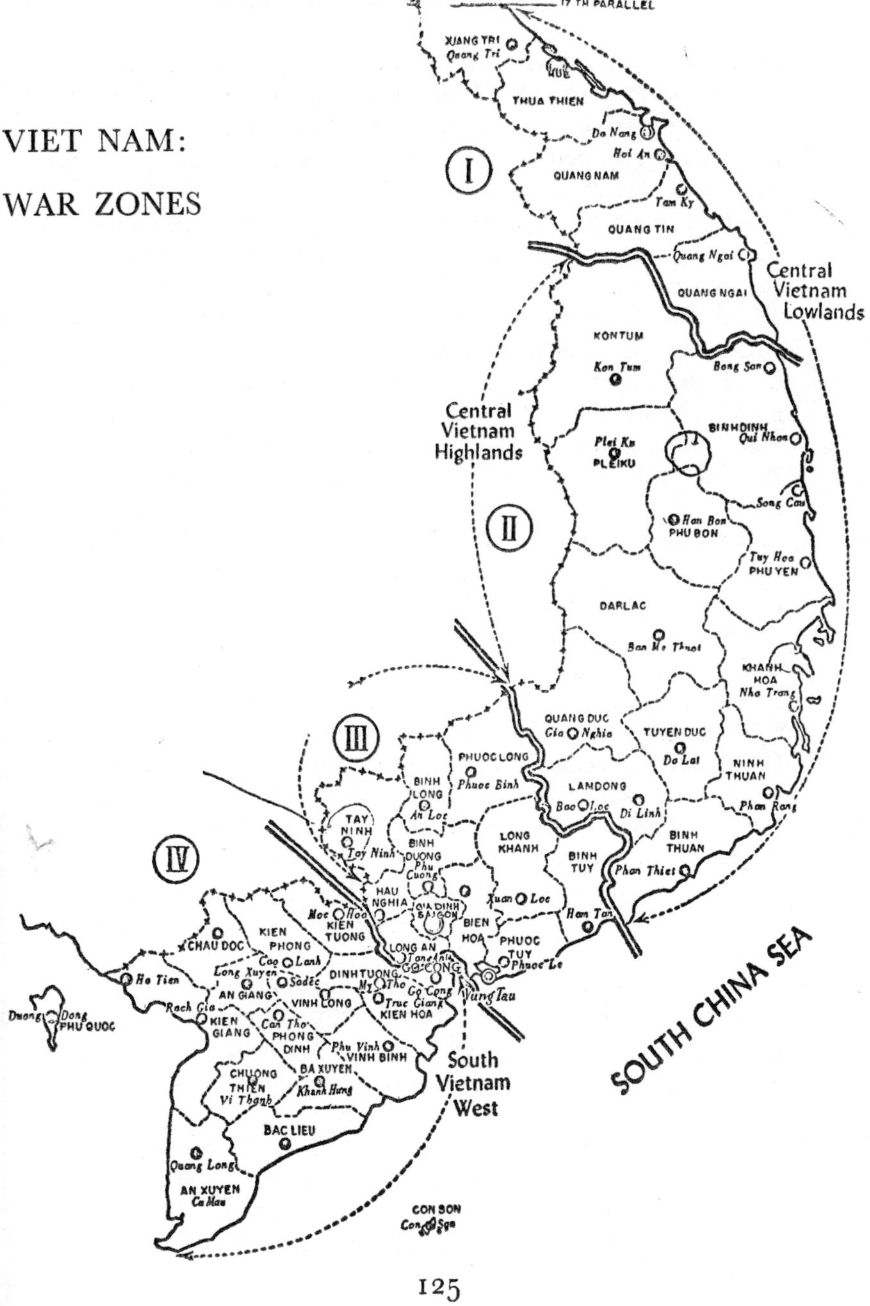

the Province Chief has a direct liaison with the local Divisional Commander. He has the Civil Police under his authority and a Popular Force of local militia in the villages and hamlets. He also has a regional force under his command which he can deploy as and when required.

There is close co-operation between the Province Chief and the Divisional Commander. If, for example, an operation is in progress, the Divisional Commander may require part or all of the Province Chief's regional force. Equally, if the Province Chief has a sudden flare-up in an area, he can call upon the Divisional Commander for help. There must be close liaison between this quasi-military set-up of civil administration and the local military commander. Almost all of the Province Chiefs are members of the armed forces. So also are the District Commanders. Although the provinces have had elected advisory Councils since May 1965 the Province Chief has an over-riding authority, essential if he is to take command in a crisis.

The four Corps come under the Vietnamese Minister of Defence, and the exact link between him and General Westmoreland is not clearly defined. General Westmoreland is Commander-in-Chief of all American forces operating, and is Commander-in-Chief of the Free World forces. Thus his relationship with the Commander-in-Chief of the Republic of Korea's Army, or with the Australian Task Force, is complicated. A simple analysis would be to say that the internal administration and discipline of units other than American, i.e. Korean or Australian, is the responsibility of the National Commander.

The chain of command is further complicated by the fact that all the aerial and most of the artillery support is supplied by the Americans, as indeed is the transport. Thus, an operation which requires the use of helicopters, for the transport either of men or materials, has to rely on the Americans.

One of the results of this complicated chain of command is that each nation has a particular way in which it fights a battle. Once a task has been allotted to a unit it is up to them to carry out that task in the way they believe to be best.

THE WAR IN VIET NAM

The Korean Army has three divisions operating in different areas. From South and North they have the Tiger Division, the White Horse Division and the Marine Division; 45,000 troops; a number rising steadily and with a possible ceiling of perhaps 60,000.

The chain of command between the Americans and the R.O.K. (Republic of Korea) forces is that the R.O.K. forces are given a task to carry out, and it is up to the R.O.K. forces Commander to decide in detail how that task is to be carried out. There is a slight difference in the internal chain of command in that the R.O.K. Field Headquarters gives a task to the R.O.K. Division as a general instruction. Then, for some reason, the detailed orders given to the Divisional Commander have to be countersigned by the R.O.K. Field Headquarters. They may be amended, altered or merely countersigned.

This is very different from the British Army, where once the Commanding General has been given an order it is up to him and his staff to transmit these orders as an operational instruction to the troops involved. A British General takes complete responsibility for the conduct of operations and does not normally have his orders countersigned by a higher authority. This higher authority of approval of orders is something which is special to the R.O.K. forces.

This does not mean to say that the R.O.K. forces are independent. Far from it, because they have not sufficient helicopters for transportation, nor have they artillery and air support. So any operation that is launched requires that the Americans should allocate sufficient transport and air and artillery support. Once again, an operation requires close liaison between the Americans and the R.O.K. forces. Sometimes the allocation of helicopters, etc., may be a difficult problem for the Americans, for it may well be that they themselves require them in other parts of the country. In general, the allocation of fire power and transport to the R.O.K. forces works reasonably well, and this is another example of how various nations can work together in a campaign.

General Westmoreland commands the various American

field forces which operate in the Corps Areas. To make it more complicated, there is a I Field Force, II Field Force, and III Marine Amphibious Force. The III M.A.F. is operating in the first Corps Area, the I Field Force in the second Corps Area, and the II Field Force in the third Corps Area. There are virtually no American forces in the fourth Corps Area to date.

Considering the complexity of command and the numbers of nations fighting, it is surprising that such a high degree of co-operation exists.

An illustration of the close measure of co-operation prevailing is a practical incident which occurred in the Australian area of command. Here a particularly efficient Province Chief had at his disposal some regular units of the South Viet Nam Army. The Viet Cong had decided to launch a surprise attack on the Australian positions, by a quick march through a clear, undefended area. The Province Chief, who was an extremely efficient officer, had independent reports of the advance. He immediately took command, as Province Chief, of all the Vietnamese forces at his disposal, and achieved a spectacular victory against the Viet Cong, who would undoubtedly have inflicted severe casualties on the Australians.

The Australians were originally attached to an American formation but felt that they would prefer to be given not only an actual task, but a clearly defined area of operations. Once again, this is a tribute to the degree of co-operation between the Americans and the other fighting forces. The Americans responded by giving them Phuoc Tuy Province.

This Province had been entirely Viet Cong dominated for the ten years before the Americans arrived, in July 1966. In a way it is ideal for operations as far as the Viet Cong are concerned. Most of the villages are on the coast, and behind them lies an area of hills and unpopulated jungle. The Viet Cong strongholds are in this hill and jungle area, but their weak point is supplies, as these have to come from the coastal villages.

Brigadier Graham, apart from a charming personality, has a realistic approach to war, particularly to the tactics which

1. The Author on patrol in an American personnel carrier

2. The Author with American Advisers to A.R.V.N.

3. Hidden tunnel

4. The Author's first patrol with the Americans

5. The Author lunching with officers of the White Horse Division

6. Cambodian Border: Viet Cong Escape Route

7. Australian soldier playing with Vietnamese crippled child

8. Vietnamese soldier with his family

9. Korean soldiers help with the harvest

10. Premier Ky handing out Land Certificates

were used by the French in the Algerian campaign. Here the French erected a wire and mined barrier along the whole length of the Algerian-Tunisian frontier. This, together with good intelligence on the Algerian side of the frontier, rendered it almost impossible for the regular F.L.N. troops stationed in Tunisia to reinforce their brothers in Algeria. For even if they did penetrate the fence on occasions, intelligence reports gave away their movements and they were captured by the French. The fence was electrified (and the writer nearly got killed on it when, whilst he was attached to the French Foreign Legion, his jeep skidded in the early hours of the morning, when under fire). Brigadier Graham has got his force to erect just such a fence, the object being to cut off the Viet Cong supply lines from the villages.

Recently, Operation Portsea was launched against a Viet Cong stronghold at Xuyen Moe and here units of the American Air Cavalry supported the Australians. Almost a year's food and large supplies of armaments were captured.

Within their area the Australians have developed an excellent technique when a village has been pacified. Quite rightly, they hand over to Vietnamese administration, but they will not tolerate maladministration by the Vietnamese and insist on retaining some measure of control over the administration of the pacified villages. This is difficult because they cannot interfere with the day to day administration without it becoming apparent that it is the Australians who rule the area and not the Vietnamese. They are endeavouring to get the right type of arrangement, which should be an example for other units and forces operating in Viet Nam, as to how to handle Vietnamese administration in the pacified areas.

The Australians treat the Vietnamese in their area in the British way of "fair play", but there is one snag which they can never overcome, and that is the intrinsic suspicion with which the Vietnamese regard all Europeans. The Australians have put their finger on the most difficult of problems, which is how to ensure that American aid is channelled through Vietnamese sources but is not appropriated before it is given to the villages, and, secondly, how to judge what degree of interference is necessary to steer Vietnamese village administration along honest lines, i.e., to encourage the really good Vietnamese administrators, but not hesitate to censure the black sheep who are always present in any community in the world.

Here again the legacy remaining from a background of occupation by the Japanese is one of bribery and corruption. When a nation is occupied and under the heel of a cruel ruler, corruption and bribery follow naturally, and in cases where it operated against the interests of the Japanese the participants were classified as patriotic. To destroy such legacies takes time; nor should one forget that the standard of public administration in Viet Nam cannot possibly be compared with that prevailing in Europe. Their history has allowed the Vietnamese little chance of developing their own administration; it is easy to criticise, but sometimes it would be wiser to reflect on the difficulties of setting up a new civil administration overnight, and guiding the administrators in the difficult task which has befallen them.

The necessity for close co-operation between military and civil forces, of which the above is an illustration, is the reason why some members of the Vietnamese military junta feel that Province Chiefs must have the power of command in their areas, so as to be able to deal with any serious situation as and when it should arise.

The members of the military junta holding this view have suggested that whilst the country is still at war, a democratic government is unsuitable. There is substance in this argument, but the disadvantages outweigh the advantages in that it is essential that the process of instituting a democratic government in South Viet Nam should not be delayed. There is no reason why the Province Chiefs should not exercise military command when the necessity arises, and provision could easily be made for their powers to over-ride the civil rights in an emergency. This would leave the civil administration the task of carrying out the day to day work in their villages and hamlets, leaving the Province Chief free to act in an emergency.

THE WAR IN VIET NAM

Summary of the Military Operations

It is impossible to isolate the military campaign from the political situation because no victory will be achieved without a combination of these two factors. From a purely military standpoint the ultimate defeat of the Viet Cong forces in South Viet Nam will depend on:

1. Killing or capturing a high proportion of their forces.
2. Cutting off their sources of food supplies.
3. Stopping Viet Cong reinforcements by local recruitment.
4. Preventing reinforcements of men and war materials from North Viet Nam reaching Viet Cong Units situated in South Viet Nam.

The success of each one of these is dependent on the internal political situation and the degree of co-operation which can be obtained from the population of South Viet Nam.

The Viet Cong forces must be located before they can be killed, and the only satisfactory way of doing this is by means of information obtained from friendly villagers. To cut off major food supplies the main roads have to be controlled by the military, but the job cannot be done properly unless the villagers themselves cease to co-operate with the Viet Cong by refusing to give or sell to them or their agents the necessary food supplies. Infiltration by North Viet Nam soldiers carrying arms and essential medical supplies will not be stopped by bombing North Viet Nam. The Ho Chi Minh trail along which the bulk of these supplies is moved is in neutral territory, but even if it could be bombed the bombing would be ineffective, as movement along it could take place at night. The only effective way of stopping this flow is to do so after it reaches South Viet Nam. This requires the operation of an efficient system of identity cards to control all movement, and the co-operation of the villagers so that any North Viet Nam infiltrators are handed over to the police.

Of all these factors the most important is food supply, without which the Viet Cong could not live nor reinforcements be fed. Unlike arms and ammunition, rice is a bulky commodity which except for short hauls must be carried by road transport.

Ode to the White Horsemen

> Here they are, the invincible men,
> The White Horse Hill Heroes,
> With the banner of the vanguard of justice.
> When the White Horsemen march out,
> Justice is for you.
> When the White Horsemen march out,
> Peace is for you.
>
> Here they are, the ever-winning warriors,
> The White Horse Hill Heroes,
> With the banner of crusaders.
> When the White Horsemen march out,
> Justice is for you.
> When the White Horsemen march out,
> Peace is for you.
>
> *Song of the 9th ROK Inf. Div.*

The attack on the Korean Marine Division by the Viet Cong took place in 1967 during the State Visit of the Korean Prime Minister to South Viet Nam and occurred on the day before the Prime Minister was due to pay a ceremonial visit to the Division.

This was an unusual battle in that it was rare for the Viet Cong to launch a full scale attack and thereby commit their forces directly against the enemy. The Viet Cong actually entered the Koreans' defence perimeter, so that the battle which ensued was to a large extent hand to hand fighting. This is the type of fighting to which the Koreans are particularly adapted, both by training and mentality.

News of the attack flashed through the compound with great rapidity, and within seconds the Korean Marines were ready for counter-action. A long and bloody, hand-to-hand struggle went on throughout the night. The Viet Cong had been engaged so rapidly that their hit-and-run tactics could not be employed and they were compelled to fight hand-to-hand or, to put it more accurately, to fight a difficult rearguard action aimed at extricating themselves with the minimum number of casualties. They had probably overestimated the value of a surprise attack and underestimated the ability of the Korean forces to mobilise in strength at very short notice and launch a counter-attack almost immediately.

This particular type of battle is a rarity in South Viet Nam, and if more battles of this nature took place, in which the enemy launched their forces in major operations, the war in South Viet Nam might be over very quickly.

A more typical sort of war is being fought on a daily basis by the Koreans, for example the White Horse Division, which is in fact the 9th Republic of Korea Army Infantry Division. This Division was raised on October 25th, 1950, immediately after the outbreak of the Korean War, and was involved in many operations from 1950 onwards. In 1951 it resumed the defence line at the White Horse Hill in Central Korea; it was here that the Division fought the Communist Chinese 38th Division and, in the fifteen ensuing battles, killed over 13,000 of them.

After a period of retraining, on June 1st 1966 it was transported to Viet Nam, and by October 1966 the entire Division was in a position to launch offensive operations against the Viet Cong. In the few months in which the Division has been in place and operating on National Route I, between Cam Lan and Tuy Hoa, it has succeeded in clearing nearly 3,000 square kilometres of previously Viet Cong dominated territory.

It is surprising to many outsiders that the Division has been able to achieve this with very little bloodshed and, at the same time, has built up a very friendly relationship between themselves and the local Viet Nam villagers.

The value of Route I is not so much the use to which it can

be put by the Allied Forces, who have an alternative supply route by air; its importance lies in the denial of its use by the Viet Cong to supply their guerrilla forces with essential food. In addition to this, the psychological effect of permitting civilian transport to move freely between the villages is of great importance. Whilst a single vehicle could never previously be guaranteed security even in the hours of daylight, the degree of security now provided is sufficient to allow a reasonable amount of free movement on this road.

In their area of responsibility the Koreans launched operations against enemy-held concentrations. In Operation Horse Head, the Regiment attacked Nui Ho Mon, 8 kilometres south of Tuy Hoa. In this area the Viet Cong had been rampaging over the mountain-side and had regarded themselves as being in occupation of an impregnable area. White Horse Division was not daunted by this legend. It surrounded the area and, by February 7th, had killed 153 Viet Cong and captured 144 small arms, 119 grenades and 20,000 cartridges.

During these activities it discovered in the Kyho Valley an army repair workshop beside a waterfall. It was estimated that one rifle a day could be produced from the repair shop by a small team of eighteen Viet Cong.

The Division's results up to 16th February, 1967, are as follows: 753 enemy killed, 161 captured, 466 suspects, 377 returnees, 782 small arms, 5 AR, 31 LMG, 3 57mm RR, 1 81mm mortar, 1 M79 grenade launcher, 134,247 cartridges, 188 live shells, 533 grenades, 281 sacks of rice, 13,247 different documents and 13,809 other articles captured.

The psychological effect of these rapid operations and high casualty rate was twofold. First, the villagers were convinced that the grip in which the Viet Cong had held them for many years was beginning to break. Many of these villagers had believed that nothing could smash this vice-like hold which the Viet Cong had consistently exerted over them. The second effect was on the morale of the Viet Cong, who had hitherto believed themselves to be invincible in this area. Having by their reign of terror lost any respect which they had built up, the Viet Cong morale within its own forces had been reduced.

How were the Viet Cong to endeavour to re-establish themselves except by a major offensive in an area where their forces were still intact? The operations carried out by the Koreans had been so successful that the Viet Cong deemed it necessary to engage in a major military confrontation in order to re-assert their authority, and the attack on the Rock Marine Division was probably motivated by this.

The White Horse Division was in the process of carrying out an operation on a number of small villages situated within a radius of 5 kilometres and with a hilly, wooded area in the neighbourhood—the sort of jungle through which it would be impossible to pass except by hacking one's way foot by foot through dense undergrowth.

The Korean battleplan was simple. They gave the enemy very little warning. On D-1, they assembled at an area some distance from the operation. The operation began at 0400 hours on D-Day with a short bombardment. By 0600 hours, troops were already in location and by 1100 hours on that day, by using 50 helicopters each capable of carrying 9 men, the entire force was in position at the base of the hill.

The actual number of troops involved was four battalions of the 9th Division supported by 2 Batteries, one American and one Korean, both 105 millimetres. The area involved was 8,000 square metres. Two battalions formed a block round the wood to prevent the enemy escaping, while a further two battalions moved inwards, driving the enemy like beaters towards the infantrymen and the two static battalions. The battle lasted several days and resulted in the complete annihilation of all the Viet Cong forces in the area.

What was interesting to see was the reaction in the villages towards the Korean attack—dumb, silent, hostile, anxious—a real Viet Cong dominated village—dehydrated of any juice of freedom, sceptical of any army that was prepared to fight in what they had regarded as impenetrable jungle.

Whoever and whatever people are, they have human feelings and these villagers were no exception. The sudden bombardment, the sound in the night of the Korean troops moving to battle with lust for victory—these strong, tough men—would they murder, would they kill the villagers' brothers, uncles and cousins who were members of the Viet Cong organisation hiding in that little jungle? They could not see the course of the battle because the jungle was too thick. All they could hear was the sound of the shots ringing out. Each time they heard the bullets they could well imagine that it might be some of their relations whose bodies were being penetrated by those bullets.

In a village like this, whose spirit had been broken completely by the Viet Cong, which had been disciplined to ask no questions, pay their taxes to the Viet Cong and supply them with food or anything that the Viet Cong demanded, it is not surprising that there was no one left in that village who dared to speak out against the Viet Cong, whether they liked them or not.

After years of domination by the Viet Cong, it is going to take a long time before these villages are converted to a new way of life. Kindness by the troops, help with threshing and the building of houses will not be the passport to success, for the Viet Cong have made many promises with regard to land tenure. In many cases, the land has already been parcelled up and pseudo land certificates, purporting to give land to peasant families, issued by the Communists.

The whole pacification programme will collapse unless these families are given the land in pursuance of Premier Ky's declared policy. It would be fatal if the land were to be returned to the landlords, whether they be the Catholic Church, the French landowners or absentee Vietnamese. Why should the peasants go through all this just so that the clock can be put back and they be again dominated by absentee landlords demanding their pound of flesh? Would they not be better off, in their own estimation, serving the Viet Cong, believing their land to be their own and paying their taxes to the local guerrillas?

The sheer audacity, battle-worthiness and efficiency of the Koreans combined with the complete defeat of these local Viet Cong guerrillas was sufficient to destroy the hold which the Viet Cong had hitherto had over these villagers. The Koreans are Asiatics; they understand the feelings of these people and they have made it quite clear that they are not there as conquerors to replace the French or Viet Cong, but there to liberate fellow-Asiatics who are suffering the same fate as they themselves suffered in Korea.

The bloodbath of battle over, the Koreans do not just vanish. Instead, they fire their second barrel—civic action. Armed with their interpreters they go into the villages and try to get the people to understand that, in the first place, the sheer strength of the Allies, and secondly their determination, will result in the eventual elimination of the Viet Cong forces: that the Viet Cong is not unbeatable.

Then they go on to show that in practical ways they have every intention of encouraging village life and helping in the day to day tasks to rebuild these villages and to make good the damage which has been done by so many years of hostilities.

This is not just a psychological war of talk, parley and nothing else, but a practical demonstration of what it means to be free from the Viet Cong. The Korean soldiers help the villagers in their financial and family problems, call on the households of the Viet Cong and explain to the families the futility of their husbands carrying on the struggle.

Those of the Viet Cong whom they have captured and who want to return to their families are given free conduct passes through the Korean lines to enable them to return to their families.

Korean medical standards are not very high, and of course they are short of doctors, male nurses and orderlies, but they give the Vietnamese treatment equivalent to that of their own soldiers and they set up village dispensaries manned by their own military medical personnel.

In order to show their feeling towards the local people they give parties for the children and the older folk are also entertained. Even more practical examples of their goodwill towards the local people are provided by gifts of food and clothing to the poor. Where labour has been short, the Korean soldiers are the first to go into the villages and help rebuild the houses and go into the fields and assist with the harvest. The building of orphanages, the repair and construction of bridges, gifts and loans of farm machinery are all part of a practical demonstration of help to the Vietnamese people. Quite a few of the Korean officers are learning Vietnamese so as not to have to rely on Vietnamese interpreters.

During his tour of Viet Nam, the Prime Minister of Korea visited the new school in the Tiger Division area. (I was the only European war correspondent invited to join his party.) Most of the buildings had been constructed by the engineer battalion of the Tiger Division and had been made as a gift to the Viet Nam Government. This particular school housed no less than 1,700 pupils. It provided a high school education for boys, and some of the pupils were still living in areas dominated by the Viet Cong. The Prime Minister summed up the whole of the attitude of the Koreans to this War—"*We are fighting not only with our soldiers' lives, but also with their all-out efforts to help the people in their task to build a new life in Viet Nam*".

It has been said that Koreans are cruel and tough on the villages. Certainly they do not permit any outbreaks of pro-Viet Cong sympathies once a village has been pacified. Why should they, for they have guaranteed the people security from the Viet Cong and it is part of their bargain to stamp out any attempt by the Viet Cong to re-assert their influence in such villages.

Apart from their attacks on known Viet Cong military strongholds, they have also had to deal with the villages where there are Viet Cong present, and in these cases they have developed a novel technique of conquest, without unnecessary killing. They surround the village completely and give it warning that they are present, but will allow any non-Viet Cong villagers to leave the village and go without hindrance to a temporary camp. Thus the first villagers come forward and are taken to a centre where they are fed and looked after, and when, after a period of possibly days, the ultimatum has expired, all that are left in the village are the die-hard Viet Cong. It is at this point that operations start. The Koreans move in to destroy the Viet Cong, but even at this point, they give them a further series of warnings and if they give themselves up with their arms they are treated as Chieu Hoi.

The hardened Viet Cong may either try to get out of the military line by declaring themselves Chieu Hoi, or they may stay and fight it out. If they do stay to fight it out, then as a last resort the Koreans move in and clear them up. They carry out a complete search of all the underground stores, and the usual result is the capture of a large amount of enemy weapons and material.

Army of the Republic of Viet Nam (A.R.V.N.)

The Vietnamese Army numbers three quarters of a million. This figure includes all local and popular forces and every Vietnamese in the country who is actually under arms.

The four Corps Areas come under the Minister of Defence and the Vietnamese are responsible for administration within the areas. The Fourth Corps Area is the only one in which there are no other troops besides Vietnamese. Here the Viet Nam Corps Commander in the fourth Corps Area controls military operations, subject of course to the necessity of employing air and artillery and transport from American sources. Thus, if an air strike is required for an operation, or aircraft are needed to transport troops to the scene of the operation, American aircraft have to be employed.

In the other Corps Areas there is close liaison between the Vietnamese Corps Commander and the Task Forces operating in the Corps Area. The language problem has been overcome by having American advisers attached to the Vietnamese formations. These officers do not normally advise on military tactics except possibly in the senior echelons but are available for general advice about such matters as fire power, weapons, the time required before an air strike can be called down, and similar technical matters. Their great value is that they have their own wireless network and can therefore be in contact with the Vietnamese with whom they are serving as well as with their own chain of American communications.

These staff advisers go right up to Corps level. Thus, if it is decided either before or after an operation that an air strike is required, or artillery barrage is necessary, they can pass on to the American force concerned the details of what is actually required.

The American advisory teams consist of officers and N.C.O.s, and they do a very valuable job of work. Each has the advantage of being a small independent unit command. Their work may be with a battalion or regiment, but the great disadvantage is that they are lonely commands, especially for the non-commissioned officers. A typical team might consist of two American officers, an American N.C.O., a Vietnamese interpreter and perhaps one Vietnamese who acts as cook, batman, etc.

Not many of the teams are in the happy position of being able to speak Vietnamese, but many of them volunteer, possibly because the command is independent and responsible and they are dealing with high level Vietnamese officers of experience. In many cases those who apply for this particular type of job usually like the Vietnamese people. It has its disadvantages, not only by reason of loneliness but also because at night movement by road is very restricted and in some cases quite impossible. Villages to which one can travel in the day time would be death traps at night.

It could be that a particular route or village is used frequently without any unfortunate results. But on the 99th day an ambush could be laid and the officer and his companion be killed or wounded. No one in the village would be prepared to give information about the attacker, who would probably have disappeared from the scene by the time help had been called for.

The top echelons of the Vietnamese Army have officers of high calibre. Many of them have been trained in French military establishments, have excellent military knowledge, good standards of discipline and a sense of patriotism and dedication to the task ahead. Quite a high proportion of them, in fact, come from North Viet Nam, where they have left members of their family and have had to abandon their property in that region.

THE WAR IN VIET NAM

The Vietnamese Army has expanded rapidly, and whilst the officers in the higher command would compare favourably with those of any other nation, yet there is a gap both in the young officers and N.C.O.s this is only to be expected when one realises the speed with which this army has had to expand, and also that education in Viet Nam is excellent up to the primary stage but has thereafter a gap which will not be filled for many years to come.

The quality of the army and its equipment has steadily improved under American guidance and there is no reason to suppose that it will not go on advancing in the future.

General Westmoreland said in his address to Congress on 29th April 1967, that in 1965 the Republic of Viet Nam had had fewer than thirty "combat ready" battalions, and that that figure had risen to 154 in the intervening two years. He also drew a parallel to Korea in 1952. At that time there were many who doubted the ability of the Republic of Korea to produce a first class fighting force, and yet today the Korean units in Viet Nam have proved to be not only the best fighters, but the most effective in civic action. "When I hear criticism of the Vietnamese armed forces, I am reminded of that example," he said.

In an effort to make a surprise attack, the Vietnamese adopted a novel procedure. Security to them is always a difficult problem because the language permits the villagers to be more closely in touch with the Vietnamese troops than with any other units fighting in Viet Nam. What is often forgotten is that many of the Vietnamese soldiers have their wives with them and, even if the troops are moved, often this retinue of married families follow the soldiers, rather like camp-followers. It is not surprising, therefore, that information regarding impending attacks is liable to leak out. This is no criticism of the individual soldier for talking too much, but clearly if he gets himself ready for a battle it is inconceivable that some of the married families should not realise that there was an impending operation. Knowing the rough location of the Vietnamese units and the disposition of the Viet Cong within striking distance, the enemy, by a simple combination of these two facts, can get a fairly shrewd idea as to the date and time when the A.R.V.N. forces are likely to launch their attack. This gives the Viet Cong a chance of dispersal from their area before the attack is launched. This leakage of information is an important factor, for it removes the element of surprise which is so vital for the success of these operations and, in the case of the Australians, they have gone so far as to suffer considerable discomfort in their daily lives by dispensing with the services of Vietnamese to carry out the daily chores which require to be done in any camp.

The troops of the 5th A.R.V.N. Division wanted to achieve an element of surprise. That there was an impending operation could hardly be concealed, and D-Day must have been already known by the local inhabitants. The Corps Commander, who was a highly educated officer whose training had been carried out in the French army and who had been a student at a French Military Academy, decided that he would endeavour to try a trick to put the enemy off their guard and deceive them as to the exact time when the attack would be launched. He came down the previous day; the troops of the Division were assembled for a G.O.C.'s inspection, and a large party followed. The local girls were brought in to dance and amuse the troops and the whole atmosphere was of gaiety. The idea was that the Viet Cong would think it most unlikely that after a celebration of this nature an attack would be launched the following day.

The Corps Commander then ordered that D-Day should be advanced 24 hours and that the men should go almost straight from the celebrations to the battle field. (Perhaps his military studies had included an account of the Duchess of Richmond's Ball prior to the Battle of Waterloo!)

The area which had been selected for attack was conveniently near to the location of the units and the battle plan was quite simple, consisting of surrounding the area which was known to contain Viet Cong units. The A.R.V.N. troops' job was to block three sides of the defined area. Two sides of the square were held by units of the 7th A.R.V.N. Infantry Regiment, and the third side by the 1st of the 18th Infantry (American). The fourth side, which was open, was left to the 1st Company of the 2nd Battalion, 34 Armoured Support Infantry, 1st of the 18th. Tactical Headquarters, commanded by Major Chuong, was to be conveniently sited and was given an armoured cavalry troop of A.R.V.N. to provide local protection for the Headquarters and also to be utilised as mobile reserve if required.

Early in the morning of the 5th of February, we heard the tanks rumbling. A cry went up from the American advisers to the A.R.V.N. "Those blank blank tanks will give away the plan." They had started up on their move forward before the infantry was in position.

Tactical Headquarters was established in a forward position by 0600 hours and information was received that by 0655 hours the Infantry were all in position. The troops had moved out early under cover of darkness and it appeared that the local villages through which the units passed were surprised.

Tactical Headquarters was set up. The American Armoured Support Infantry continued their advance with the object of flushing the enemy out and forcing them through the three-sided infantry ring which had been set up. Unit Divisional Commanders were all airborne in helicopters watching the battle, landing at different places and supervising operations. Later in the day, as the battle progressed, from the air one could see the armoured support vehicles weaving and interweaving through the thick country, firing their guns and clearing the area as they went.

By lunch time it was clear that very few Viet Cong troops had been found in the area, and the actual casualties at the end of the day proved to be very few. By 6 p.m. the operation had been called to a halt.

None of this should be interpreted in any way adversely against the A.R.V.N. forces' fighting capabilities but as a clear indication of the tremendous difficulty of security. Given the right circumstances, the A.R.V.N. troops are only too delighted to get to grips with the Viet Cong, and the brilliant occasion when a large Viet Cong force endeavoured to attack the Australian Task Force is but one illustration of their heroic deeds.

The observation post which had been used by troops to make sure that any attempt by the Viet Cong to attack the adjoining villages could be spotted immediately. But what they had failed to observe was that the Viet Cong had slipped the net, and by the time this well-planned operation had been launched, the Viet Cong had disappeared from the area.

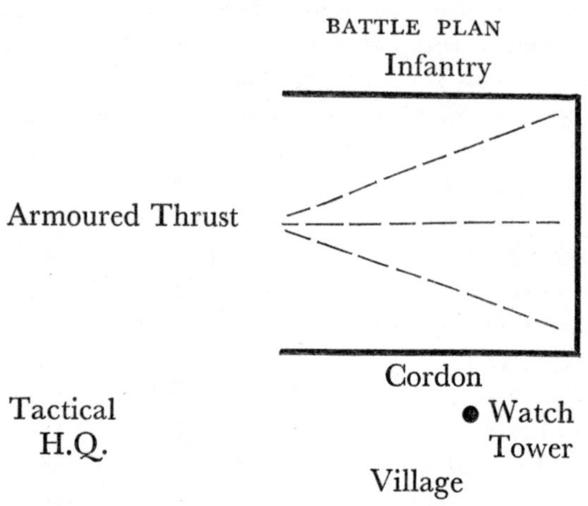

The Parachute Units of the Vietnamese Army have a very fine battle record and as soon as information has been obtained to enable the disposition of Viet Cong Units to be located the Parachute Units are only too delighted to become airborne and to drop their men in the Viet Cong infested area. From that moment on, these A.R.V.N. forces get to grips with the Viet Cong and fierce hand to hand fighting results. Some spectacular victories on operations of this nature have been achieved. In the air the Vietnamese pilots have also played their part alongside their American fellow airmen and have taken part in long range bombing attacks on targets in North Viet Nam. Premier Ky himself when he was on the active list of the Vietnamese Air Force actually led some of these successful attacks, taking part in the action himself. Ky is a born leader and does not expect his subordinates to do anything which he himself is not prepared to undertake.

The great problem which confronts the Commanders of the Vietnamese Army is the deployment of their forces, the overall strength of which is three quarters of a million. This figure takes into account not only the Units but also the Popular Forces. Once a village or Province has been pacified it is essential that the protection afforded to the inhabitants of that area should be undertaken by soldiers of the Vietnamese Army and not by Americans, Australians or Koreans. Any one of these, with the possible exception of the Koreans, smacks of colonialism and is a vivid reminder to the Vietnamese of their period of occupation by the French and the Japanese. The job of the Allied forces is to defeat the Viet Cong, and in this role the Vietnamese Army must make its contribution in order to sustain the whole concept of the war against Communism. Free World forces are in Viet Nam at the invitation of the South Vietnamese Government to help the Vietnamese people and their army to defeat Communism.

The role of the Vietnamese Army is twofold. In the first place it must take its share of the war, fighting the Viet Cong alongside its Allies. In the second place it must ensure protection of the villages after pacification. This second role is by far the more important, but can give rise to criticism of the South Vietnamese Army by the insinuation that the Allies do the fighting and that the role of South Viet Nam's armed forces in the war only occurs after the main battles have been fought and is confined to providing local protection.

This is the dilemma in which the rulers of South Viet Nam, and indeed the Commanders of the Free World Forces, find themselves. The only solution to this problem is a compromise whereby units of the South Vietnamese army continue to take their part in active anti-Viet Cong operations whilst the remainder undertake the essential tasks of protecting the inhabitants of areas which have been pacified. This is a delicate balance which requires explaining to those who attempt to denigrate the fighting capabilities of South Viet Nam's Armed Forces.

Too little publicity is given to the major actions to which South Viet Nam's Army is contributing. A good illustration of this is afforded by the description of the action taken by the Province Chiefs in the Australian theatre of operations already described.

The risks to which the members of the Popular Forces in the villages are exposed are far greater than those which soldiers face when fighting in units against the Viet Cong. Once the villages have been pacified they are left with a few men who are armed and whose duties are patrol and protection of the village or hamlet. These men are rather like Territorials in England or National Guardsmen in the United States, and are essentially part-time soldiers who perform ordinary jobs as carpenters or manual workers at all times except when they are called upon either to patrol or, if the village is attacked by Viet Cong, to put up resistance against armed attacks which may be launched by forces far superior in numbers to their own. The Viet Cong are unlikely to attack a village unless they already have a superiority of force. Members of the Popular Forces know that if the village should be overrun they will be the first victims of Viet Cong reprisals, which always assume the same pattern of murder, torture and mutilation. Far from being the second echelon in the war, they ought to be regarded as the spearhead of any defence system in the country.

The Americans

With the recent addition (1967) of troops allocated to General Westmoreland American Forces operating in Viet Nam will be over the half million figure, but only a small proportion of this number are actually taking part in the fighting as combat troops. A very high proportion are used in the various echelons of supply and transport. The American Army is equipped with every modern device for the destruction of enemy forces. Apart from nuclear weapons they have at their disposal the finest armoury that any nation possesses. This, combined with the high educational standard of the individual soldier, should make their Army one of the finest in the world.

When American soldiers go to war they expect to be

provided with a standard of comfort similar to that which they enjoy in civilian life. This in itself poses enormous problems of supply and locks up an unnecessary number of men in non-combatant duties. But the greatest difficulty which the American Army faces is its lack of experience in this type of warfare, the tactics of which bear no relation to those employed in the Western Hemisphere in the Second World War.

The final objective of war must be to destroy the enemy on the ground or to deprive him of essential supplies of men and material and force him to surrender. In a guerrilla type of warfare this means that American soldiers must come to grips with the Viet Cong, and destroy them in what amounts in many cases to hand-to-hand fighting. The Americans have yet to learn that bombs and flame throwers are not the answer in this war and that it can only be carried out successfully if the American nation and its political leaders are willing to accept the plain fact that a war of this type necessitates the acceptance of casualties, killed and wounded, among the American Forces.

In one particular operation journalists were instructed to be at Tan Sanut in order that they might be flown out to an area to witness a major battle in which American forces would play the predominant role. Pressmen and cameramen all assembled and duly arrived at the headquarters of the battle area to be briefed by the Brigade Commander. The operation itself was only part of a major thrust against what was believed to be a large concentration of enemy forces. We all listened with great respect to the detailed briefing to which we were treated. The only major questions which occupied our minds were whether the information upon which this operation was planned was accurate and whether the vast preliminary barrage by artillery and aircraft would provide the enemy with sufficient warning of the impending allied attack to enable them to slip through the cordon of troops which was deemed to be sufficient to prevent their escape. The Commander himself assured us that this was not likely to happen and that we would witness a major slaughter of Viet Cong.

This assurance boosted the morale particularly of the television men, who had brought with them heavy loads of camera equipment with which incidentally the pressmen had to give them a hand. The experienced pressman carries as little as possible, restricting himself to the essentials such as a toothbrush, razor, soap and spare pair of socks and possibly a light woollen pullover, all of which could be stowed in the deep thigh-pocket of a British battle dress.

From then on the party split up into groups of two or three, so as to fit into whatever spare seats were available in the helicopters flying supplies between base headquarters and the operational area. It was therefore a matter of luck as to which area any group of correspondents landed in. In our case we were fortunate, the distance from the helipad to the unit was a reasonably short march. The troops on the ground consisted of infantry and cavalry units, and naturally, as a cavalry officer, I made sure of attaching myself to the cavalry and immediately made contact with the young Lieutenant in command. But, as he was having trouble with the tracks of his personal tank, it seemed wise to get aboard one of the tanks which was fully mobile. Apart from looking at the map of the area it was hardly necessary to be briefed as it was clear that the armoured vehicles were to be used for close support of the infantry, whose job it was to search the area and to destroy or capture any Viet Cong. No sooner had we arrived than the units began their sweep forward to fulfil their task. This particular area consisted of a few isolated farm houses and a number of groups of mud and reed houses built around a communal well.

The infantry units advanced slowly from mound to mound and feature to feature with the armoured vehicles in constant radio touch almost on their heels. As the day wore on and the searches continued it became apparent that very few, if any, Viet Cong were left in this area, and it was clear that the search was not going to be very thorough and the troops became bored by the prospect of a fruitless routine search.

Almost all of the settlements had been badly damaged by aerial and artillery fire and were practically deserted. Routine searches of what remained of the houses included the removal of floor boards to see if there were access to underground tunnels. One particular incident brought the whole of the human aspect of this war home to the observer: a woman and three children were standing round the entrance to a tunnel, the opening of which had been carefully camouflaged but which had been discovered by one of the patrols. The woman spoke no French, nor were any of the party able to converse in Vietnamese. She simply stood there silently with her children at her side whilst the search took place. It was clear that this was the mouth of a tunnel which probably ran for miles under the ground. Other sections operating in the area also discovered openings, some of which were only just above water level in the wells, and these entrances were no more than three feet in diameter. It did not necessitate a knowledge of the Anglo-Saxon language for the woman to realise what the American soldiers were doing. They placed explosive charges in the mouths of the tunnels and pushed them along inside as far as possible, leaving only the fuses to be set off. Once the charges had been laid the units retreated to a safe distance to set off the fuses. All this time the woman with her children had been watching the process until she was told to move back with the troops to a safe place. Her face was twisted with emotion, and the question that was obviously foremost in her mind was, how far would her husband be able to get along the tunnel before the charge exploded? The very fact that her interest had centred round this particular hole, which was adjacent to her home, indicated that probably her husband had been one of the last to escape through the tunnel. This war in Viet Nam is fought in and around the homes of the Vietnamese so that the hazards of war are shared equally by the families and dependants of the soldiers. It is the same for them whether it happens to be the Allies seeking to destroy the Viet Cong or the Viet Cong wreaking their vengeance on families who have failed to support the Viet Cong. The only difference is that Allied troops, unlike the Viet Cong, do not commit atrocities against the civilian population.

After the dull thud which shook the earth, uprooted small

trees and bushes and closed the entrance to the tunnels there was little more that could be done except to feel sympathy towards the woman and her family whose only crime was that the husband was obviously a member of the Viet Cong, or he would not have taken refuge. Early on in the search it became apparent that this was going to be a slow process and that there was no advantage in riding on the tank after we had reached the point where the "search and kill" operation was to start and that one might as well join an infantry patrol. During a lull in the operations the two of us who were on this particular operation decided that we might as well have a good look round on our own in the area, but naturally we were careful not to get out of sight or range of the patrol. By pure coincidence we went down a track which had already been searched by the American soldiers and found some twenty sheets of paper folded in a bundle and lying by the side of the track. Inspection of these sheets showed that they were a set of plans exhibiting the entire layout of the underground tunnel system in the area and were drawn to scale: a set of plans which would have been a credit to a junior regimental officer.

Although the plans did not indicate the exact depths from the surface of the ground it appeared that some of the tunnels went down to something in the neighbourhood of forty feet and that as soon as the first bomb had been dropped, or artillery shell delivered, it would have been possible for the entire male population of the area to have gone into hiding. This could have been done in one of two ways: either they could have remained in this labyrinth of tunnels, which from the plans were shown to be fully ventilated, or they could have escaped through the system and out of the area which was being subjected to the search. Once the troops had passed over the area there would have been nothing to prevent the refugees from returning. Those women, children and old people who had been left behind could well give the male members of their families the all-clear signal. The plans which we discovered concerned part of the area in which this large operation was taking place. These tunnel systems were all linked up, so that even when in possession of plans like this it would not be possible to predict with any accuracy exactly what points the Viet Cong might choose as their escape routes.

As the day wore on it was quite clear that very few Viet Cong would be captured, and apart from those prisoners who had been taken by the sub-units operating with us, we discovered on return to base the remainder of the prisoners who had been captured in other areas confined within a barbed wire perimeter in a **P.O.W.** cage. That day we were extremely fortunate in being able to get on a "chopper" which was returning from the area of operation to the base camp in time to be able to attend the evening briefing conference. It was a question of "I told you so".

Commanders have been given clear instructions radiating from the Pentagon through various military channels to the effect that it is fire power which matters and that man power is to be conserved—but what had been the results in this particular day's fighting? The Americans had laid down a vast barrage in order to kill as many Viet Cong as possible before the ground troops moved in, and thus reduce the number of casualties to a minimum. As soon as the first shell had exploded and the hum of aircraft overhead was audible the Viet Cong in the area took refuge in their tunnels. The moment that they had gone underground the effect on them of shells and 500 pound bombs was negligible. The most that these might **have** achieved would have been a few casualties at the beginning, before the bulk of the enemy had managed to get into the tunnel system. As usual, they had taken with them their dead and wounded so that there should be no evidence of casualties inflicted as a result of the bombardment. Charlie had slipped through the net once again. There was no point in rubbing salt into the injured pride of the Americans, but we did have an opportunity of a quiet private talk with the Brigade Commander. If this particular operation were to achieve success it would have meant that after the search operation sufficient troops would have had to remain for a considerable time in order to prevent the Viet Cong reappearing in the area. This could mean a long wait, as the tunnel system is fully equipped with rice and water in order that the Viet Cong can remain for long periods underground.

The basic tactics of this operation would have been sound in a conventional war. A perimeter had been manned by troops of the allied nations and information had shown that in the centre of this area there were concentrations of Viet Cong. An American Brigade had been allocated the task of driving the enemy towards the northern perimeter so as to force them against troops aligned in pre-arranged positions. Where the plan failed was that this was not a conventional war, fought under conditions similar to the Second World War in the western theatre of war; it was essentially a guerrilla type war complicated by the existence of this vast ramification of tunnels. The preliminary barrage had caused few casualties among the Viet Cong forces and no damage to the tunnels. All that it had achieved was to give the Viet Cong adequate warning of an impending ground attack and dig deep into the American tax payer's pocket.

The only way to defeat the Viet Cong is to launch an attack without warning and to fight with troops on the ground. The possibility of destroying the tunnels themselves has been the subject of an investigation by the Americans, but as yet no solution has been found and no new explosive capable of destroying them completely. When American soldiers are lowered down on a belt through the mouth of these tunnels their efforts are almost always rewarded by having one or other of their limbs blown to pieces by the Viet Cong, firing at short range. Even if the American serviceman is not attacked, and is able to lay his charge in the mouth of the tunnel, the resultant explosion only damages a short section of the tunnel which can later be dug out with surprisingly little effort and restored to its original condition. The soil is of such a nature that this unbelievable ramification of deep and ventilated tunnels is capable of lasting for unlimited periods without any form of riveting or reinforcement.

Although the object of the operation, which was to destroy the Viet Cong, had not been achieved, the Americans had without realising it succeeded in breaking up Viet Cong units which intelligence reports had suggested were going to make an all out attack on the base area, which in this case was the supply area for large numbers of troops and had been built up by the Americans over a very long period by air supply. If this could have been destroyed, it could have been marked down as a significant success on the part of the Viet Cong.

The lesson remains. If they wish to defeat the Viet Cong, American troops must accept that they will have to dig out and fight the Viet Cong who except on rare occasions will not commit their force to a major all-out conventional fight.

In recent months the Americans and other Allied forces have had a better opportunity of fighting the Viet Cong at close quarters. As a result of losses which they have sustained, the Viet Cong have launched a series of direct attacks, the main object of which has been not so much to kill Allied troops as to restore confidence to their own forces by displaying the Viet Cong's ability to attack major military installations and units.

The Viet Cong are extremely good at removing their wounded and dead from the battlefield. This is part of an almost religious fervour to ensure that the dead are properly buried and the wounded adequately treated in their own hospitals, many of which are underground. At the same time it hides their real casualty figures from the Allies. There is no doubt that the medical treatment received by Viet Cong wounded is of a high level, nor is there any doubt that they make sure that the widows of those killed in combat not only get meritorious recognition, but receive some form of monetary payment for the loss of the breadwinner.

None of the shortcomings described so far can be attributed to, or should be interpreted as, a deficiency in the fighting qualities of the American Army. Rather is it an illustration of the difficulties of fighting a war against a guerrilla force which can make its escape before contact can be made. Nor is it the fault of the soldier that his superiors are reluctant to accept casualties and place so much importance on air strikes and artillery barrages as a substitute for armed combat at close quarters.

American units fighting in the Mekong Delta have suffered appalling casualties. Here the fields are laced with *pungi* stakes and mines. The uninitiated often feel that it is easier and quicker to use the paths which lie alongside the fields but invariably these are the most dangerous areas and contain a greater number of mines. They are also selected as points along which Allied forces will most probably pass, and have been accurately plotted so that fire can be brought down at selected points as and when required. Viet Cong soldiers have merely to lie in wait and pull the trigger to see their victims fall like ninepins. The adjoining fields are equally unpleasant in that they represent an ideal place for hiding those sharp bits of bamboo which until recently were capable of piercing American servicemen's boots and which, since they had been treated to an impregnation by faecal material, gave rise to gangrene. The Americans now equip their soldiers with protective boots lined either with metal or plastic, thus preventing a high proportion of casualties from this source.

During a fierce hand-to-hand battle the casualties suffered by both sides are appalling. One of the worst features is the tumbler bullet, which enters the side of its victim with a comparatively small hole but leaves the body on the other side together with most of the internal organs of the body. Its damage puts the dumdum bullet of the First World War into the shade. The Americans when under fire behave impeccably and do not panic, but proceed to carry on with the task which has been allocated to them. Their senior officers would certainly rank as equal to British, German or French counterparts, and their senior non-commissioned officers exhibit a very high example of efficiency and leadership. If there is to be any criticism it would lie with their officers of Captain and Field rank, especially in the non-combatant units where promotion has perhaps been too rapid.

One of the miracles of the war is the rapid evacuation of casualties from the front line. When out on patrol one day the American soldier next to me was badly wounded and, as soon as the firing was over and first aid had been rendered, he was taken back on an armoured personnel carrier to the Unit headquarters of the Company. The wireless operator had radioed back to Company Headquarters informing them of the nature of the casualty, and the doctor on this information had asked for a helicopter. No sooner was the casualty taken out of the armoured vehicle and a quick medical inspection made than he was aboard the helicopter, back to base and on the operating table, well within an hour of the time the original injury had taken place. The field hospital was the last word in medical achievement, and although of a temporary nature it carried every modern piece of equipment in an air-conditioned theatre such as one would expect to find in a first class city hospital. It is the rapidity with which a casualty can be transported from the forward areas, to a base hospital, which is responsible for reducing the number of fatalities. MEDIVAC in Viet Nam is one of the most efficient organisations. Hospitals in Viet Nam are not over-crowded with casualties because the Americans make sure that places are always vacant by moving certain categories of casualties to base hospitals elsewhere, such as Japan.

The patrol to which reference has just been made was an illustration of the efficient way in which the Unit operated, even though the patrol itself consisted of only twenty men. The operation was in Tay Ninh in an area adjoining the Cambodian border. Until recently there had been no Allied troops in the area at all, and all the Units were new to this type of country. Company Headquarters was within two miles of the Cambodian border which at this point was clearly identifiable as it consisted of a river measuring about 65 yards in width at this time of year. (See photograph.)

This area was the responsibility of 196th United States Infantry Brigade, which was part of the 25th Division. General Knowles reminded me very much of the French General Massu and it was entirely due to his kindness in lending me his personal aircraft that I arrived in time to join the patrol. General Knowles knew the location of all his forward troops and the names of the officers who commanded the Units. He had just been visiting the 1st Battalion Mech 5th Infantry Battalion and told me that Colonel Rodgers was about to send out a daylight patrol, so before leaving I asked him if I might have his permission to join that patrol, at the same time lodging a complaint that one of his senior officers had refused to take the risk of allowing correspondents to go to the front line.

Unfortunately, on my arrival at the air strip there was only time to get briefed and no time to get issued with a weapon. The first part of the patrol was carried out in an armoured personnel carrier. The moment that we dismounted it was quite clear that the senior N.C.O. with whom I was travelling knew his job perfectly: without saying a word he made sure that the only unarmed man in the party was covered—he immediately moved to the rear of the party himself. Discipline and movement of the patrol was excellent, and when we eventually came under fire there was no panic and the patrol continued their search of bunkers as though nothing had happened, the wounded being placed in a position of comfort whilst the work of the patrol continued. The fascinating object lesson of this patrol was not only the rapidity of MEDIVAC I have already described, but the tactics adopted by the enemy. The previous night the units had been subjected to heavy fire from the area which we had attacked, and the pincer movement we had just executed left them only one route of escape—over the river and into Cambodia. From the river bank it was clear, by looking through field glasses, that there were recent tracks on the opposite bank of the river which were almost certainly those of the Viet Cong who had escaped. What we were unable to find out was whether the Viet Cong had fired on us from the Viet Nam or the Cambodian side of the river. This operation was evidence that the enemy had taken sanctuary in neutral Cambodia.

We are all Americans

The negro population is approximately just over 10 per cent of the United States population. It would not be unreasonable to expect that a somewhat similar percentage should be found in the troops serving in Viet Nam or indeed in the armed forces of the whole United States.

The American standing army has reached the figure of something like three million men, of which over 500,000 are serving in Viet Nam. The proportion of negroes fighting in Viet Nam is far higher than the proportion of negroes in the civilian population in the United States.

Critics might maintain that this is colour discrimination, pushing the burden of fighting in Viet Nam on to black backs. However, there are special reasons for this.

The negroes are probably at least as physically fit as, if not more than other Americans, but their exemption from military service is obviously less, because the proportion of negroes at universities or in specialised jobs is very much smaller. Again, the standard of living of the average negro is very much lower so that possibly he is reluctant to claim exemption. But the third, and most powerful, reason is that the Services represent to the negro the unique opportunity of living in an American society where there is absolutely no colour bar whatsoever. Negroes can be officers or non-commissioned officers commanding white troops. They eat the same food, sleep side by side and share the perils of a soldier's life. Bullets do not discriminate between colour or race, and the negro is certainly no less brave than any other American.

But this is one corner of American life where the negro, with his lower standard of living and background, is capable of making a way for himself in life and defeating the national colour prejudice which exists in the United States. If you talk to American negro soldiers their outlook is very similar to that of any other American. Somehow nobody seems to notice their colour in war; and even going to and from a battlefield, either in a helicopter or in any other means of transport, conversation flows easily and barriers are non-existent.

When wounded, whether mildly or severely, they behave with fortitude and bravery, and do not seem to regret that this is a white man's war against oppressed coloured people, although I do not think the Vietnamese would care to be

described as negroes. They have perhaps acquired the sentiments and feelings of the rest of the American army, which is
that the war must be carried on if Communism is to be defeated.
In a curious way they have become, if not more American
than, certainly as American as, the average American. Very
little good comes out of war, but it may well be that the
Vietnamese war has broken down the colour barrier which
has hitherto existed in so many of their minds.

The recent race riots in America are beginning to assume a
more organised pattern and are becoming para-military
operations. The White House must be concerned at the
effects which demobilised negro soldiers may have on what is
already an explosive political situation.

The negroes in the army are now first class battle troops,
accepted as equals whilst fighting the war in Viet Nam alongside their white brothers in arms. When they return to the
United States for good, their attitude towards the negro
problem could alter the course of American history.

There would appear to be three possible courses, any of
which individual negro soldiers might adopt. On return to the
States some of them might well decide on a neutral position,
and take no part whatsoever in racial disputes. The second
is that they might have pressure brought to bear on them by
other members of the negro community, to throw in their lot
and to put at the disposal of the negro population the
military skills and experience which they have acquired as a
result of the fighting in Viet Nam. The last and probably the
most likely course, and certainly one which would harm the
United States race relations less than either of the others, would
be if they decided to integrate with American whites with
whom they have been sharing their everyday lives in the course
of their duties in Viet Nam.

This last course of action must depend on what degree of
acceptance is offered by white Americans. In view of the
magnitude of the recent disturbances the white population
would be well advised to do everything that is possible to help
these soldiers to become assimilated into the life of the United
States.

IV

PROGNOSIS

DOES TORTURE PAY?

TO BOMB OR NOT TO BOMB

ECONOMICS

WILL DEMOCRATIC GOVERNMENT WORK IN SOUTH
VIET NAM ?

SELLING DEMOCRACY AND VICTORY

Does Torture Pay?

THROUGHOUT history atrocities have been committed both in peace and in war. The Communists in Russia from 1917 onwards, the Bela Kun régime in Hungary in its attempt to overthrow the legal government of Hungary after the First World War, the Nazis in Hitler's Germany—these are all examples.

Stalin repeatedly gave orders for crimes to be committed against humanity in order to extract information or take vengeance. But to assume that only the Communists are capable of these crimes would be to neglect the facts of history. The Inquisition itself was supervised by Catholic priests, though indeed those practices ceased some centuries ago, as did mutilation and torture under British law. Probably the last person to undergo torture legally in this country was Guy Fawkes.

Great criticism has been levelled at the Japanese for the way in which they treated their prisoners. To the Japanese it was an unforgivable crime to surrender. In their philosophy you should either be killed fighting or commit *hara-kiri*. Many British and Commonwealth prisoners perished on the death railway and road through lack of food and from the routine work which their physique was incapable of withstanding. The Japanese did not, as a rule, use these methods to extract information from prisoners of war. In the case of the Germans in the Second World War, most of the inhuman acts were committed against those brave people who formed the resistance movements and were not party to any international convention concerning prisoners.

The fact that the Gestapo's main activities were directed against people who had no protection or status as prisoners-of-war, and were in many cases against their own nationals, both Jewish and Aryan, in no way lessens the crime they committed against humanity.

The Viet Cong treatment of those captured in war is in fact probably better than that meted out to the unfortunate civilians living in villages which have supported the South Viet Nam government. The following incidents reveal practical examples of Viet Cong terror.

On 3rd August 1961, in the Long Dien village in Dinh Tuong province, the wife and daughter (aged 8 months) of a self-defence man were murdered in cold blood in their living quarters.

On 20-21st May an innocent villager had her left fist chopped off, her left leg hacked and her neck and breast stabbed.

The parish priest of La Ma church in Kienhoa province paid a heavy price for his adherence to the Catholic creed when he was murdered in his bed on 6th April 1960.

The wife of the Chief of Long Thoi hamlet in Long An province was sent her husband's head on the 1st February 1961.

A simple farmer attending a Communist Viet Cong meeting had the audacity to complain that the taxes levied by the Viet Cong were too high and that it was hard enough to make ends meet without the additional burden of their taxes. Vo Van Lanh subsequently had his hands tied behind his back and was silenced for ever.

None of these crimes was any less wicked because the victims were civilians. But the conduct of the Viet Cong in cases like this illustrates to the world the sort of mentality prevailing in the Viet Cong Communist force.

Most of the victims of Viet Cong terrorism have been selected at random, but the principal targets in the rural areas have always been the village Chief, the policeman, and the Government adviser who is trying to help farmers improve their lot under the Land Reform Act. It is these small men who have been kidnapped, tortured, mutilated and murdered. It is estimated that since 1958 no less than 70,000 people in South Viet Nam have suffered.

The Communist grip on South Viet Nam is based entirely on terrorism, ill-treatment, and reprisals carried out by the Viet Cong against any citizen who co-operates with the South Vietnamese Government. Any villager who fails to pay his respects to the Communist creed or to pay its toll in money, men or rice, will be subjected to the same treatment.

By committing atrocities, whether it be on civilians, in concentration camps in Russia, under the Nazi régime in places such as Belsen, or in innocent villages in Viet Nam (at the instigation of the North Viet Nam Government), these nations have made themselves the object of deep-rooted hatred and sowed the seeds of distrust. Who could trust any nation which has so recently degraded itself?

Great Britain in 1940, after the fall of France, had practically no German prisoners, but many of the British and Allied prisoners who had been captured by the Germans were manacled like criminals. The British Military High Command ordered raids to be carried out on the German-occupied mainland of Europe, the sole object being to capture German soldiers. When this had been achieved Great Britain was in a position to ensure that our prisoners in Germany were properly treated. The manacling of prisoners by the Germans was a violation of all international agreements, but until such time as we had some German prisoners they had ignored the provisions of international agreements.

There is no declared war between North and South Viet Nam, nor between the Americans and the North Vietnamese. South Viet Nam and America are parties to the conventions regarding the treatment of prisoners-of-war, but North Viet Nam is not a signatory. South Viet Nam allow their prisoner-of-war camps to be visited and inspected by the International Red Cross, but this is not so in the case of North Viet Nam.

When American airmen and soldiers are captured they are treated not as prisoners-of-war but as criminals. Photographs have been shown of American soldiers with yokes round their necks, being led like oxen from village to village and pilloried in front of the populace. This sort of treatment has not enhanced the stature of North Viet Nam in the eyes of the West, and once again the petty advantages of propaganda which had been achieved in the villages by this barbaric treatment are certainly offset by the international repercussions of such actions.

Today, as soon as a prisoner reaches a prison camp in South

Viet Nam, he is nearly always guaranteed treatment as a prisoner-of-war. There is however one very serious loophole in the position of prisoners who are captured by third nations, that is to say, by Koreans, Australians or Americans. After a short period of interrogation they are handed over to the Vietnamese authorities. This action is in accordance with a provision in the Geneva Agreement on Prisoners which allows it to take place, always provided the capturing nation is ultimately responsible for the treatment of the prisoners. These three nations have in fact maintained a list of prisoners who are actually handed over, so that they can trace them when hostilities have ended.

The exception to this rule has always been that if the Americans capture prisoners at sea, and not actually on South Viet Nam territory, they retain them as American P.O.W.s, presumably with the object of exchanging them with American servicemen captured either while flying over North Viet Nam, or in military operations in South Viet Nam.

This passing on of prisoners is not a very satisfactory procedure as there is always the chance that they might be ill-treated before they actually got into the Vietnamese prisoner-of-war camp, perhaps by those who have suffered at their hands or whose village has been the object of an attack by a force to which that particular prisoner belonged. Premier Ky assured me that this was something to which he was giving his personal attention, as he agreed that any short term advantages of extracting information by brutality was inhumane, morally wrong and, in the long term, against the interests of South Viet Nam.

From this account so far it might appear that everything in the garden in South Viet Nam is rosy and that North Viet Nam is the only one at fault. Unfortunately, this is not the case.

There are many instances where prisoners have been tortured by Allied nations including the Vietnamese in order to get information from them.

Once, when visiting a Vietnamese unit and talking with American officers, I was horrified to hear two officers discussing the fate of a captured prisoner-of-war. On learning my identity they endeavoured to pass it off as careless talk, with no foundation whatsoever. However, the descriptions were too vivid for the imagination and had obviously been backed up by practice. The Americans suddenly became ashamed and worried.

In the case of prisoners taken by the South Vietnamese it must be remembered that many of them do not wear uniforms and have no badges of rank or insignia of units, nor indeed do they wear any form of recognised uniform. Some of them may have a black pyjama suit, but the practice is that, whatever they may be wearing when captured, the South Vietnamese have decided that they should be categorised as prisoners-of-war.

General Westmoreland assured me that any proven instances had been severely dealt with by Court Martial and that he had every intention of ensuring that any departure from the conventional treatment of prisoners-of-war would be treated by the United States army as a very serious offence, and punishment awarded accordingly.

The Koreans had a bad reputation when they first arrived in Viet Nam for the way in which they treated their prisoners, but they soon learnt that it was a short term advantage. By treating their prisoners as human beings, and giving them the same food and accommodation as the Korean soldier, they have shown the villagers that they are humane. This leads to a comparison between themselves and the Communist Viet Cong, who are well-known by the villagers for the atrocities they have committed.

The fact of having captured a man in battle and knowing that he is in possession of information which would enable you to save the lives of your own forces in attacking a position puts a heavy onus on the nation or individual who captures the prisoner. Brutal treatment will probably reveal the location, strength and details of the enemy unit, and enable the position to be captured with the minimum amount of loss of men. But once having brutalised this man the capturer has two alternatives, either to kill him after he has given the information, and so bury his own mistakes, or to let him go free to talk to other prisoners-of-war and, probably, in the end to the International Red Cross. It is the intervention of this last element, the International Red Cross, which may to some extent curtail this type of activity. It could of course be argued that selected prisoners, having divulged the information, are more likely to be quietened by death.

The most dangerous period for a prisoner-of-war is immediately after he has been captured, because it is at this time that the information which he has would be most valuable. If he is not high ranking, it would be of no value after the first 48 hours. It is at this stage that it is essential for the Red Cross to interest itself in the fate of the prisoner. There will always be those sadistic people who will continue to perpetrate these vile practices in spite of instructions which are given by their army commanders. Premier Ky and General Westmoreland, on whose shoulders the blame must ultimately rest, have both made up their minds to do all in their power to stamp out these brutal practices.

To publicise these cases and to show the punishments which they have received by Court Martial should not be interpreted as a sign of weakness, but one of strength. Strength and courage to show to the world that every nation has a sadistic black sheep in its ranks, but the Governments of South Viet Nam and the United States are determined that wherever this occurs it will be treated as a criminal offence and the sentence awarded be appropriately severe.

To Bomb or not to Bomb

The United States Air Force is now actively engaged in destroying targets in North Viet Nam—a curious situation in international law in that there has never been a declaration of hostilities between the United States Government and Ho Chi Minh's North Vietnamese Communist State. In the Viet Nam war each side has committed its forces to attacking the other directly. Gradually, North Viet Nam has built up a strong defensive system against American aerial attack. This counter-measure by Ho Chi Minh, which consists of the erection of more S.A.M.'s (surface to air missiles), is taking a heavy toll of American bombers.

Few people realise that in 1965 Ho Chi Minh had not a single battery in operation. His war-making barrages lay, in fact, quite unprotected and could have been wiped out with but few casualties on the Americans' side. Once again, for political reasons, the Americans were limited in their targets for aerial attack.

At this time the D.R.V.N.'s Air Force consisted of a few sub-sonic MIG's, which were sitting on an air strip with no protection whatsoever. The political order was given that only aircraft in the air were to be shot down; no sitting ducks were permitted as targets. But these aircraft could have been completely wiped out, and the lives saved of thousands of servicemen fighting in Viet Nam. No such scruples existed on the other side. Brave members of the Viet Cong attacked the main U.S. naval base outside Saigon, Tan Sanut. The casualties were 26 aircraft, over 150 wounded and about 8 dead. The cost to the American taxpayer is estimated to have been in the region of some $10 million.

North Viet Nam have set up about 200 S.A.M. implacements, many of which are operational. Since these implacements have been set up, the cost to America has been something in the neighbourhood of 500-600 planes. All in all, the anti-aircraft defences of the North Vietnamese are so highly developed that only one choice is left to United States pilots flying over North Viet Nam. They can either fly high and face a murderous attack from the S.A.M. missiles, or they can fly below the S.A.M. missile level. But if they do the latter they are subjected to a well organised barrage from ground fire.

As time goes on, the anti-aircraft defences will increase in efficiency and fire-power and the Americans will be faced with running the gauntlet over a country whose anti-aircraft defences will be as highly developed as Nazi Germany's were during the Second World War.

China and Russia are continuing to supply North Viet Nam with MIG fighters, and the North Viet Nam military command have ensured that their aircraft potential is scattered over a number of fields.

To many Americans whose sons are fighting in Viet Nam, a policy of anything but an all-out attack on North Viet Nam appears to be ridiculous. After all, the real test is that there are members of the North Viet Nam Army in formed units and in North Viet Nam uniform actually fighting the Americans in South Viet Nam so that a *de facto*, if not a *de jure* state of war exists between the two countries.

American casualties up to April 1967 amount to 10,000 dead and 52,000 wounded. The cost of the war amounts to something in the region of $20 to $30 billion a year.

The United States had, on a number of occasions, ceased the bombing of North Viet Nam in an attempt to bring Ho Chi Minh to the conference table. But what has been the result? During the 1965-1966 37-day truce North Viet Nam was able to erect surface to air missiles without let or hindrance. During the truce in 1967, the Viet Cong were able to move supplies in the region of 25,000 tons, according to conservative estimates.

What, in fact, is the United States attempting to achieve by the bombing of North Viet Nam? There can be only three main justifications for its action.

The first reason, which has been given, cannot be compared with the second and third reasons, now set forward. The theory was that heavy bombing of North Viet Nam would force Ho Chi Minh to come to the conference table. What is far more likely is that it will harden the opinion of the North Vietnamese to fight what they regard as a cruel aggressor and will serve to unite the North Vietnamese in their determination, not to give in, but to continue the fighting.

The second reason is that North Viet Nam is supplying three to four thousand soldiers a month as reinforcements for Communist armies fighting in South Viet Nam. The bombing is an attempt to stop these reinforcements arriving in South Viet Nam. But here it is questionable what degree of success can be achieved. The Ho Chi Minh trail runs through neutral

Cambodia and the Pathet Lao part of Laos. Reinforcements have proper staging camps and are capable of dispersing, moving by foot, bicycles and trucks. They are not easy to destroy, as they are moving in neutral territory and probably infiltrating at points on the frontier between Viet Nam, Laos and Cambodia, a distance of well over 1,000 miles.

As to whether concentrations of troops in North Viet Nam might be attacked, that is another matter. But it is clear that casualties from aerial attack on the Ho Chi Minh trail represent only a fraction of the number of reinforcements actually entering South Viet Nam. The same applies to arms and ammunition coming into South Viet Nam, the route for which is the same, i.e. the Ho Chi Minh trail. Most of the frontier between Viet Nam, Cambodia and Laos is undefined and in many places lies in thick jungle. This means that the likelihood of capturing the infiltrators is very small indeed, as also is the possibility of capturing large-scale caches of arms.

The third military reason for aerial attacks would be the destruction of arms dumps and of factories manufacturing war materials which are supplying Communist troops in South Viet Nam. This is a better bet, but here again the source of supplies must be divided into two main categories.

First there are the supplies coming from China and Russia overland, and secondly there are those coming in by sea, mainly into the port of Haiphong.

Until 1965 the two North Vietnamese railroads which connected with the Chinese and Russian systems were narrow-gauge. This created a great problem because both China and Russia have broad gauge railway systems, so that supplies had to be transhipped, but again it is necessary to be realistic about this. Transhipment might have been a time-consuming operation, but in a Communist state where labour is directed, there is no shortage of coolies to perform such a task.

North Viet Nam has now built an additional rail which permits the operation of narrow or broad gauge systems and allows the free flow of ammunition and weapons across the border from China into North Viet Nam. The bombing of railroads, marshalling yards, etc., would certainly have an effect on the supplies being delivered to Communist forces in South Viet Nam.

The best place to bomb would be at the points where the railroads cross rivers or ravines by bridges. An attack on the bridge over the Red River leading into Hanoi would have a devastating effect, for trucks from the North, as well as freight from the railroad lines, pass over this bridge.

The United States Government have dragged their feet and wasted valuable time. Had they not been so squeamish, and attacked these targets earlier, they could have wrought havoc in the transportation system without suffering many casualties themselves. All these bridges and railroad points are now heavily defended and the United States will suffer severe casualties when attacking them. In 1965 they could have been wiped out with practically no casualties.

Supplies for the war effort in South Viet Nam are also passing by sea to North Viet Nam. The port of Haiphong is the most important in that a high percentage of all sea traffic comes through this port, to a large extent from the iron curtain countries. Vital fuel supplies, and possibly 85 per cent of North Viet Nam's essential supplies, wind their way through a narrow sea passage several miles in length, before they reach Haiphong. It would not be very difficult to block this port completely.

Apart from the port of Haiphong, there are targets in North Viet Nam the destruction of which would curtail the supplies flowing into South Viet Nam. If the electricity-generating plants and the transmitters which distribute current could be cut, then much of Viet Nam's industry would be brought to a standstill. This, combined with the steel mill at Thai Nguyen, would reduce the amount of exports available to send to China in payment for arms and ammunition.

Too much emphasis should not be placed on this last point because, clearly, even if the arms and ammunition were not paid for or part paid for, China would still almost certainly continue that supply because it forms an essential part of their programme for the fulfilment of Mao's ideal—the Communisation of South East Asia. Nevertheless it would have a severe disrupting influence on North Viet Nam's army.

PROGNOSIS

The main targets of importance would be the air-fields in North Viet Nam, but this would require a massive attack so that they could all be wiped out in one operation.

The moral case for bombing was clearly set out by General Westmoreland in his address to Congress on the 28th April 1967, when he said: "A typical day in Viet Nam was last Sunday. Terrorists near Saigon assassinated a 39-year-old village chief. The same day, in the delta, they kidnapped 26 civilians assisting in arranging for local elections. The next day, the Viet Cong attacked a group of Revolutionary Development workers, killing one and wounding 12 with grenades and machine-gun fire in one area, and in another they opened fire on a small civilian bus and killed three and wounded four of its passengers. These are cases of calculated enemy attack on civilians, to extend by fear that which they cannot gain by persuasion.

"One hears little of this brutality here at home. What we do hear about is our own aerial bombing against North Viet Nam, and I would like to address myself to this for a moment.

"For years the enemy has been blowing up bridges, interrupting traffic, cutting roads, sabotaging power stations, blocking canals and attacking airfields in the South, and he continues to do so. This is a daily occurrence. Bombing in the North has been centred on precisely these same kinds of targets and for the same military purposes—to reduce the supply, interdict the movement and impair the effectiveness of enemy military forces.

"Within his capabilities, the enemy in Viet Nam is waging total war all day—every day—everywhere. He believes in force, and his intensification of violence is limited only by his resources and not by any moral inhibitions."

Having had this straight from the shoulder of their Commander-in-Chief, who is responsible for the day to day conduct of the war, why should the American Government hesitate? It is certainly not the doves or Senator Fulbright which is holding them back. The war in itself has alienated a certain section of the American electorate's opinion and the stepping up would not result in a great deal more antagonism to it. So what is holding the Americans back? There is a much more important reason lying behind this apparently "pussy-foot" attitude of the White House.

To date, the entire United States and Allied Forces are operating in South Viet Nam without any aerial opposition whatsoever from the enemy. The helicopters and transport aircraft upon which the Americans depend almost entirely for the supply and movement of troops in South Viet Nam, have only to face ground attack from Viet Cong Units. They have not got to face what could be attack by enemy fighters.

Could it be that the Americans believe that an all-out attack on North Viet Nam would result in Ho Chi Minh deciding to use his aircraft to attack American airfields and aircraft, both in the air and on the ground? If Ho Chi Minh were to do a "Pearl Harbour" on Tan Sanut and other airports and railways, the whole character of the war could change overnight.

Perhaps this is holding the Americans back, for they might lose more than they would gain in an all-out attack on North Viet Nam targets, and it could result in their having to take on guerrillas not only in South Viet Nam but in North Viet Nam as well. If they cannot beat the Viet Cong in South Viet Nam, they can certainly never beat them in North Viet Nam as well, and even if they did, they would then be presented with the undesirable result of having a direct frontier between the United States and Communist China.

The strategic decision, as to how far they can save American casualties by escalating the war, and at the same time not going so far that they are subjected to attack by North Vietnamese aircraft in South Viet Nam, must rest with the White House.

Economics

In a war of the type which is raging in Viet Nam, one must look at the basic economy of the country to see whether, if the guerrilla threat was overcome, the country could survive either with or without American aid. Viet Nam is being given a higher per capita rate of American aid than any other country in the world and there is at the moment no doubt that if this were withdrawn, whether the guerrilla threat had been overcome or not, the country would not be able to survive economically.

To assess the economic viability of a country a large proportion of which is under direct military threat or, in some cases, Viet Cong control, and a considerable part of its agricultural potential is lying idle (as a direct result of hostilities), is an impossible task.

In 1961 a report by the State Department entitled "A Threat to the Peace", claimed that between 1956 and 1960 an economic miracle took place in Viet Nam, and the April 1961 issue of the Malayan economic review *Ton That Thien* asserted that South Viet Nam was poised ready to take off. A more realistic view was put forward by the Dean of the Saigon Law School, Vu Quoc Thuc. In the April 1962 edition of *The Times of Viet Nam Magazine* he listed 1961 as a critical year, but made it quite clear that the economic crisis in Viet Nam was entirely due to the insecurity prevailing in the rural areas of the country. This is probably the best appraisal of the situation, and Professor Milton Taylor, who was a former adviser to the South Vietnamese Government, came to the conclusion in 1961 that after six years of massive American aid, Viet Nam was still in the state of a patient requiring permanent medication in order to remain alive. (Author's words.)

There is no real barometer. Accurate documentation on key factors is lacking, and in many cases is liable to be biased. No statistics could be accurate because they would only take into account an economy which was completely overshadowed by military operations.

The creation, in 1954, of the 17th Parallel divided the nation into North and South. This brought a further problem in that over three-quarters of a million refugees from the North had to be absorbed into the South Viet Nam economy. The insistence, by South Viet Nam, that the remainder of the French army should withdraw in 1956 also had its effect because France was spending no less than $500 million a year, and more than 120,000 Vietnamese were serving in the French armed forces. In addition to this considerable figure there was an army of Vietnamese staffing the logistic support for this army, whose jobs disappeared with the evacuation of the French army.

The effect on the country was similar to that on a patient who suffers the sudden denial of a drug to which he had been addicted for a number of years. South Viet Nam was suddenly faced with the problem of more than 150,000 Vietnamese previously employed by the French army, for whom there was no immediate hope of work. The Vietnamese army itself could not absorb all of these, and could only take a small fraction of skilled men. But the immediate post-partition years had left South Viet Nam one of the world's greatest producers of rice, and the rubber plantations were producing more latex than they had done in the years prior to the Second World War.

By Asiatic standards South Viet Nam had very good roads, but as a result of the war many of these had been damaged or destroyed, and later, under Viet Cong threat, became virtually unusable.

In the years immediately prior to the war both Viet Nams together had a population of $16\frac{1}{2}$ million, but by 1961 it had risen to nearly 30 million. Pre-war rice production amounted to more than seven million metric tons, whereas, with almost double the population in 1960, production then was only just over eight million tons.

The easy way to understand these statistics is to say that if Viet Nam was ever to preserve pre-war standards of living, and assuming there was no large-scale change in staple diet, i.e. movement away from rice eating, then in 1961 there would have been just about enough rice produced in South Viet Nam to feed the South Vietnamese. What this book makes clear is that until peace is restored in the villages, American aid will be required, not only to fill the immediate gap in food production but also to develop other crops, such as sugar, fruit, vegetables, peanuts, corn, tea, coffee, soya beans, etc.

Rubber production is an important item, and although the level of production in 1954 was higher than it was pre-war, we have to consider that since 1954 French management has been working under tremendous difficulties and in many cases has been obliged to pay protection money to the Viet Cong in order to be allowed to continue production of the rubber. It also has to combat Government hostility for paying this toll to the Viet Cong, but as has been mentioned in another part of this book, the rubber planters know that unless they can maintain their trees in a reasonable state the trees will go to waste and, short of replanting, could not be brought back into production.

South Viet Nam's essential exports for many years to come would have to consist of the two R's, Rice and Rubber.

The most up-to-date statistics available are contained in the Government's National Institute of Statistics in a publication entitled *The Economic Expansion of Viet Nam in 1965*. This Government-sponsored pamphlet is a realistic appraisal and makes no attempt to exaggerate economic expansion.

Of the two main products, rice is by far the most important. The 1965/66 production of rice was affected by drought, which also had an adverse effect on their mid-season rice crop. Fortunately, seasonal rice, which is planted much deeper, did far better in the adverse conditions of drought.

The general picture is somewhat depressing because the total area under cultivation in the entire country in the year 1965/66 was almost the same as it was in 1954/55 (no appreciable increase in ten years). In other words, the effort which the Government has made to redistribute whole areas of population which were subject to Viet Cong attack, together with the immense pacification programme which has been carried out throughout the country, has not in fact resulted in any substantial increase in the areas cultivated. A graph from 1954–1966 shows an almost steady acreage except for a slight increase in 1956/57. In areas which are not yet pacified and where the rural population is disillusioned with their treatment by the Viet Cong there has been a movement of agricultural labour towards the cities. The short term problem is of course unemployment in the cities, but a far more important effect will be felt in the long term. Will those who have left the land be willing to return to it even if they are offered their own holdings and substantial Government help? Time alone will answer this question. Suffice it to say that the drift from the countryside could be serious. Counter-balanced against this factor the use of machinery in farming could to some extent reduce the labour force required, but here again, South Viet Nam, in its move towards a property-owning democracy, has reduced the size of the holdings so that mechanisation will not have as great an effect as it would if the holdings were larger.

But, depressing as the acreage-under-cultivation figures appear, there is one positive factor which is of considerable importance and that is the yield of paddy per hectare. In 1954, out of a cultivated area of just over two million hectares, approximately two and a half metric tons were produced, which represented a yield of 1.23 metric tons per hectare, whereas in 1965, just under two and a half million hectares under cultivation produced over four and a half million tons, corresponding to a yield of 1.98 tons per hectare.

But the rice having been produced, its movement within South Viet Nam to the cities is still a serious problem. Until the roads are opened and the Viet Cong threat removed there will continue to be severe restriction on the movement of rice within the country.

The second product of primary importance is rubber. Here again, the internal security threat developed by activity against the Viet Cong has resulted in a fall not only in the area under cultivation since 1962 but also in actual production. Rubber is even more susceptible to internal security than paddy because the estates on which it is grown are far harder to defend. The number of planters who are willing to continue under the threat of attack, or are prepared to continue their protection payments to the Viet Cong is diminishing.

A typical case was recounted to me by a French rubber planter who had been in the business for many years and was an expert in rubber cultivation. "I have two alternatives, sir; one is to pack up the plantation completely, which could only result in the trees becoming useless within a few years, or to co-operate with local Viet Cong elements. In the long term interests of Viet Nam I believe that we ought to keep these trees going, and it is no use trying to rely on any form of Government protection either for myself or for my workers on the plantations because sooner or later protection would fail and we would have to pay the price, which would be a slit throat. The Viet Cong have come to an arrangement with me: after work, before the weekend I leave all my vehicles full of petrol with the keys in the ignition and instruct my workers not to appear anywhere near where the vehicles are garaged until Monday morning. The Viet Cong use the vehicles for essential transport and return them before Monday with their petrol tanks almost empty. Not only does the plantation have to pay normal taxation, but it also has to give use of its vehicles and some protection money to the Viet Cong for the privilege of being allowed to continue the production of rubber and the maintenance of the trees."

Secondary crops, including vegetables, have, in general, remained static or in some cases increased; thus, in the case of sugar cane, although the cultivated area decreased in percentage in 1964 the use of improved types of cutting made up for the loss of area.

The South Vietnamese Government has put through a pilot project the object of which is to increase pig production; this has proved very satisfactory, but here again, a local increase in the number of pigs is quite useless unless transport facilities enable them to be taken to other parts of the country.

The number of people practising fishing has remained static at just under $\frac{1}{4}$ million, and most of the fleet consists of light junks. However, the quantity 375,000 tons of fish produced in 1965 showed a marked decrease compared with the two preceding years, in spite of the introduction of more mechanisation and better methods. Part of this decrease was due to floods and part to increased military activity and a tendency for some of the fishing boats to be used for transportation only and not fishing.

In the industrial field, again the Government has tried to create new industries. One of the most successful attempts in this field has been the textile industry. When the North was split off at the 17th Parallel, South Viet Nam was left with almost no industry, as most of the projects were sited North of the Parallel. The tragedy is that if normal trade relations could exist between the two parts, even if they were to remain under separate Governments, one economy would be complementary to the other: rice from the Mekong Delta could be utilised in North Viet Nam, since partition supplies from its Red River Delta have been insufficient to feed North Viet Nam's population. Purchase of South Vietnamese rice by North Viet Nam would enable the South to buy more of the North's industrial products.

From what has already been said it will be obvious that the importance of transportation cannot be over-estimated. Not only are the roads insecure but what is far more alarming is the decrease not only in passenger traffic but in freight actually moved by rail. There has, of course, been a large increase in the internal air traffic, both for freight and passengers, but this does not compensate for the fall in rail transport, and costs are proportionately higher.

Motor vehicles have shown an increase, in particular the light motor cycle, Lambretta type, on account of its very low costs both in purchase and running.

Apart from the Government appraisal of the economic position, Professor Lilienthal, who was responsible for the Tennessee Valley project, is doing a separate independent survey at the invitation and expense of the South Vietnamese Government.

Security, however, is the key word. Planning, and improvement of techniques are all a help which should not be minimised, but what the country needs is the security not only to be able to continue cultivating the rich land still available in South Viet Nam but also to permit free movement by road and rail so that its products can move at low cost without let or hindrance. Surveys are a help, but security is the key to success.

Another important aspect of South Viet Nam's economy is the export and import position. Since 1961 exports have halved in value, whereas imports have increased by 50 per cent in the same period. In round figures, Viet Nam imports ten times more than it exports; nearly half of her imports come from the United States, whereas 33 per cent of her exports still go to France. According to these figures it must be assumed that, for many years to come, South Viet Nam will be dependent on donor nations for her survival. Of these nations the United States will be the major contributor.

Help from other nations, although it may not amount to very much, does show that there are other countries in the world who feel that South Viet Nam's struggle against Communism and its desire to survive as an independent nation merits their help.

Premier Ky is fully aware of the need for industrialisation and land reform and he told me that one reform which he was carrying out was intended to benefit both. Instead of giving land compensation in cash he is giving part of it in the form of industrial equities. If the owners of such equities keep them for a reasonable time the equities should show considerable appreciation and thereby make up for the loss which their owners have sustained by receiving a comparatively low price as compensation for their land holdings. It also has the advantage of channelling wealth into the essential industries.

Land Reform

North Viet Nam had very little trouble about this, as over 90 per cent of the holdings were 12 acres or less. Here, land reform was a comparatively simple operation as almost all the large landowners had departed, and the Viet Minh simply parcelled out the properties and gave them to the sitting tenants and at the same time issued certificates of land ownership to the new holders. The departure, after the 1954 Agreement, of about 800,000 workers from the Red River Delta gave Ho Chi Minh a further million acres for distribution. In whole areas everyone, from bishop to bullock boy, packed up to flee from the Communists. This mass exodus was encouraged by the Americans and by the Church, the latter in many cases indicating that the Church had gone South and deserted the North. The French Fleet, assisted by the American 7th Fleet, helped this movement to the South.

In the years immediately following this distribution the North Vietnamese Government was wise enough to make relatively few demands on the new holders for rent or taxes. Land reform was started in the North in 1945 and had virtually ten years start over the South. By October 1950, almost four years before France's final defeat at Dien Bien Phu, the Viet Minh had occupied almost the whole northern half of North Viet Nam. Even so, it was no painless operation in the North. Ho Chi Minh, after the 1955 Geneva Agreement, was not satisfied with the progress he had made and wanted a more radical reform on the lines of Mao Tse-tung's doctrine. About 100,000 farmers and agriculturalists who stood in the way of these Communist agriculturalist methods were exterminated, and, as an example, in Interzone IV, Ho Chi Minh had to employ an entire division to put down a revolt by the small farmers, 2,000 of whom were killed or removed to other areas.

The whole process of land reform was carried out in typical Communist tradition, the first step being the extermination and expropriation of landlords, a process in which the landlords' tenants were only too willing to participate in order to acquire land for themselves. Then, to keep the peasants quiet, periods of varying length were allowed during which no rent or toll was demanded, and the impression thereby given among the new holders that life under the Communist Government had every advantage for them: their own land, and virtually no taxes. Following this, taxation and the final Communisation, in many cases, took place. A reference to the Constitution of North Viet Nam shows a class classification which would startle any democratic country. Acting under it, Peoples' Agricultural Reform Tribunals were set up. Under this, an arbitrary system of redistribution, not only of the land but also of personal chattels, agricultural machinery and all livestock, was re-allocated according to the whims of the Tribunal. At the same time classification of the population was carried out, each member being named in one of the five degrees, varying from landlord to agricultural worker. Disturbances (like Interzone IV) were put down ruthlessly and the final result was that the holdings became so small that they were uneconomic. Private ownership and small holdings had not been abolished by law; they had, by a stroke of the pen and through the operation of the Agricultural Reform Tribunals, deliberately been reduced to such a size that the worker was left with a unit which by careful calculation was too small to sustain the simple life of himself and his family. The only choice left to these wretched peasants was to work for the Government or seek agricultural employment in some form of Communist co-operative farming enterprise.

In the South, sloth and inactivity in the field of land reform prevailed. A start was made by the Cochin Chinese Autonomous Republic in 1947. At this time they promulgated a law which aimed at the gradual reduction in farm rents, many of which were as much as 50 per cent of the annual output of the land.

In 1951 the Emperor Bao Dai realised that there was cause for alarm. The French Union forces and the Vietnamese troops were beginning to reduce the guerrilla threat. The Emperor's Government had come face to face with an important human problem. Since the threat of the Viet Minh had been removed from the village and law and order restored, an ideal opportunity was presented to the former French and Vietnamese landlords to leave their apartments in Paris or their villas in Saigon and to return in the wake of the armed forces to claim back their lands. Instances occurred where the armed forces were actually assisting landlords to claim part of the crops and in some cases went so far as to assist the landlords in endeavouring to get payment in money or crops owing from previous years. It should be remembered that in these "previous" years the country had been controlled by the Viet Minh and the landlords had abandoned their property.

The law which the Bao Dai Government promulgated in 1951 was deliberately vague. The peasant was to be entitled to the crops but not to the actual title of the land, which would still remain with the landlord.

In the South a combination of the return of the landlords, aided and abetted by military force, with a system of legislation which favoured the landlord at every turn, had the effect of making the average villager detest and mistrust the South Viet Nam Government. Once again the Viet Minh was outbidding the Government.

In North Viet Nam the French Union forces had had strict instructions not to allow the return of landlords to certain of the forward areas. This was a wise move but in the long run made no difference to the history of that part of the country. Had this policy been adopted in the South it might well have affected the number of villages embracing the Communist faith.

In 1952 the opportunity for agricultural tenants to purchase their land was established. This was, however, far too small a programme to tackle what had in fact become a major national problem, for by this time many a Vietnamese farmer had got a title to his land in the form of a certificate issued by the Viet Minh. Quite apart from this, most of the Vietnamese small-holders held the view that they had acquired the equivalent of squatters' rights to their land since it had been virtually abandoned by the landlords and was under the direct control of the Viet Minh force. The peasant, therefore, had two claims: one by virtue of his squatter's rights and the other on the grounds that the land had been conquered by the Viet Minh who then became the owners and were in a position to distribute to the smallholders. With a great flourish the Emperor pro-mulgated new ordinances in 1953. Farm rents were to be reduced and more Government machinery set up to allow farmers to purchase their own land from the landlords over an extended period of time, and finance was to be available for the tenant to buy the land. But what tenant wanted to pay good money for the land on which he was squatting and to which, in his view, he already had a title of ownership?

A further boost to land reform came in 1958 when the French Government was helped by the offer of a loan of over three million dollars to purchase about half a million acres of land from French holders. How much of this was actually paid to French owners is not known but from the only statistics available on this subject it appears that by January 1961, French owners had sold over half a million acres at an average of thirteen dollars a hectare against a current market valuation of about two hundred dollars.

In the first seven years of land reform nearly two million acres had been acquired by the Government but how much has been distributed, and to whom, is unknown, though it is thought that the figure is about a quarter of the total which was made available. Some of the land purchased must have been in areas still controlled by the Viet Cong.

The great tragedy was that Diem's Government was made up to a very large extent of men whose financial interests were enmeshed in land holdings Diem and his wife were no exception. It was not surprising that there was resistance inside the Government to any land reform which permitted the wider ownership of the soil.

Under Premier Ky the pace has been accelerated. He has realised that land reform is probably the most essential subject which he must tackle if he is to win support from the majority of villagers in the country. It is a brave step, because there are still men at the top who do not approve of land reform. Premier Ky made it quite plain to me that he had no intention of letting anything stand in the way of this essential reform. He summoned the Press of all nations of the world and personally handed out bundles of land certificates to district chiefs at a public ceremony*. The aim of this particular operation was to give out about 100,000 hectares, to be distributed among about 42,000 farmers, but who knows what the basis of distribution will actually be? It is a heavy responsibility to be handed a bundle of land certificates, and in any country it would be hard to imagine what the subsequent distribution would be in relationship to family, friends or acquaintances.

*See Illustration No. 10.

Will Democratic Government Work in South Viet Nam?

The Americans always assume that a government modelled along the lines of the United States Constitution is the pattern upon which all other governments should be run, and believe that such a type of government is suited to South Viet Nam.

Premier Ky is prepared to go along with the Americans because he is convinced that he must be the head of a democratically elected government in order to demonstrate to the rest of the world, and particularly to the Communist-dominated part of Viet Nam, that he is the leader of a modern state which is based on election by universal suffrage, not only for local government, but national government as well.

A military junta operates directly through the provinces and districts down to the hamlets and it has been argued by members of this junta that a direct form of government is far more suitable whilst operations of war are in progress. There is a substantial weight of argument in favour of this opinion but, of course, it does not take into account international considerations.

Presuming that the war will one day be won, a time must be chosen to start the development of democratic institutions and Premier Ky's government has done the right thing by getting the National Assembly to draw up a new Constitution and to set in motion the necessary machinery for elections throughout the country.

Once elected, the National Assembly made a strong attempt to perpetuate its own authority and to convert itself into a National Parliament. This was resisted by the military junta, who pointed out that the sole function of this elected body was to draw up the Constitution. It was not for its members to assume the function of a nationally elected parliament. To date, the recommendations of the National Assembly have been for the institution of an Upper and a Lower Chamber. The Chairman of the National Assembly has, in fact, allowed his name to go forward as nominated for the Presidential Election, along with Ky. Whichever of these two eminent men is elected, he will have the right to nominate the Prime Minister.

Premier Ky has on many occasions said that he would rather remain an Air Force Commander than take part in politics, but it is probable that he would rather accept the post of Prime Minister than President, for the real power lies in the hands of the Prime Minister and not the President.

When the elections for the two Houses of Parliament are held it must inevitably result in the diminution of the powers at present exercised by the military junta.

The Electoral Roll was prepared for the early elections which took place for the Provincial Advisory Council, in May 1965. The same Roll will be employed for the election of President, both Houses of Parliament, hamlets and villages.

With many parts of the country still threatened by the Viet Cong, how will it be possible to hold these elections? The first principle essential to a fair election is that the people should be able to go and place their name in the ballot box without fear, either from the Vietnamese Army or the Viet Cong. The Viet Cong's attitude is that the election should be boycotted, and they will do all they can to prevent the electorate from casting their votes at the appropriate time.

The Vietnamese answer to this problem is that it is only a mechanical difficulty; it means that the elections will have to be staggered so that sufficient troops can be moved to wherever the election is being held, to preserve law and order and to allow the people to exercise their franchise without let or hindrance.

The country has been notionally divided into areas which are regarded as safe, relatively safe and unsafe, and, of course, those areas which are under reconstruction. That is to say, people from areas where the population has been evacuated completely and is about to be resettled in new geographical locations, will have to wait for their elections until such time as they have been rehabilitated.

The 1st September 1967 will see the election of the President and the Upper House, and on the 1st October elections for the Lower House will take place.

As a result of these elections and the long process which is required to establish a democratic form of government, Viet Nam is faced with one of its greatest problems—where to find men of the right calibre to fill the positions. So far, most of the administration has been carried out by Provincial Governors, almost all of whom are members of the armed forces. Some, indeed, are quite young.

Whilst elementary education in the country, established by the French, is good, there is, as in any developing country, a shortage in the number of graduates equipped with higher educational qualifications. Premier Ky, or whoever may follow him, will find a difficulty in providing sufficient qualified teachers. It would take something in the nature of 20 years before there are sufficient schools to produce enough recruits of the required educational standard to fill the places.

Some of the blame for this situation must be placed upon the French, and yet at the same time, credit must also be given to them. Primary education was encouraged by the French and a number of excellent schools were set up, either independently as religious schools, or as State schools, but the number of people who were able to partake of higher education was very small indeed.

For the better-off members of Viet Nam's community it was possible to get this education in Viet Nam, and, of course, many of them elected to send their children abroad (mostly to France) and pay for their education. French military authorities permitted Vietnamese officers to be trained in their academies, and some of the most reliable and best qualified senior officers today owe their position to the fact that they were educated at French military establishments.

It was part of the French colonial pattern to give most of the administrative jobs to Frenchmen. This policy was carried out to a ridiculous extent in countries such as Morocco, where even the local postman was recruited from France. The regrettable aspect was not so much that it created a type of poor white society in the French colonial administration as that it barred local people from these jobs. The inevitable result was that when independence was achieved there was a lack of trained people, even in the humbler government posts.

British colonial policy had many faults, but it did encourage, over a period of years, the employment of local people in the lower grades of administration and even permitted posts such as District Commissioners and Magistrates to be given to qualified local people.

The average villager in Viet Nam is not really interested in the reasons which motivate other nations to fight in his country, for by bitter experience he and his fellows have learned that reprisals have been taken against those who in their turn sided or co-operated with the French, the Japanese or with the South Viet Nam Government. Too often, perhaps, they were prepared to do a deal with their Japanese masters in the village, perhaps to obtain some advantage or favour, but that advantage or favour was of a transient nature. No sooner had the Japanese been expelled than reprisals were taken against these villagers for their co-operation with the enemy.

This is how, in Viet Nam today, a village is pacified. The headman and the senior members of the families in that village decide that they will no longer co-operate with the Viet Cong, but throw in their lot with the South Viet Nam forces. On the advice of the headman of the village some members of the community are armed and assume the mantle of a local defence force, whether it be the armed policeman or the Popular Force member. Rifles are loaded and bayonets are fixed, ready for the attack. The days go by, the weeks go by, the Regular forces of the Viet Nam army may withdraw, believing the village is safe, and so it is for a time. The headman sleeps with his family in his house, rejoicing in the new freedom he has found. No longer is he compelled to pay tribute in rice and tax, or in recruits for the Viet Cong army. He and the members of his village are able to pursue their normal lives and till their fields, and go about their daily business.

Without warning, with no blast of trumpets or beating of drums, a sizeable unit of Viet Cong, supported by Regular soldiers of the North Vietnamese army, descend rapidly upon the village. They have been lurking perhaps ten miles, even five miles, away in their hideouts. Suddenly they attack the village. The headman is their chief target, as indeed are the members of the Popular Force. A short and sharp action results. The headman is lucky if he is murdered and not taken away alive to suffer a fate which is worse than death. He is lucky if his wife and children are not murdered. Suffice to say that terror reigns in that village. But how can they trust this government, which has been unable to supply sufficient forces at the right time, to reinforce their own local unit?

Could this have been avoided? asks the innocent visitor. The answer is obvious. One of two methods might have been adopted to ensure that this attack did not take place. A hard one would have been to see that the Viet Cong units in the area had been completely destroyed before the main Vietnamese Army, or other Allied forces, left the area. The second method would have been to ensure that that village, by wireless communication, had been able to summon immediate reinforcements by helicopter, to surround the area before the Viet Cong could do their dastardly work.

There can be one of two solutions for ensuring security in the villages. The first is the long term one, the complete annihilation of all enemy forces in South Viet Nam. A long process of elimination is required to achieve this. The second is the disposition of forces in such a way that mobile reserves, capable of being alerted immediately, can be dropped into an area within the space of minutes, like a Fire Brigade. Such forces would at first reduce, and eventually eliminate, the possibility of counter-attacks by the Viet Cong.

Few but the bravest and most idealistic of the South Vietnamese will be prepared to throw in their lot with the South Viet Nam government until such time as one or other, and preferably both, of these security measures have been adopted.

No country can institute democracy at the drop of a hat,

but a date must be set for the commencement of this process. The sooner it is put into operation, the sooner it will work. Premier Ky has forced the pace because he knows that, in this as in so many other problems, time is not on his side. No one can judge how long it will take before the new form of government is established and working throughout the country. It would be impossible to guess, because there are so many unknown factors. The most important of these factors is how long it would take for the Allies to defeat the Viet Cong completely. How long will it take for the Viet Cong to realise that they cannot win the war?

At some time or other the North may realise that from a military point of view they may be able to hold the country to ransom and create a stalemate within it, but that they will never achieve actual victory. Ho Chi Minh's best plan would be to accept overtures of peace from any third party and to endeavour to win the battle of the people's minds by allowing the Viet Cong to give up their arms and return to the villages. Once back in the villages, the Viet Cong could infiltrate into the political system, build up strong Communist cells within the community, and use their powers of persuasion, accompanied eventually by terror, to overcome the democratic government. Or even get themselves elected to that government and so bring influence to bear on the South Vietnamese Government.

In this respect, it should be remembered that there are still vast areas in South Viet Nam which are completely Communist dominated, and in these areas it is highly probable that even if the elections were free, some Communist candidates would succeed in being returned even if they were to stand on a non-Communist ticket.

It is difficult for some people outside to realise why Premier Ky will not allow Communist candidates to stand, but perhaps not so difficult to appreciate when one realises that both Premier Ky's Government, the Americans and the Allies are actively at war with the Communists; and clearly the last thing that any of these parties want is infiltration into the Government by Communists.

Corruption

The Vietnamese are essentially a simple people and are not particularly fond of those asserting authority over them, whether they be the local tax collector, appointed by the South Vietnamese Government, or, indeed, the Viet Cong. To the Vietnamese each of these represents a force whose only function, in their minds, is to extract money from them in the form of legal or illegal taxation. In the case of the Viet Cong it was always an illegal tax. But frequently this was also the case with the Government's representatives, who used their jobs and positions to amass fortunes for themselves and to pass on some or none of the money they collected. The Government official could perfectly easily say, after he had collected the tax in full, that the area was riddled with Viet Cong and he was quite incapable of collecting the tax which had been levied by the South Vietnamese Government. This could very easily result in an innocent village receiving a surprise attack by soldiers to root out the Viet Cong, who in fact had never existed.

But not every village had a wicked and spiteful tax collector appointed by the Government, and many honest and good people took on these jobs at great personal risk and fulfilled them with a degree of honesty comparable to that of a Western civil servant.

But in all these things South Viet Nam had to contend with a tremendous shortage of qualified and dedicated men as a result of the vacuum left by the evacuation of the French administration. Also a country which until very recently had virtually no communications at all was a paradise for the dishonest official, whose dishonest conduct would probably never be discovered, or which he could quite easily cover up by an excuse, the authenticity of which was incapable of being checked.

The spheres of corruption were certainly not confined to the local tax collector; it went right through Diem's administration to the top. Importers who had goods in the bonded warehouses in Saigon were quite capable of organising armed thugs to loot the warehouse and then to claiming the compensation from their insurance company. After a decent interval the thugs would probably turn over the stolen goods to the importer who could then sell them. This was a well-known racket in Saigon and one which Ky endeavoured to stamp out.

But the difficulties of clearing out such undesirable practices are great even in a civilised Western community equipped with a modern system of crime detection and Courts which administer the law with impartiality. How could one expect the same standards to be applied in an Eastern nation, and particularly one which had been at war continuously for nearly a quarter of a century? The Americans, in their minds and in their actions, endeavoured to apply standards of behaviour which it would be easy to carry out in a United States city but quite impossible in a war-torn country like Viet Nam. Small wonder that the American tax payer is worried as to how much of the aid programme actually finds its way into projects rather than into the pockets of senior Vietnamese officers. Certainly the local officers responsible for handling the vast sums of money involved in the aid programmes are always worried as to how free a hand they can give to the Viet Nam officials who are working with them.

This is one of the dilemmas in which the United States finds itself: how to ensure that the Vietnamese have some say in the use to which aid is put, and, at the same time, ensure that unscrupulous individuals do not divert part or all of the money allocated for these projects to their own personal use.

Forced Removal—Notice to Quit

Operation Cedar Falls was a surprise attack launched by the Americans in an area popularly known as the "Iron Triangle". For many years the whole area had been completely dominated by the Viet Cong. The object of the operation was to transplant the entire population to another part of the country and re-settle them. There had, of course, to be an intermediate stage during which the people would live in temporary housing in a hutted camp until such time as the new permanent houses had been constructed and the reception area was ready to receive them.

The operation was given no previous publicity whatsoever and the whole area was surrounded by troops so as to form an iron ring through which neither villager not Viet Cong could pass. It was an immense task to undertake the resettlement of an entire area with its equipment, furniture and livestock, not forgetting the most important element, the villagers and their families. This huge exercise was carried out in three stages, and all forms of transport were employed: air (CH 47), road vehicles and barges.

The first phase was the light removal stage, in which people and light equipment such as cooking utensils only were taken to the new staging area. In the second stage the heavier equipment, including the wooden beds and much of the personal furniture and belongings, was transported. This left the final and third stage, when even the carts, cattle and the young boys with their buffaloes were moved to their new area.

The four hamlets in the area of Ben Suc were moved bodily to the new temporary camp in Phu Cong. Here the local officials were ready to meet them and explain the mystery of water coming through a galvanised pipe and out of a tap. Around the camp, areas had been set out where the villagers could graze their cattle but provision had of course to be made by the Government to provide rations since the new area was only a temporary residence.

Out of a total of six thousand people there were 1,600 women but only 700 adult males. It was quite clear that most of the members of this community were active participants of the Viet Cong, who were not in the village at the time when it was encircled by the troops. The only explanation for this was that either their Viet Cong bands were on patrol or, what was much more likely, the Viet Cong kept part of their force in the very close country surrounding the area. A third, but less likely possibility, was that the Viet Cong had broken the security and knew that the operation was about to take place. But whatever the explanation, the men simply were not there when the time came (*prima facie* evidence that they belonged to the Viet Cong).

The Viet Cong probably thought that they would be able to make use of the villages again, but they were wrong. Before leaving, the Americans brought in bulldozers and completely demolished the whole area so that there was no sign of any of the villages left when their job was completed.

But what about the new camp where the refugees had been moved? Tidy looking tentage, water points conveniently located and surrounding areas reserved for the grazing of their cattle meant better living conditions than they had previously enjoyed in their villages. But to understand the people's thoughts and their reaction to this new life it was only necessary to put a few questions to them in simple words.

Yes, conditions were better where they were living now than in the villages from which they had come; but it was not their village, to which they were accustomed, and they had not had any desire to move from their homes.

Asking about their husbands was interesting, particularly in the case of those wives whose husbands were not with them. In their new surroundings they had already adjusted themselves to the fact that the Viet Cong were no longer in control. The wives were at pains to prove that their husbands were at no time Viet Cong supporters, and even those who were widows made it clear that their dead husbands had not been killed on a Viet Cong patrol and had not in any way been associated with the Viet Cong.

Having asked them for their views on their recent move, I went on to interrogate them very closely on the next move it was proposed they should carry out. The Government had made it quite clear to all of them that this was a temporary move and that they were finally to be taken to an area where they would be provided with new houses, would be allocated their own small bit of farmland and given many other advantages. But the more I questioned them the more it became apparent that they were quite incapable of visualising a new area which they had not seen with their own eyes. The majority of these villagers had never left their own village. This new life into which they had been precipitated was strange, and it was not possible for them to imagine what their new homes would be like.

What was clearly worrying the wives more than anything else (though it was perhaps not made much of in their conversation), was the whereabouts of their husbands. How were they to know whether their husbands would elect to remain with the Viet Cong guerrillas in the old area, or defect from that organisation and re-join them either at the camp or later at the permanent area? Where would their loyalties lie if their political views became hopelessly enmeshed in Viet Cong philosophy? Would their family ties prevail on them to return to family life? From the authorities' point of view, even if some of the husbands gave themselves up under the Chieu Hoi Open Arms Programme and returned to their families, could they, the authorities, interpret this as a conversion to the Government cause, or was it just a temporary domestic convenience? Curiously enough, there were some such husbands in an adjoining Chieu Hoi Camp, and after great difficulty I got permission to talk to some of them. Many expressed a desire to start a new life in the area to which their families were to move. But all these sentiments expressed by former Viet Cong members must be considered suspect. Only a long period of surveillance will prove the loyalty or otherwise of these people.

The ordinary Vietnamese peasant has very strong ties both as regards his family and the soil. It is not surprising, therefore, that many who live in Viet Cong controlled villages have no desire to be moved to secure areas unless the conditions in their own areas are very bad indeed. It is going to be a long and laborious task to persuade these villagers that they are in fact better off in their new surroundings.

These New Life Hamlets were borrowed from the British model set up in Malaya during the Emergency, but conditions in Malaya are in no way comparable to those in Viet Nam.

PROGNOSIS

In Malaya most of the subversion came from the Chinese section of the community, and in a country where there was a natural dislike by most Malays for the Chinese it was not surprising that Chinese Communist propaganda fell on moderately deaf Malay ears. There were exceptions, as for example when dissatisfied Malays were actively working as Communist agitators, but that proportion was small. When it came to the re-settlement of Chinese in the New Life Hamlets the Chinese attitude towards such re-settlement was completely different from that found in South Viet Nam. The Chinese who were re-settled in Malaya were largely squatters who had little attachment to any particular region. One bit of land to them was as good as another. In fact, the legal rights they acquired as a result of Government re-settlement in the New Life Hamlets put them in a better position than they had been in previously, when their rights had been tenuous and akin to squatters' rights.

This lack of attachment to any particular area was one of the factors which enabled the Government to make a success of re-settlement. South Viet Nam's problem, on the other hand, was the reverse. In this case the affinity of the peasant for the land was almost unbreakable. It cannot be too strongly emphasised that the whole Vietnamese way of life in the village was bound up with family ties and land tenure. Throughout the centuries these strong feelings had enabled the community to throw off the effects of one conqueror after another.

In some villages the Viet Cong demands on the villagers had succeeded in weakening and in many cases breaking these ties; and in a village that had suffered for a long time from Viet Cong domination the effects were beginning to show. In the first place, the taxation levied by the Viet Cong may have become so oppressive that the whole village was reduced to a state of serfdom, its entire output going into the coffers of the Viet Cong either in the form of goods or money, leaving the villagers themselves with less than enough to subsist on. In most cases the Viet Cong's hand was light on the village in the first instance, but as time went on their demands increased. In the early days their entrance into the village was heralded with pleasure and accompanied by the re-distribution of land; the removal of the necessity to pay Government taxation and rents to landlords were factors calculated to win over the hearts and minds of the local people.

As time passed the Viet Cong became more and more dependent on local supplies, for which they had no money to pay. They were forced to exact higher rates of taxation, particularly as the size of the forces was constantly on the increase and reinforcements were arriving regularly from North Viet Nam. The amount of rice eaten by a North Viet Nam soldier fighting in South Viet Nam was certainly not less, and was probably considerably more, than that required by the ordinary member of the Viet Cong.

While the Viet Cong consisted only of South Vietnamese, the villagers had a stronger urge to feed them voluntarily. They were after all, in many cases, members of their own community, being fed from the resources from the village in which they lived.

The Viet Cong was faced with a double supply problem: the numbers to be supplied from a given area were on the increase as a result of the arrival of North Vietnamese reinforcements, and at the same time the local population was being asked to supply "foreign" North Vietnamese soldiers. The supply position has become the Achilles heel of the whole Viet Cong campaign in South Viet Nam.

Little by little Viet Cong pressure upon villages intensified, to persuade them to increase their contribution to the anti-Government military forces. It was not only supplies that they demanded, but also reinforcements of men from the villages. Simple demands for information about troop movement were stepped up, and a situation arose where the villagers were working and digging defences for the Viet Cong.

Refusal to comply with their demands, or even hesitancy in accommodating their wishes, was followed by rapid reprisals: murder and public disembowelment of the village headman, the school master and the doctor. The village became terrorised and completely under the heel of the local Viet Cong. As a result of Viet Cong pressure many villagers' loyalty has changed.

But for a family to escape from such a village as refugees

was no easy matter; it required a brave man to leave with his family and without goods or chattels to remove to an entirely new re-settlement area. American aeroplanes have dropped leaflets by air explaining to villagers how they might escape from an area and move to a new Government controlled fortified zone. If the man were to leave on his own and reach safety, he could be sure that the family he had left behind would be murdered. If he took courage and moved his entire family by night he might be lucky and miss the Viet Cong patrols; if he should be caught, death and the murder of his family would be a happy release, but, knowing the brutalities of the Viet Cong, he would be aware that the route which they took to the grave would be long and painful. However, many families have made the break and been re-settled in a New Life Hamlet on a plot of land allocated to them by the Government. They receive approximately 3,500 piastres (which is about £30 at the official rate or £20 at the black market rate). This is just about enough for the man to build a house, some of the materials for which are supplied by United States A.I.D. (Agency for International Development). In addition, he and his family receive a daily allowance of rice until such time as they have become self-supporting.

An Giang was a province which until recently was Viet Cong dominated but has now become one of South Viet Nam's "show" pacified provinces. The villages were equipped with their own local defence force and links with the Provincial force but, in spite of this, during the night of May 21/22, 1966, armed elements of the Viet Cong invaded the village of Vinh Hanh, in the Chua Thanh district of the Province. They machine-gunned labourers employed in the construction of the Tra Kiet canal. Twenty-three people were killed in their sleep, including, of course, women and children. An incident like this represents a major set back. Doubt arises in the villager's mind as to the ability of the Government and their local force to protect his life from the Viet Cong. It takes a long time to build up a sense of security. To the Western mind this senseless and barbaric attack on innocent women and children might be interpreted as something which would antagonise the villagers towards the

Viet Cong, but the average villager merely wonders if he is in fact supporting the stronger side.

An Giang's main problem until pacification was that the population of a half-million was isolated in groups with no adequate means of communication. Since pacification, roads and bridges have been constructed utilising local labour and materials supplied by America. But, to give some idea of the cost of this programme, one million American dollars were required to finance these projects in the province.

The great advantage of a scheme of this nature is that although the Americans are supplying the material it is the hands and bodies of Vietnamese people which are doing the work. This is the origin of the satisfaction felt by the people in their achievement of building up a new society and way of life. Villages like this, which have lived under the cruel oppression of unbridled domination by the Viet Cong, are beginning to think for themselves. Even the more ignorant cannot help but be impressed by the way that a pile of concrete blocks, sand, cement and other building materials becomes transformed over a period of weeks or months into a building of modern design capable of housing a new school or medical unit. Whilst the villagers are building their houses, all around them a new community is developing so that they themselves can take pride in a tremendous stride forward in both the social and economic fields. Agriculturally, the help which American tractors and other essential machinery are giving has rendered their task much simpler. But even so, American aid has its limits and there is a great deal to be done by manual digging, not only to get the irrigation in the fields going but also to repair bridges and widen the roads, both within and without the perimeter of the villages.

Nothing succeeds like success, and in villages like this there is no shortage of volunteers coming forward for the essential administrative posts such as that of village headman. But the work which is being carried out has still to be co-ordinated with military operations and particularly with defence, both local and national. The American Government has recently decided to try and get the U.S. Aid and the military channels of command working in tandem. The Americans have a very good working arrangement whereby the projects themselves are approved by the Province Chief and therefore have the full weight of the local hierarchy behind them before they start. This is a two-way movement of ideas. It might be that the Americans consider the damming of a local river is the first step to be taken, or this idea could just as easily come from a Province Chief who knows the area or has local advisers who are aware of the details. Very serious consideration is given to the projects. A Province Chief who chairs the meetings between his own officials and the representatives of U.S. Aid, having decided that the project is worthwhile, then proceeds to sketch out the details and make out a timetable. All of this work must be done in very close co-operation with local people, and the Americans have achieved an extremely good working arrangement in order to get the job done.

All over the country there are Americans handling large sums of money and administering considerable sized projects. It may be a source of surprise to many people that the standard of honesty in this corps is so high, considering that the temptations put in their way are great. The reason is that there is a sense of dedication and purpose in their lives and a genuine feeling of having achieved something, literally out of nothing.

But, having said this, it is important to be realistic and to understand that every system has its imperfections. In the case of South Viet Nam the success of these civil projects depends on a number of factors. The first essential is the willingness of the American taxpayer to continue to carry the burden. It looks as though America is so heavily committed that she will continue for a number of years to participate in South Viet Nam's military and economic affairs.

Given the money and the materials, the next hurdle to be overcome is the distribution of the aid itself and the decision as to the priorities of the projects. In a country which is still in a state of major civil war the allocation of funds and materials and the priority for their use must be made to a very large extent at high level discussions between American representatives and officials of the South Viet Nam Government. A balance between the various economic surveys being carried out and the military requirements has to be struck.

At the provincial level there will of course always be conflicts of local opinion and loyalties but, in general, at this level it is comparatively easy to achieve harmony. The Province Chiefs are military men appointed by the Government, and persons of a fairly high calibre are chosen. A new difficulty will arise later on, when a Government has been elected. Locally elected members will feel that they have to push their own particular projects in order to justify their local nominations. A time will then be reached when the whole of the distribution of economic aid might have to be reviewed.

Until a democratic Government is achieved, the donor nation, America, is obviously going to have a far greater say in how the money is spent than it will have after South Viet Nam has a fully elected Government. American aid to South Viet Nam may well pass out of the direct management of America and become more like post-war Marshall Aid.

It is unlikely that the Americans will be prepared to accept this and they will probably continue to exercise the right to have a considerable say in how aid should be used.

But by far the greatest difficulty is going to be in the lower echelons. The success of all the projects in the end will depend on the leadership provided at village and hamlet level. Unfortunately, South Viet Nam is desperately short of men and women of the right calibre, a situation not helped by the fact that this tiny country already has three quarters of a million men under arms.

Turning to the villages themselves—whether they be New Life Hamlets, pacified areas, or any other category of area over which the South Viet Nam Government has control—the problem will always be the same: security. Each type presents a different degree of security problem. Where the villagers have voluntarily moved into a new area there will be little or no internal trouble from the Viet Cong. Their problem is a simpler one: to provide adequate defence by armed police and Popular Forces capable of resisting attack from the Viet Cong. Thus the New Life Hamlet will be protected by barbed wire and have semi-military forces in the form of armed police and probably two platoons of Popular Forces. The weak link in the chain is how to get the regular provincial forces to back up these local elements if the village or hamlet should receive a full-scale Viet Cong attack. Until every hamlet and village has a radio contact with the province no system of defence can be regarded as satisfactory.

What is required is a fire brigade system, equipped with helicopters and flares, capable of coming to the immediate help of areas under attack. Such a system is a long way off and would also be dependent on complete knowledge of the movements of local Viet Cong forces. Once again the need for liaison between civil and military operations becomes apparent. All the work carried out by U.S. Aid—the new schools, houses and irrigation projects—can be completely destroyed overnight when one of the hamlets is overrun by the Viet Cong, and its leaders and inhabitants become victims of murder and torture at the hands of the Viet Cong.

The South Viet Nam Government has for a long time encouraged a programme of open arms, known as Chieu Hoi. Under this programme anyone who wishes to leave the Viet Cong forces and come over to the Government side is at liberty to do so. They go through a process of screening and are subsequently allowed to return to any part of Viet Nam which is under Government control. Where there are no Chieu Hoi, and in an area such as the one that has been described, the internal security problem is small and probably confined to a few known or unknown communist agents living within the community.

The line taken by Prime Minister Ky is that the best practical way of exhibiting solidarity within South Viet Nam is to give a free pardon to all those former members of the Viet Cong who are prepared to disassociate themselves from the activities of the Viet Cong. This presents a direct contrast to Communist policy, which sets out to divide one section of the community from another whether that division be one of religion or of social position. When the programme was initiated the Viet Cong were at the climax of their power and the response was slow. The main reasons for desertion from the ranks of the Viet Cong have been their loss of grip over the local population, combined with the heavy casualties they have sustained as a result of the stepping up of military activity throughout South Viet Nam. Many of the Chieu Hoi adherents admit that food supplies have become more difficult, and living conditions are of course very poor. Who really wants to live for long periods in a tunnel 40 feet deep on inadequate rations? Their only change of scenery is when they are thrown into battle and their lives put at risk.

The tremendous increase in the numbers coming forward under this programme must be taken as a clear indication that the Viet Cong are at the losing end of the war.

The present system gives the Chieu Hoi recruit a short period of rehabilitation before allowing him to return to his family. He is watched for a period of three months, the statistics for the number of successful converts being based on the findings of this three month period of probation. It is becoming accepted in the higher echelons of the Government, including the Prime Minister, that this is far too short a period of time. In one area where the programme has been operated by an Australian officer he argued that it was essential that when the converts returned to their villages they did so without any stigma attached to them and were to be regarded as ordinary members of the community. When I suggested that no judgement could be formed in such a short period I was almost blown out of his office by a heated exchange of words. To anyone familiar with South Viet Nam it would seem most unlikely that the reasons for a man's absence from his village would not be known by the entire village. Most families supporting Viet Cong activities are known to other members of the community, and the officer's argument was just another example of the inability of the West to understand the Eastern mind and way of life.

The whole of the Chieu Hoi programme must stand or fall, not on the numbers of its recruits but on the numbers which can be shown to be loyal over a long period. That period might well have to be anything ranging between one and three years. During this time it is a vital duty of the police and security agencies to watch the activities of those released under the Chieu Hoi programme.

Desertion from the Viet Cong could result in brutalities not only against the individual concerned but also against his family and relatives. The pressures which can be brought to bear are considerable, and a long period of active surveillance is essential. The Chieu Hoi are not barred from military service, either in the National Army or the Militia (Popular Forces). This latitude has not gone unchallenged by some of the military commanders who doubt the loyalty of these recruits. As one tank commander put it to me, very bluntly, while we were temporarily halting between advances: "How would I know that a Chieu Hoi, if I had one in the tank, was loyal? Just as I'm looking down the gun sights he could easily cut one of the essential electric cables and render the whole tank immobile and a sitting target for the Viet Cong. You may laugh and think this is unlikely but in fact something like this did occur. Two Chieu Hoi actually made off with a couple of tanks. The Regimental Commander was fairly quick off the mark and as soon as he realised jumped into a tank and ordered a crew which was on guard to follow the escaping tanks. The Tank Commander managed to fire at one of the escaping tanks, hit it and put it out of action but, believe it or not, the other tank escaped and has never been seen since."

Loyalties, especially in Viet Cong dominated areas, may well be thin but many soldiers are not happy about former Viet Cong serving alongside them in action against the Viet Cong. In any new hamlet or rural development area where there are Chieu Hoi being integrated with the population there is always the danger that they may be used by the Viet Cong; if not actively, then certainly in a passive role as suppliers of information. Such a village has a double security problem; direct attack from without, and the possibility of espionage from within.

There is no doubt that as Government forces get the upper hand the likelihood of former Viet Cong members returning to the Viet Cong is reduced. The only real guarantee that they won't return is to ensure complete protection in the villages after they have been pacified so that the Chieu Hoi recognises the plain and simple fact that by remaining loyal to the Government he is on the winning side.

Selling Democracy and Victory

"In most of your villages, Prime Minister, you have got people who have never travelled outside their area, and in spite of all your efforts to visit the countryside there are millions of people who have probably never seen you. Why can't you have another television network with a range throughout the country so that every village and hamlet understands what is happening, and particularly the importance of a forth-coming election?"

Premier Ky replied: "I have been trying to persuade the Americans that this would be the best investment in South Viet Nam. We have got one station, but of course its range is limited. What we need is stations throughout the country which could bring into the villages and hamlets, face to face on the television screen, the problems which confront our country, and the tasks which our people and the government have to tackle together."

The practical implications of this policy of course are immense, especially where you have a country which is very hilly. Once again, Prime Minister Ky's whole idea that things cannot be done overnight applies to this problem as to so many others.

It would mean that a television receiving set would have to be supplied to the village or hamlet chief, placed in a public position, and villagers encouraged to come in and watch the programmes.

Curiously enough, it would probably have more effect than the supply of large numbers of sets to individual homes. For by coming to a central area and meeting place it would focus the importance of the local government and encourage the people to move freely in the area.

PROGNOSIS

Nothing works better than success, and slowly but surely those villagers who are frightened of exposing themselves to attacks by Viet Cong would understand the dangers of this organisation and be more likely to stick together to fight it.

Subtle programmes exposing the activities and methods of the Viet Cong would enable the villagers to set their own problems into the general picture.

As an example, let us consider taxation. Frequently villagers are forced to pay taxes to the Viet Cong if they want to avoid the consequences of default. Default in payment always has the same effect: the wives of offenders are mutilated, their children kidnapped, or they themselves subjected to brutal torture.

Again, the giving of rice to the Viet Cong merely results in a village having insufficient supplies for its own needs.

If these sort of incidents could be subtly shown on the television screen the people would realise that they were not isolated incidents of Viet Cong terrorism but a state of affairs which existed throughout South Viet Nam.

On the other side of the picture, the government would be able to show how this could be avoided by the villagers sticking together and standing behind the local civilian authority backed up by police and local military forces.

This medium could also be used to show how the Communists have purported to issue land certificates to the peasants but that in North Viet Nam, where these certificates are also issued, the peasants have found themselves landless. The so-called certificates mean nothing if a Communist Government imposes such heavy taxation that the peasants are unable to carry on as individual cultivators and are compelled, either economically or by other means, to join a collective.

On the propaganda side, pictures should be shown not only of the ceremony in which Premier Ky gave away land certificates to the various provinces, but, what is far more important, how these parcels of land were in fact given to local people. Really subtle propaganda would be for the local landlord, especially when that happened to be the Church, to appear on the programme and explain that he had given up his land in exchange for Government compensation, so that his right to the land had terminated for ever. It would be foolish to expect that national affairs should dominate the programme. As in all television programmes throughout the world, the authorities would have to present attractive and amusing programmes, and the local stations in particular could devote a considerable amount of their time to the activities of local institutions and individual farmers.

The initiative in all this would rest with South Viet Nam. North Viet Nam would probably not be able either to compete or to interfere with these programmes. The mountainous nature of parts of the country has a disadvantage from the South Vietnamese point of view because it necessitates having a very large number of stations with a limited range of viewing area. But this has the advantage in that North Viet Nam would not be able to jam these stations.

Geographically South Viet Nam is a narrow strip of country, and distances from North Viet Nam are great. Even if China and Russia were prepared to spend money by setting up stations in Viet Nam's westerly neighbouring territories, Laos (Communist-dominated eastern Laos-Pathet Lao territory) and possibly Cambodia, it is doubtful if they would have much range unless they were to set up very powerful transmitters.

This leaves South Viet Nam at a positive advantage in the television field. Psychologically there is a world of difference between listening on a radio set and actually seeing something on a television screen. Villagers seeing their own areas on the screen could be educated to believe and trust the television programmes.

Devastation and death by means of aircraft and five hundred pound bombs are cruel weapons of war, and when launched against an enemy which is in some cases entrenched 40 feet under the ground, has little effect other than killing a few weeds and burning some scrub.

If some of the money which is spent on these vast military operations and equipment was devoted to explaining to the nation what was happening, it might be possible to begin to build up a feeling of national coherence and determination to defeat the Communist aggressors.

V

INTERESTED PARTIES

LAOS AND CAMBODIA

THAILAND

KOREA

JAPAN

WHAT IS THE ROLE OF TAIWAN AND
CHIANG KAI-SHEK?

INFILTRATION INTO LAOS

Laos and Cambodia

BOTH Laos and Cambodia had been colonised by the French at the end of the nineteenth century, and remained part of Indo-China together with Viet Nam until their complete independence was finally recognised by France and ratified at the Geneva Conference. The text of the Agreements is important and a summary of them was included in the chapter on the Geneva Conference.

Laos and Cambodia play an important part in the Viet Nam struggle for two reasons, one political and the other geographical. Politically, their future will to a large extent be determined by the outcome of events in Viet Nam. Should Viet Nam go Communist, then both Laos and Cambodia would find it difficult to resist Communist infiltration and aggression and would eventually go Communist themselves. The second and even more important reason is their geographical position as neighbours of Viet Nam. Laos on her eastern frontier is contiguous with North and South Viet Nam, whilst Cambodia's eastern frontier runs alongside South Viet Nam. By virtue of this geographical fact North Viet Nam is able to send supplies of men and munitions through Laos and then into South Viet Nam, or through Laos into Cambodia and thence into the Southern part of South Viet Nam. Both Laos and Cambodia are theoretically neutral, so this route, known as the Ho Chi Minh Trail, cannot be directly attacked by American or Allied troops without breaching the neutrality of these two countries.

After the fall of France, French control from Paris of Indo-China ceased. The French Governor General of Indo-China signed agreements with the Japanese on the 22nd September 1940 and the 29th July 1941 which permitted the administration of these countries to continue under the French. During the Japanese occupation all Indo-China's resources were placed at the disposal of the Japanese. The degree of control over Laos and Cambodia by the Japanese was less than that exercised over Viet Nam.

French resistance to the Japanese gradually built up in Indo-China and by the beginning of 1945 it had reached such a peak that the Japanese decided on the 9th March 1945, to overthrow the French Administration. In Viet Nam the Emperor Bao Dai signed an Agreement with the Japanese on the 12th March 1945, which replaced French authority by Japanese. Three days later the King of Cambodia proclaimed his country's independence, and the King of Luang Prabang acted similarly in Laos. In all three territories French authority had disappeared, but the Chinese under the Potsdam Agreement were still in occupation of Laos, north of the 16th Parallel.

In all three of France's colonial possessions resistance movements had sprung up, but it was the Viet Minh, founded by Ho Chi Minh, which was the most influential. By August 1945 the Viet Minh had linked up with the Khmer Issarak (Free Cambodians) and the Lao Issara (Free Laotians).

Cambodia in 1945 did not fall within the Chinese sphere of influence but after the displacement of French officials in March 1945 power had fallen into the hands of Son Ngoc Thanh, who had been installed as Prime Minister by the Japanese. He was known to be violently anti-European, a fact which was soon discovered by the British officer who had been sent there to take charge of the Japanese forces. This officer informed General Leclerc of the position and as a result Son Ngoc Thanh's arrest was ordered and he was removed from the country. Six years later Son Ngoc Thanh returned to Cambodia and joined the Communist militants who were grouped in the western part of the country. In 1945 the Provisional French Government proclaimed that Indo-China should consist of a Federation of five territories with a Federal Assembly. The powers of this Assembly were strictly limited, and effective control was still to rest in the hands of a Governor General advised by a Council of State whose members were to be nominated by the Governor General. France's solution to her colonial problem was presented too late and was not accepted. The countries concerned had already secured nominal autonomy and had no desire to return to colonial status. This was France's classic error in Indo-China—she offered too little too late. The reaction to this was mixed; Viet Nam was adamant in her refusal, but Laos and Cambodia proved more co-operative and in the long run their conciliatory attitude enabled them to achieve independence and retain unity whereas Viet Nam is still divided, with half of the country controlled by the Communists and the southern part still at war with the Viet Cong. By January 1946 Cambodia was recognised as an independent autonomous kingdom although in fact the French Commissioner and his assistants retained control. The Free Cambodians, as they called themselves, recognised the deported Son Ngoc Thanh, but their resistance to French authority met with little success.

Cambodia was not to receive her Independence until after the French defeat at Dien Bien Phu; her Independence was recognised at the Geneva Conference. Under the French, Cambodia was an elected monarchy and by a queer turn of fate Admiral Decoux passed over many of the candidates for the throne and appointed through the Crown Council a student of eighteen, Prince Sihanouk. Throughout his career this member of the Royal Family has displayed a brilliance for timing and compromise, as a result of which his country has remained neutral. In 1953, when his appeal to President Auriol for independence failed, he immediately shifted his ground and canvassed for support in the United States and finally set up an autonomous area in the centre of the Khmer Empire and simply sat tight until the French gave in to his demands. His master-stroke was to abdicate from his throne in February 1955, instal his parents in his place and enter the arena as the supreme and unchallenged political leader of his country. Considerable criticism has been levelled against Prince Sihanouk on the grounds that he is on good terms with the Communists and is prepared to accept aid from whichever quarter it is offered. At the same time he very wisely accepted American Economic Aid. Up to 1961, about two-thirds of American Aid went in supporting the armed forces and the remainder to development projects. Prince Sihanouk's policy with regard to American aid has been divided between expenditure on capital equipment, the building of schools and the education of some of her citizens abroad. The greatest danger to the economy of Cambodia is a tendency for a drift towards the cities, thus depriving the countryside of essential labour.

Sihanouk's manual labour campaign smacks of Chinese Communism but in fact what he is trying to achieve is to show by example that by joining in the business of manual labour, all classes of Cambodian society demonstrate the importance of agriculture in the Cambodian economy. The lighter side, and one which shows the sense of humour in Sihanouk's character, is the way in which visiting statesmen and ambassadors are invited to toil for a few hours, after which they are rewarded by a first class party at which their dancing partners are selected from among suitable members of the Royal Ballet.

Sihanouk is no fool and he realised that although China's historic domination of South East Asia may have been halted for a time she is quite capable of extending her influence, in the form of Chinese Communism, if the Western Powers pull out of South East Asia. If the American electorate became bored with Viet Nam and withdrew their support from the South Vietnamese Government it would only be a matter of time before Communism obtained control of Cambodia. The bonds of personal friendship between Sihanouk and Chou En-lai would probably ensure Cambodia's freedom, but personalities are not immortal, especially in Communist states, and the time might well come when Cambodia could no longer depend on Chinese policy towards Cambodia being moderated by Chou En-lai.

At home, Cambodians regard Sihanouk with the reverence they accord to members of the Royal House; even though he has stepped down from the throne he is to them still their king and leader. In the international field it was his persistence which enabled the conference on the neutralisation of Laos to take place.

It was through no fault of Sihanouk that the attempts made by the British Government in 1965 to promote an international conference on the neutrality and territorial integrity of Cambodia did not succeed; the intransigent attitude of the Soviet Government was to blame.

The only real criticism which can be levelled against Prince Sihanouk is that he has allowed North Viet Nam supplies of men and material to pass through his country into South Viet Nam. It is no secret that Viet Cong guerrillas have bases in Cambodia from which they can launch attacks on South Viet Nam. Having launched these attacks they can then retreat and claim the protection of neutral Cambodia. In the first action in which I took part in South Viet Nam the Viet Cong when attacked retreated over the river to Cambodia. Cambodia's frontier with Viet Nam is in many parts undefined, and it would be impossible for the Cambodian military forces to patrol this frontier even if they wished to preserve strict neutrality. No doubt if they took a stricter attitude to this infiltration and restricted it in any way whatsoever, the aid which they are at present receiving from Communist sources would be substantially if not completely cut off. Cambodia under Sihanouk prefers to walk the tight rope of neutrality and receive aid from any nation willing to give it.

Laos

Unfortunately, the situation in Laos was fundamentally different from that prevailing in Cambodia. Under the Potsdam Agreement the Chinese were still in occupation of that part of Laos north of the 16th Parallel. When the Chinese departed, early in 1946, French forces moved in rapidly, replaced the Chinese, and re-established themselves in the country. The Free Laotian Government in exile exerted little influence and the country was united under the King of Luang Prabang. Neighbouring Viet Nam was going through a civil war and the French in the Elysée Agreement recognised Bao Dai as a rival to the Democratic Republic of

Viet Nam in the north. It was a collateral effect of the Elysée Agreement which gave a form of independence to Laos and Cambodia. After the Elysée Agreement was ratified in January 1950 Great Britain recognised Laos and Cambodia as associated states within the French Union, and at the same time the United States recognised them as independent states within the French Union. Unfortunately, after the 1949 Agreement, most of the so-called "free" Laotian leaders had returned from Thailand and took part in the country's political life. A group led by Prince Souphanouvong went to Viet Nam and joined the Communists of Viet Nam, establishing a "Government for Laos". By 1952 they had organised themselves sufficiently well and had been able to join up with Viet Minh forces to such an extent that they were able to launch an attack on the Laotian Government forces, and all but succeeded in reaching the capital of Luang Prabang. Prince Souphanouvong established his Government at Sam Neua on the 19th April 1953. He controlled and still continues to control a large part of the country. His Government is known as the Pathet Lao, or Laotian Nation.

The Geneva Conference on Indo-China was concerned principally with implementing a cease fire between the French Union Forces and the Viet Minh, and the defeat of the French at Dien Bien Phu made a settlement essential.

The fighting in Viet Nam was so intense that military action which took place in Laos and Cambodia was eclipsed. Details of the Agreement on the cessation of hostilities in Laos are included in the chapter on the Geneva Agreement.* Article 14 had stipulated that pending a political settlement the fighting units of the Pathet Lao should move into the provinces of Phong Saly and Sam Neua. The Government of Laos had agreed to special representation of the Pathet Lao in the Administration of these two provinces pending a General Election. In a typical Communist way, the Pathet Lao construed these provisions as giving them exclusive control of the two provinces. The International Control Commission

---

* See page 52.

endeavoured to reach a settlement between the Laotian Government and the Pathet Lao, but without success. When the Elections were held in 1955, they did not extend to the provinces held by the Pathet Lao. In fact the claim that the Pathet Lao had complete control of these provinces was not strictly correct, as there were still loyal detachments of Government troops stationed in both of them.

The co-Chairman representatives had been invited by the International Commission to take up the issue, but no success was achieved. The Pathet Lao showed no real desire to reach an agreement so long as Katay Don Sasorith remained Prime Minister. Katay was a vigorous patriot, and his anti-French attitude ought to have enabled him to have common ground with the Pathet Lao, and had the latter wanted it there is no question that a political settlement could have been achieved. Katay was defeated in the National Assembly in 1956, and he handed over the Premiership to Prince Souvanna Phouma. If anybody could have made a lasting settlement with the Pathet Lao it was Prince Souvanna, who was Prince Souphanouvong's half brother. Almost immediately after his appointment as Prime Minister he visited Peking and Hanoi. By the end of the year the two Princes had signed a joint declaration making a Coalition Government a possibility. Difficulties between the two Princes appeared immediately afterwards, and Prince Souvanna lost patience and resigned, but three months later was persuaded to accept the Premiership again. November 2nd 1957, saw the signing of the Vientiane Agreement with the Pathet Lao. The new Government included Prince Souphanouvong and Phoumi Vong Vichit. It was agreed that the two provinces should be transferred to the Royal Government and that a number of the Pathet Lao followers who held administrative posts should be allowed to continue in office. On the military side, 1,500 Pathet Lao troops were to be integrated into the Laotian army and the remaining 7,500 to be demobilised.

Following elections, Prince Souvanna Phouma lost a great deal of his support and finally Phoui Sananikone became Prime Minister, in August 1958.

The situation was complicated because the Laotian Prime Minister had informed the Chairman of the International Control Commission in Laos that the Geneva Agreement had been fully executed, and as soon as the supplementary elections had been held he asked that the Commission should be dissolved. Finally it was decided by members of the Commission (the Polish Member dissenting) that it should not be dissolved, but adjourned, its legal status being retained.

Within months of the departure of the Commission, North Viet Nam forces began infiltration into Laos. Alarmed by events Phoui Sananikone demanded and obtained special powers from the Assembly, which put itself into recess for a year. The integration which was to take place between the Royal Army and the Pathet Lao troops was handled in an extraordinarily clumsy way and eventually some battalions of the Pathet Lao decamped from their position in the Plaine des Jarres and moved to an assembly point close to North Viet Nam. Any possibility of compromise had vanished and the Government placed the Opposition leaders, including Prince Souphanouvong, under arrest. Civil War had started again.

Phoui Sananikone's conservative attitude was challenged by a political group called the Committee for the Defence of National Interest (C.D.I.N.) at whose instigation Government buildings were surrounded by the army, and on New Year's Day 1960 the Prime Minister resigned, leaving the solution of the country's problems to the army and to the monarch. An interim Government was formed, and elections took place on the 14th April 1960. The results surprised nobody. It was an overwhelming victory for the C.D.I.N. and candidates sponsored by the army. The new Government was headed by Prince Somsanith. Souvanna Phouma returned from his position as Ambassador to France to take his place as President of the Assembly.

Whilst the new Government was in the process of being formed, Prince Souphanouvong and his fellow political prisoners escaped on May 24th. They had been in prison for fifteen months and were to be brought to trial. By being so negligent over the custody of their prisoners the Government were responsible for restoring to the Pathet Lao their Leader, without whom the movement would probably not have survived.

On August 8th the Prime Minister and all his Cabinet left Vientiane for Luang Prabang in order to supervise the arrangements for the funeral of the King. They had left orders that a Parachute Battalion commanded by a certain Captain Kong Le should embark on an operation against Pathet Lao forces. Captain Kong Le decided that it would be far easier to take over the city of Vientiane, and much more comfortable than enduring the hazards and discomforts of guerrilla warfare. His *coup d'état* would have been quite useless if he could not obtain some semblance of authority—so he turned to Prince Souvanna Phouma. Souvanna Phouma's motives for co-operating could have been personal ambition or simply an attempt to use his undoubted influence to prevent this spontaneous uprising from getting out of hand.

The troops, accompanied by unorganised groups of the population, marched on the National Assembly and broke into the Parliament Building. Souvanna Phouma announced from a balcony that the Deputies (very few of whom had the courage to remain in the building) had passed a motion of "no confidence" in the Government. Somsanith's Government resigned and the young King called on Souvanna Phouma to form a Cabinet, but the constitutional position was unresolved since the new King, who remained in Luang Prabang, withheld his formal sanction from Souvanna Phouma. The King sat tight in Luang Prabang surrounded by the members of the deposed Government, among whom was the ex-Defence Minister General Phoumi. General Phoumi set up his Headquarters in Southern Laos and began a leaflet campaign whose effect on the population was negligible. But what was far more effective was the action taken in Luang Prabang on General Phoumi's orders against a messenger sent by Prince Souvanna Phouma requesting the King's approval for his Government. The messenger was arrested and his aeroplane confiscated. Souvanna Phouma was then faced with a serious military threat, since most of the Royal Laotian Army was still loyal to General Phoumi. Souvanna Phouma decided that the only course of action open to him was to confer with the Opposition (the deposed Government). He borrowed an American plane and flew South to Savanna khet. On his return Souvanna Phouma announced that agreement had been reached on all problems. On the morning of August 29th 1960, Prince Souvanna left for Luang Prabang, and 34 Deputies of the National Assembly and other dignatories departed for the same destination.

After considerable delay a so-called settlement was worked out at Luang Prabang, but events proved this solution to be of a transitory nature. On September 10th, General Phoumi announced that he had formed a Revolutionary Committee under Prince Boun Oum. Civil War had broken out again, with pro-Communist Pathet Lao guerrillas emerging from their jungle hide-outs to re-capture and occupy Sam Neua.

In Vientiane, Souvanna Phouma was being pushed further and further to the left and at his invitation the Soviet Government had agreed to send an Ambassador to Vientiane; at the same time he was alienating American support by his open embrace of Communist help. But far more important was the fact that food was running out and the blockade which the Thai Authorities had imposed against what they realised was a pro-Communist Government, was rapidly taking effect. Prince Souvanna gave up the struggle, and on December 9th he left Vientiane together with some of his Ministers and supporters and flew direct to Phnom Penh in neutral Cambodia.

General Phoumi organised his forces for a major attack on Vientiane against Kong Le's forces, which consisted mainly of the Parachute Regiment and some armoured units. General Phoumi's superior force won the day and it was not long before Kong Le was driven out of the town. This was the signal for the new King to dissolve the Souvanna Phuoma Government and appoint Savannakhet's Committee as a provisional Government headed by Prince Boun Oum as Prime Minister. Unfortunately, General Phoumi made no serious attempt to pursue and destroy Kong Le's forces which were allowed to retreat to the Plaine des Jarres, their retreat being accompanied by drops of supplies and food from Russian aircraft. Once installed in Pathet Lao territory Kong Le issued an invitation to Souvanna Phouma to visit his "loyal troops". A Russian aircraft was put at his disposal and a *rapprochement* was reached between Prince Souvanna Phouma and Prince Souvanouvong in the Plaine des Jarres. After the ceremonies were over Souvanna Phouma returned to Phnom Penh, where to his surprise General Phoumi, representing the Boun Oum Government, called on him in the hope of achieving a settlement with the rebel prince before events had gone so far that a reconciliation would be impossible. From his hide-out in the Plaine des Jarres Prince Souphanouvong condemned the proposed agreement and insisted that his half-brother Prince Souvanna Phouma had been the victim of an imperialist plot.

Having failed to take the initiative and destroy Kong Le's forces, General Phoumi now sat back nursing the belief that his National Army was capable of destroying the Communist forces located in the area of the Plaine des Jarres. Fighting again broke out between the two sides. The Pathet Lao's forces were now reinforced by Kong Le's forces.

It was clear to the Western World that the pro-Communist forces located in the Plaine des Jarres were likely to remain a thorn in the side of the Laotian Government and represented a direct military threat to Boun Oum's Government. With this in mind they proposed that Great Britain and the Soviet Union should reconvene the Geneva Conference after having made an appeal to both sides for a cease fire, that cease fire to be supervised by the International Control Commission, whose return to Laos should be requested. The Russians sat tight, and once they realised that the SEATO powers, who had published a communiqué on March 29th, were unwilling to fight for Laos and had decided that any solution would have to be through peaceful means, they were not slow to use this information. Why should they hurry themselves if they knew that the Western powers were not going to force the issue; time was on their side and enabled the joint forces of Prince Souphanouvong and Kong Le to improve and consolidate their military positions.

Prince Souvanna Phouma had set out on a tour of the

Communist and non-Communist capitals to canvass his neutralist solution for Laos. Unfortunately, his schedule had to be altered and the United States were compelled to tell him that, as he had postponed his visit to them, there would be an inevitable delay in his appointment to meet President Kennedy and Dean Rusk, both of whom were committed to long standing engagements which could not be disturbed at such short notice. In a fit of pique Souvanna Phouma cancelled his visit. Whether a meeting between this basically non-Communist Prince and Kennedy would have achieved any results must remain a matter for speculation but certainly the meeting could have done no harm. Day by day the military situation, as far as the Royal Laotian Government were concerned, was deteriorating.

Instead of concentrating on the war the Laotians were side-tracked in their efforts by arranging for the last rites of the late King, whose funeral had been delayed in order that it should be carried out in the presence of foreign guests and the Diplomatic Corps. They had even used aircraft which could and should have been used to their full capacity for military supplies. There were two conspicuously vacant seats at the ceremony—for the two members of the Royal House, Prince Souvanna Phouma and Prince Souphanouvong. The most important guest to attend the ceremony was Prince Sihanouk of Cambodia who was directing his efforts and using his very considerable influence to persuade all concerned that the only solution to the problem would be an international conference at which the differences of attitude could be resolved. Sihanouk was not sparing in his criticism of all three Princes. Souvanouvong for his co-operation with North Vietnamese Communists, Souvanouvong's half-brother Souvanna Phouma for allowing himself to become a lackey of the Russians, and last but not least Prince Boun Oum for his reliance on America. As a result of Sihanouk's diplomacy Boun Oum agreed to meet the other two Princes and after considerable argument it fell to Sihanouk to choose the meeting place, Zurich.

The second Geneva Conference assembled on the 16th May 1961, at Geneva. As co-Chairmen the United Kingdom and Soviet delegations played the principal role and as in the

1954 Conference acted as Chairmen at alternate sessions but, unlike the 1954 Conference, the Foreign Secretaries, Lord Home and Mr. Gromyko, only attended certain sessions; otherwise Mr. Malcolm MacDonald and Mr. Pushkin acted on behalf of the co-Chairmen. The 1954 Conference had been confined to nine delegations, but in 1961 the scope was increased on Sihanouk's suggestion so as to include Laos's other neighbours, Burma and Thailand, and also representatives from those countries providing the supervisory teams: India, Canada and Poland. The work of the Conference was held up for various reasons, the most important of which was the co-operation of the three Princes concerned. It was Prince Sihanouk's initiative which overcame this hurdle; on the 22nd June 1961, his diplomacy prevailed and the three princes issued a joint communiqué agreeing to establish a provisional Government of National Union which was to send a single delegation to the Conference, a delegation which was to pursue a neutral foreign policy. It was not until October 1961 that an agreement was reached in Laos between the three Princes whereby Prince Souvanna Phouma should be Premier, but they were still unable to agree on the Constitution of the Cabinet. Again the Conference was held up. Although the three Princes had agreed in Zurich on a cease fire, fighting between the armies continued. On the 2nd December 1961, the co-Chairmen made a direct approach to the three princes urging them to carry out the provisions to which they had already agreed. Again on the 6th January 1962 the co-Chairmen invited the three princes to come to Geneva to resolve their differences. This proposal was accepted, but the three were still incapable of reaching agreement on the details.

Conditions in Laos reached a peak of danger on 6th May, 1962, when Pathet Lao forces occupied a town near the Thai border. Two days later President Kennedy ordered United States armed forces to Thailand, backed up by an R.A.F. squadron and contingents from Australia and New Zealand. On the 7th June 1962, negotiations between the three Princes were resumed in Laos, and five days later they agreed on the composition of a provisional Government of National Union which was to take office on the 23rd June. At last a united delegation was sent to Geneva, and on the 23rd July the Conference issued a Declaration of Neutrality of Laos and adopted a special Protocol which laid down the role of the co-Chairmen and of the International Commission. From then on the Commission in Laos became an instrument of the Conference, a position which it had never previously held. The co-Chairmen were to receive reports from the Commission and were at the same time given powers to issue general guidance to the Commission. Unfortunately the new position which had been laid down between the co-Chairmen and the Commission could only be made applicable to Laos, since the Conference's terms of reference were confined to that country, but it did have the effect of strengthening the co-Chairmen's functions in Viet Nam and Cambodia although by implication only.

The three rival Princes in Laos were unable to co-operate, and the Government of the National Union was never really effective. Each of the rival elements had retained his own armed forces and gradually the country reverted to a state of general civil war, with each sector receiving military aid from the Government which supported it. All efforts on behalf of the British Government, acting as one of the co-Chairmen, to persuade the Soviets to assist in a solution proved fruitless, but the co-Chairmen were able to join in condemning a military coup which was attempted in Vientiane in April 1964.

In May 1965, SEATO Council condemned the presence of North Vietnamese forces in Laos and also the use of Laotian territory as a channel for sending men and material to the Viet Cong operating in South Viet Nam. It regretted that the International Control Commission was unable to act effectively against violations of the Geneva Agreement which were taking place in Communist held sections of the Kingdom. At the same time it expressed its support for the 1962 Geneva Agreement and the efforts of the Government of the National Union under the Prime Minister, Prince Souvanna Phouma to preserve the independence and neutrality of Laos.

Both Laos and Cambodia are regarded as neutrals, and they would probably not tolerate any interference in their internal affairs. It is, however, clear that the utilisation of their territory for the passage of men and materials to South Viet Nam is contrary to the Geneva Agreement. If and when South East Asia has a new treaty of protection, then the Control Commission which is still working in Laos could be given teeth so that the activities of the Pathet Lao and North Viet Nam in respect of their use of Laotian territory could be curtailed. Far from being contrary to the spirit of the Geneva Agreement, this would be adhering to its provisions.

The political difficulty over this would be that the Control Commission takes its orders through the co-Chairmen of the Geneva Agreement and it would not be easy to persuade Russia to co-operate unless at that particular time she had some other motive for wishing to co-operate with the West.

The great international effort which was made in 1962 to bring the three Princes together succeeded in setting up a United Government which ought to have survived and enabled the country to pursue a neutral policy. The very fact that they retained their own forces was an ill omen for a lasting settlement. The Provisional Government of National Union was formed in June 1962 under the leadership of Prince Souvanna Phouma. The pro-Communist Minister of Foreign Affairs was murdered in April 1963, and two or three months later Prince Souphanouvong returned to join the forces of the Pathet Lao. From then on any hopes of a settlement disappeared.

Although the International Control Commission is still present in Laos it is hampered by a refusal on the part of the Pathet Lao to permit the Commission's staff free operation in the territory under their control. The Royal Laotian Government under the Premiership of Prince Souvanna Phouma claims to control most of the large towns and two-thirds of the country. The Pathet Lao assisted by North Viet Nam troops has been able to retain control of that part of the country bordering North Viet Nam and South Viet Nam and has repelled all the attempts made by the Royal Laotian Army to re-occupy these areas, but the Royal Army has been able to take prisoners and has given the International Control Commission an opportunity for cross-questioning them. From this it is clear that North Viet Nam troops are operating with the Pathet Lao. It is also clear that the Ho Chi Minh Trail runs through Pathet Lao territory and that the passage of North Vietnamese regular soldiers through Laos has been facilitated by the protection afforded them by military units of the Pathet Lao reinforced at times by North Viet Nam troops.

So long as the Pathet Lao controls this frontier North Viet Nam reinforcements will be able to move unimpeded from North Viet Nam to South Viet Nam and can enter the country at any point along that frontier. American and Allied forces could not possibly control this entire stretch of Viet Nam's frontier.

Cambodia

Cambodia's role in this troop movement is less important, but its significance lies in the fact that Viet Cong troops can take refuge in neutral Cambodia where they can rest and re-equip before returning to join the Viet Cong in South Viet Nam. Looked at in this light the prospect is depressing—as soon as one Viet Cong is killed by the Allies, two can easily be brought in as reinforcements via this comparatively safe route. This flow of men can only be stopped when the South Viet Nam Government in collaboration with their Allies have complete control of the country. Then and only then can they establish an effective system of identity cards which would make it far more difficult for North Viet Nam soldiers to move through South Viet Nam to join Viet Cong formations. Once this degree of control has been established in the country, and the South Viet Nam villages are given a sense of security, then an inducement, possibly in the way of a reward, may persuade villagers to hand over these infiltrators to the Government. Until these conditions are fulfilled there is no possibility of arresting insidious infiltration from the North.

Thailand (Siam)

Until recently, Siam, or as it is now called, Thailand, had a superiority complex towards Communism and was under the impression that its country was so stable that there was no risk of Communist infiltration.

The Japanese occupation during the war had been an unpleasant experience but there was a certain degree of co-operation between the Siamese and the Japanese and as a result of this Siam probably suffered less under the Occupation than the other countries in South East Asia. Perhaps its worst feature was the devaluation of the currency by the Japanese, who went as far as to print millions of notes and flood the country with paper money.

Fortunately, the young King of Siam was in exile in England during the war and he did not have to make a decision whether or not to co-operate with the Japanese, so when he returned after the war he was able to form a fulcrum around which the nation could rebuild itself.

Throughout the country there is a genuine affection for both him and the Queen, and it is this affection and loyalty which distinguishes Thailand from the other countries in South East Asia.

In the last two or three years, however, the Government of Thailand has discovered that there has been a steady infiltration of Communists taking place both from Laos and Cambodia, into what was known as the North Eastern provinces, whose capitals from South to North are Korat, Khonkaen and Udorn*. All these provinces have certain characteristics in common. Apart from the freedom route built by the Americans, which runs from Bangkok up to Udorn, the roads are very poor and in some cases non-existent. These areas were always regarded as of little benefit economically and were neglected and tended to become backwaters for the less successful provincial administrators.

*Infiltration is also coming from Malaya.

After talking to the Government in Bangkok, I learned that in the last two years information had shown them that Communist infiltration in each of these areas was a potential danger. Later, when I lunched with the Governor of Korat, it was clear that the infiltration in his particular province was not merely coming from Laos in the North down through the other two provinces into his own province, but was also coming from the direction of Cambodia in the East.

So far, the infiltrators were only in the first phase of Communism, ingratiating themselves with the people, suggesting that the Government was corrupt, and that life in a Communist society would be preferable for them. Threats and acts of violence had not yet begun, though obviously it was the clear intention that the full measure of Communist methods should eventually be put into effect. The Governor was active, and used a helicopter so that he could visit all his villages. Since there are virtually no telephone communications in Thailand it was the only way he was able to keep in personal touch with them. What he required more than anything else were better road links so that villages could feel that at all times they were in contact with the administrative capital and that, if the infiltrators gave trouble, the hamlets could rapidly call for military assistance which could be brought in by helicopter and by road.

In his opinion, the time was coming when the Communists would step up their activities and then it would be vital to bring in military or police assistance to reinforce them against any threats which the infiltrators might make. The minimum would be to produce forces which, at very short notice, would be capable of backing up the local police and militia.

In these three provinces, the Americans have got bases from which they are operating against targets in North Viet Nam. For some reason or another, this was kept secret for a long time, but the fact has now been made public. The arrangement under which these airfields were made available to the Americans is bilateral between the U.S. and the Government of Thailand. It is outside the scope of SEATO.

In all these states, American Aid (USIS) is being stepped up.

INTERESTED PARTIES

It is not only free advice on farming that the Americans have been giving, but aid in the form of modern agricultural machinery and tractors. It is this practical aid which will form the best defence against Communism in these areas. The U.S. Aid Programme in the Province of Korat, for example, is engaged in an extremely difficult task. They have been provided with a multitude of different types of vehicles and tractors, a gift which has brought in its train considerable problems, especially with regard to spare parts and maintenance. Why, one might ask, were they not sent standard vehicles of identical type, so that the spares problem would be much easier? The answer, of course, is that the Americans are paying for this, and are using a certain amount of secondhand equipment which they have secured from a number of different sources. There is also a further complication which applies particularly to any new agricultural or other equipment. American business interests are very sensitive, and if only one make were imported, then it would certainly lead to a large number of questions in the United States as to why this particular firm should be favoured.

One might think the answer to this would be for the U.S. Aid Programme all over the world to be split into sectors, and equipment of a particular firm confined to that specific theatre. But again there are difficulties because, quite obviously, although the equipment which is being supplied through this U.S. Aid source is not being paid for by the recipient country, nevertheless the very fact that these vehicles are present and bear the names of the firms, does put the firms concerned in an advantageous position for selling vehicles privately within that country.

A further difficulty in this particular province arises because of the lack of roads. The Americans have been able to produce transporters, and by almost super-human efforts have been able to move very heavy agricultural machinery along routes consisting almost entirely of tracks. Most of the movement, of course, has to take place in the dry weather. The aid which is being given is the immediate aid, but really what is required in these areas is roads not only for the transport of this United

States Aid Programme, but also to open up these areas of the country so that a proper system of administration and communications can take place.

The almost complete lack of telephones in these areas makes it impossible for normal communications to be maintained. If the villages are to be protected against Communist attacks, then it is essential that such communications should be established. In their absence, the only possible system of telecommunications is short-wave wireless transmitters.*

The Communists have not, up to the present time, been violent, but this is part and parcel of Communist methods, and the Thai Government must be prepared for the second phase of activity which is, in fact, violence. When this starts, it will be even more important that the local headman in the village should have a rapid means of communication with mobile troops, who can be put on the ground rapidly to contend with these threats.

The problem in these provinces of Thailand is almost exactly the same as the problem which exists in Viet Nam. But the essential difference is that Communism is only just starting to rear its ugly head in Thailand, while it has been existent in Viet Nam for nearly 20 years. The second difference is that at the moment the Communists are adopting a programme of non-violence, whereas in Viet Nam they have been conducting a programme of violence and terror for many years.

If communications can be improved and agricultural development carried out, then Thailand has an excellent chance of resisting the first phase of Communist aggression.

Internationally, Bangkok is important because it is the Headquarters of the South East Asia Treaty Organisation. If Thailand were to fall victim to Communist aggression, this would represent the greatest single factor in the complete collapse of all efforts to resist Communism in South East Asia.

But what of the Thais themselves? Do they really want this protection? Again, the answer is that until recently they saw little benefit from membership of SEATO or from American

---

*Wireless has the advantage that there is no line which can be cut.

military aid, but as a result of the uncovering of Communist agitation they realised that they could not possibly resist this aggression single-handed. Perhaps the only disadvantage of American Aid and large numbers of Americans operating within the country, is a danger of inflation. This is a real worry. As soon as the numbers of American personnel increase there is always an accompanying inflation. It is not the fault of the Americans, but the fact that in a scarcity market in such simple things as hotels, taxis and even local market produce, the increased pressure raises prices. American personnel must be accommodated and a fair market price paid.

The alternative would be for the Americans to set up their own apartment blocks and have most of their supplies brought from the United States. But even this would entail increased pressure on the services which the nation can provide, and would almost certainly be accompanied by some degree of inflation, though perhaps not quite so much.

Thailand was woken up out of its dream and has realised that it could not remain independent of Communism if its neighbours were to fall victims to that form of Government. It is for this reason that Thailand has undertaken to send a token force to fight in South Viet Nam. It must be taken as a signal of their fear that Communism under Mao is determined to sweep through South East Asia.

It was originally envisaged that this token force might be increased so that Thailand's military effort towards the anti-Communist struggle in Viet Nam would be of a realistic nature. Unfortunately, when America canvassed the South East Asian capitals recently for an increase, the response was not as great as had been hoped. Thailand may well have thought that the rising tide of Communism in her own country did not warrant a reduction in her home forces. It is to be hoped that in the future she will find herself able to raise sufficient troops for internal security within her own boundaries and still send a sizeable force to Viet Nam.

This is not an unreasonable proposition, as the American Aid Programme to Thailand ought to be matched by efforts on the part of that country to defeat Communism.

Korea

Korea was one of the first countries to fall victim to Japan's expansionist policy. The chances of resistance by a little country like this were indeed small. Up to the time of Japan's occupation the country had been ruled and administered by a powerful but inefficient system of Government headed by a King.

In Korea in the time of the nineteenth century there were no schools and the only education was provided by the Pai Jai Middle School which had been established in 1894 by the Methodist Missionaries, and it was in the same year that the Sino-Japanese War broke out. Korea was a hermit kingdom, and life and conditions in Seoul were similar to those prevailing in Paris in the fifteenth century, with its narrow streets with mud thatched houses. Administration was through an absolute Monarch, justice was meted out by an hereditary aristocracy, and capital punishment was the penalty for crimes even of a minor nature. Very few Koreans had ever been outside their own country. It was against this background that Syngman Rhee was brought up.

In 1866 a French man-of-war attacked Inchon harbour and besieged Kang-wha Island; the Koreans mustered a force of 5,000 men, armed with bows and arrows and flintlocks, and beat off the attack, which had been made by only 160 French soldiers. In 1871 Admiral Rogers, at the head of a force of five American gun boats, realised that the take-over of Korea would not be possible except with a very large force.

The young King had come of age in 1875, but his mother, Queen Min, was virtually in control of the country and had been very impressed by the Japanese progress in social spheres and believed that her country would do well to follow Japan's example. She made a treaty with the Japanese and allowed their merchants to trade in the country. The revolt against the Queen in 1882 was put down with the assistance of Chinese troops.

When the Japanese invaded China, the Koreans took this as a signal that they would be free from Chinese influence, and also were encouraged by promises from Japan that she would guarantee Korea's independence.

What followed in 1895 was one of the most revolting of international incidents. The new Japanese ambassador, Viscount Miura, endeavoured to increase the Japanese influence in Korea, and soon became involved in the day to day intrigues of the Korean Court. He prepared a plot for the murder of the Queen, and for the holding of the young Monarch under Japanese control. The Queen and the Minister of the Household were murdered and a pro-Japanese Government was established. Syngman Rhee himself had been involved, so whatever his later services to Korea were, it should not be forgotten that he was involved in a plot which was the most important step taken towards Japanese control of the country. But Syngman Rhee was concerned, as is often the case, not with the cause with which he aligned himself, but with its ultimate object, which was to smash a corrupt internal Government.

In 1905 Roosevelt sent his Secretary of War, William Howard Taft, to sign a secret agreement with the Japanese which left them a free hand in Korea and Manchuria in exchange for a guarantee not to attack the Philippine Islands. Already, in 1903, England had signed a treaty with Japan recognising Japan's special interests in North Asia.

It was not until 1922 that the Taft-Katsura agreement became generally known. By the careful use of money, the Japanese were now in control of the few financial institutions which existed, including the telegraph and postal systems.

Under the pretext of military necessity the Japanese Army, which was supposed to be in Korea to fight Russia, occupied large areas surrounding Seoul and then proceeded to take over control of the whole country. At the same time they surrounded the Palace, and at bayonet point forced the young King to sign an agreement accepting Japanese protection for Korea.

Roosevelt had been persuaded by his advisers that Korea was a backward country, unfit to govern herself, and that Japanese occupation was the best medicine for her.

At the end of the First World War Syngman Rhee, the great patriot, had supposed that among Woodrow Wilson's points for the release of subjugated nations, Korea would head the list, or would be somewhere near the top of it, but, after all, Japan had joined forces with the Allies and it was scarcely likely that they were going to force her to give up any of her possessions. Japan had already forestalled such a move by having a petition circulated throughout the country. This was a declaration that the Korean people were grateful for the beneficial and generous rule of the Japanese and were rapidly becoming assimilated into the Japanese way of life. It did not appear to occur to anyone that the value of this petition was negligible, since most of the population could neither read nor write. The only person who refused to sign it was the old Korean Emperor, who died soon after under mysterious circumstances.

In 1919 an attempt was made to overthrow the Japanese. It was well organised, and for some reason the Japanese Secret Service had not discovered anything about it. It rallied great support throughout the country. The Japanese used exactly the same methods as they used in the Second World War, burning houses, murdering people, and making their customary use of torture to extract information from people. This was the last real attempt at getting rid of the aggressors, and a Government of Exile was born which was probably to be the longest Government of Exile in history, for it was not until 1945 that it returned to govern Korea.

During the Second World War Syngman Rhee and his friends endeavoured to get recognition from the Americans as the Korean Government in Exile, but the whole situation bristled with difficulties. The State Department was at first unwilling to give recognition, and wanted to delay decision until after the war; there were rumours that the British had discussed the possibility that Korea might be absorbed into the Soviet Union; President Roosevelt had suggested that Korea be placed under an International agreement, with China, the United States and one or two other countries participating.

What could Syngman Rhee do about this? The corridors of

power were closed to him for, after all, he was only a private citizen. Roosevelt was still completely unaware of the full impact of Communism, and when Rhee was asked to co-operate with a Communist-influenced underground movement in Korea he refused. The danger of compromising with Communism at this stage could mean a take over by them at a later date. Once again Roosevelt was unable to comprehend Communist intentions.

It was not only Syngman Rhee who had been pressed to compromise and join forces with the Communists; the great Chiang Kai-shek himself had been placed under similar pressure. At this stage it ought to be mentioned, in fairness to America, that the President of the United States was working flat out during the war, that like the head of any Government he had to rely on information from the State Department; that that department, however efficient it might be, could only judge facts as it saw them, and, like a tennis ball, the events were being knocked from one court to the other.

The principal allies were concerned with the defeat of the Axis Powers; countries such as Korea were merely appendices to the main agenda. America and Great Britain wished to come to grips with the problems, but not at the expense of annoying their allies. Syngman Rhee had spent his life studying the problems in this geographical area, and was, of course, more forward-looking than the Americans. Both he and Chiang Kai-shek knew that no sooner was the peace treaty signed than there would be a new enemy appearing. That enemy would be the rise of Communism throughout South East Asia, a force which would be harder to combat because it would not present a conventional force against which a direct frontal attack could be launched.

It was probably at Yalta that Stalin made it clear that part of the price for Russian participation in the war was that Soviet troops would have to be admitted to Korea. Truman at Potsdam seems to have accepted Stalin's declaration that an agreement had been reached for Soviet troops to enter part of Korea, but it was not until Russia finally entered the war, six days before the surrender of Japan, that her troops entered

North Korea, both by land and sea. Korea was divided up by the Allies just like Viet Nam.

The temporary dividing line for the occupation of Korea was formalised in the top military command in mid-August, along the line of the 38th Parallel. America intended to send General Wedemeyer to occupy South Korea, but for various reasons this was not possible and General Hodge was given the task. Hodge was an excellent military commander, but sadly lacking in knowledge of Far Eastern politics.

On 8th September 1945, he landed at Inchon, where General Abe, the Japanese Governor General of Korea, had asked Hodge for authority to maintain full police control so as to prevent the murder of 600,000 Japanese residents of the peninsula. Hodge's reply was unfortunate, and was to the effect of granting the request, accompanied by a remark that he regarded Koreans as the same breed of cat as the Japanese.

His misunderstanding of the people of Korea and their problems was reflected in a tragic incident in which Koreans who had been ordered to stay at home by the Japanese came out of their homes to welcome the Americans as liberators. The Japanese police opened fire upon them. The Japanese police were commended by General Hodge and the Koreans were pushed aside as the Japanese took over the role of official hosts. Hodge capped this by announcing that all Japanese officials would retain their places and control the country until a military Government had been established. Fortunately the American Government intervened and issued strict orders to Hodge that Japanese officials were to be replaced in the shortest possible time.

During this time the Russians had taken over North Korea and had actually advanced south of the 38th Parallel to occupy the city of Kaesong, but after the landing of the American troops they withdrew from Kaesong with their loot.

Hodge found himself in a very difficult position, with no advisers who understood the problems of Korea and very few officers able to speak the Korean language. By now the position had become clear; North Korea was occupied by the Russians, and South Korea by the Americans. In the North, Communism had been put into practice, land holdings had been confiscated, and an army organised. And by 1946 the Communist régime had been "elected"; industry had been put on its feet; but still 1,600 North Koreans were fleeing to the South every day.

General Hodge was left with a very difficult task—he was at the end of the line for supplies which passed through Japan, where MacArthur took the lion's share; the only real peg upon which he could hang a new Government was Syngman Rhee, who had annoyed him in 1945 by refusing to co-operate with the Communists to form a coalition. In June 1946, Hodge invited Rhee and others to form a Government, but Rhee refused to co-operate with pro-Communists. Fortunately in the Interim Assembly elections which occurred shortly afterwards Syngman Rhee's party obtained 43 out of 45 elected members; once again Hodge exposed his ignorance by accusing Syngman Rhee of mailed fist tactics to ensure such a result. Had this been true, it would have been an indictment against Hodge who had organised the supervision of the elections. Hodge replied by appointing 45 members nominated by a pro-Communist coalition committee.

Syngman Rhee decided to appeal to the American people direct, and over the head of Hodge. On 1st March General Hodge was recalled to Washington for consultation. His failure as a political minister was obvious to Washington. In fairness to him, however, it should be said that there are very few men in history who have been successful soldiers *and* good politicians; even Wellington, when he went into politics, was not as successful in the House of Lords as he was on the battlefield of Waterloo.

Rhee found himself very much better received in Washington than he was in Seoul, and his argument that Hodge had acted unfairly and undemocratically in making his appointments to the Interim Assembly was patently true, and Rhee had the advantage of his overwhelming success in the November elections. In spite of all this, however, the State Department lines of policy had not yet altered and Rhee found himself unable to discuss in a serious vein the future political structure of the Korean Government. It was during this period (on 1st March) General Hodge was recalled to Washington.

Hodge then performed one of his best services to America by announcing publicly that the Russians were organising an army of half a million men in North Korea; this electrified the Press, and even had some effect on the State Department, but petty officialdom and lack of coherent policy resulted in delays in Rhee's return to Korea.

The Secretary of State, George Marshall, went to Moscow, and quite unexpectedly persuaded Molotov that the Joint Commission discussions on re-unification should be resumed.

Syngman Rhee's return to Korea was followed by a vitriolic debate which resulted in Kim Koo's resigning as Chairman of the Provisional Government and Syngman Rhee being elected, and a bill was introduced into the Assembly proposing a constitution for an independent Government in South Korea.

In May General Shtikov arrived in Seoul with 38 Russian officials to re-open the Joint Commission but he failed to carry out Molotov's pledge, to admit all Korean leaders to the discussions.

Syngman Rhee could not accept Hodge's views on Trusteeship and asked in an open letter for a definition which he never got. As a result, Rhee was practically under house arrest, his telephone was removed and his weekly radio talks to the Korean people came to an end. Yet his prestige in the United States was gathering momentum.

In August 1947 Secretary Marshall had come to the conclusion that the Joint Commission was a failure. Great Britain, China and Russia were invited to join the United States in seeking some alternative. The Soviet Union rejection left Marshall with the only alternative, the United Nations. On 17th September, Marshall asked the General Assembly of the United Nations to place the Korean question on the Agenda, and by the 23rd of that month, the General Assembly accepted the question of Korea (on its Agenda). Voting on the issue took place on 14th November; for the holding of free elections to establish an Independent Government under the observation of a United Nations Commission, the vote was 43—0. The Soviet Union declared the United Nations vote to hold elections illegal, but for once the United Nations were not deterred, and on 8th January 1948, the advance group of United Nations delegates arrived in Seoul.

The first formal session of the United Nations Commission was held on 12th January 1948; letters were drafted to General Hodge and General Shtikov requesting free access to all areas in Korea. Hodge gave his immediate affirmative answer, but letters to Shtikov went unanswered. Some of the delegates expressed the view that the United Nations should have simply flown their flags and driven into North Korea, but one of the delegates said: "All right, but who is going in the first car?"

The United Nations Commission had reached the point of no return and sent one of its delegates back to Lake Success for further instructions. The real argument was whether or not it would strengthen or weaken South Korea to have an election in the country confined to that part of the country which lay south of the 38th Parallel. A delightful formula was devised by the little assembly (voting: 31 for, 2 against, 11 abstentions) "to observe elections in all areas of Korea accessible to the Commission."

On the morning of 10th May 1948, for the first time in over 4,000 years of history, Korea had its first democratic election, with American soldiers and Korean policemen watching the polling booths. Throughout the country the Communists endeavoured to frustrate the election. A poll of 92.5 per cent can only be described as an exceptional turn-out (women were admitted to the franchise). The United Nations Commission later passed a favourable comment on the conduct of the election.

In spite of all the frustration which Syngman Rhee had suffered through General Hodge's misunderstandings, Rhee was sufficiently great to pay tribute to Hodge publicly at the first session of the Assembly on 27th May. Syngman Rhee was elected Chairman of the Assembly on 31st May by a vote of 189—8 and the Assembly worked on the draft of a constitution.

On 19th July 1948, Rhee was elected the first President of the Republic of Korea by a vote of 180, with 16 of the members voting for Kim Koo.

The process of transition of the Government machinery from the American military to the civilian Koreans was carried out in an orderly fashion, and at the formal inauguration ceremonies on 15th August an incident occurred which was described at the time as an act of sentimentality. General MacArthur had set foot on Korean soil for the first time. He placed an arm round Rhee's shoulder and said: "If Korea should be attacked by the Communists, I will defend it like California." How wrong the Press were when they described this as sentimentality! In June 1950 American troops under MacArthur came back to Korea to defend it, just as MacArthur had promised.

Syngman Rhee then entered the most important phase of his life, which was that of establishing a free and democratic Korea. He was faced with an extremely difficult problem, for, as a result of the Japanese occupation, there were very few people in the country capable of accepting the administrative and political appointments which were necessary in order to establish the machinery of government.

Although he was now established as elected President by certain special powers, Rhee by no means had a free hand and was dependent both economically and for military aid on the United States. He was helped by the fact that the American military government had taken over former Japanese farm lands and sold them to individuals; this was certainly a help. In the Communist North Korea, the $7\frac{1}{2}$ per cent of the population who were classed as landlords, were liquidated, and their lands disposed of to Communist committees. Syngman Rhee had no intention of following the Communist example; he was in favour of free enterprise. What he wanted was to persuade the landlords to sell their land, but how could the peasants possibly afford to buy it? In any case, many of the new land-lords were represented in the new Assembly and had always been the most influential people in the country. The worst effect of the land tenure was the system whereby a third of the produce went to the landlord. After considerable wrangling, and having refused to sign the first decree in 1949, Rhee helped to draft a new bill and signed it in March 1950, and one and three quarter million acres became the property of the former farm tenants ,the landlords receiving compensation. Syngman Rhee's tackling of this problem was just as brave as President Ky's, and equally effective.

*   *   *

In 1949 the American Ambassador in Seoul told President Rhee that the United States troops still in South Korea were to be withdrawn, to which Rhee replied that the presence of United States troops was not as important as the policy of the United States. Was the United States willing to guarantee that if Korea was attacked she would come to her aid? At the same time, Rhee pointed out that the Korean army was ill equipped and only had enough ammunition to last for three days of warfare against an organised Communist attack from the North. Already attacks were occurring over the 38th Parallel which was being violated daily by the Communists. Such equipment which Korea was receiving from the United States was dependent on the South Koreans' promises not to advance within three miles of the dividing line. In the case of the city of Kaesong, whose centre was exactly three miles from the 38th Parallel, the Koreans were obliged to restrict their defences to the centre of the city. When this city was attacked in March 1949 by the Communists, South Korean troops were compelled to operate in this "forbidden area" in order to drive back the attacking forces. The Korean Government received a strong rebuke from the Americans for their action. Later in the year, 4,000 Communist troops attacked the Ongjin peninsula. The Koreans were advised not to retaliate, on the grounds that the area involved was of little use, but Rhee refused to accede to this request as he considered any withdrawal would be an indication to the Communists that the South Koreans were not prepared to defend their rights.

The American Secretary of State, Dean Acheson, as late as

239

12th January 1950, had made a statement to members of the National Press Club in Washington to the effect that Korea lay outside the United States defence perimeter. This was all the more surprising as American diplomats in Asia had been informed that Formosa might well be taken by the Chinese Communists in the near future. It was against this background that Rhee faced the impending Communist attack. The R.O.K. forces had been equipped for minor actions of a guerrilla nature, and no provision whatsoever had been made for the possibility of a major Communist attack on South Korea. The United Nations Commission had made a survey in the early part of 1950, but its observations were confined to South Korea as the Communists would not allow inspection of their forces in the North. This commission's object had been to see whether there was a major concentration of troops on either side of the Parallel. They were sufficiently naïve to commend the way in which Rhee had his troops located all over Korea and not concentrated along the Parallel. Unseen by the Commission, north of the 38th Parallel Communist troop concentrations had already taken place ready to move across the 38th Parallel. Early on Sunday, 25th June, the Communists launched their offensive east of Kaesong. As this had been the scene of an earlier minor incident it was not clear for at least two hours after the launching of the attack whether this was just another border incident or the spearhead of a major military attack on South Korea.

Rhee was in a dilemma. Either he could make a rapid peace with the Communists or he could launch a counter-offensive on his own. He had no treaty with the Americans guaranteeing military assistance when Korea was invaded and the only way that the United Nations was involved was through its Commission, which was still operating in Korea. Had Rhee surrendered, the country would have been overrun almost immediately by the Communists and the Americans would have had no legitimate reason, once Rhee's Government had disappeared, for coming to South Korea's rescue. There would have been no South Korea left. Rhee moved every possible soldier from all over the country by every possible route, and threw his hundred-thousand-man force of lightly armed men against a massive Communist attack backed by artillery and tanks. Within a few days half of his army had perished. President Truman announced his decision to intervene, but valuable time had been lost and the only troops available were the American occupation forces in Japan. The American forces which arrived under General Walker were unused to this type of war. Their action was restricted to the roads (tactics which were not dissimilar from those employed by the French Union forces in Viet Nam). The invading Communists were able to use the high points overlooking the roads and cut off the Americans. Rhee could see that the only possibility was for the immediate amalgamation of the R.O.K. forces and the United States units. The Americans with their motorised equipment could have stuck to the roads and left the guerrilla-like operations in the surrounding countryside to the Koreans. A combination of this nature might have obviated the terrible tragedy which ensued. The Americans under General Walker were too frightened to risk a unified command and had few if any interpreters and no desire on the part of their commander to create a unified command. The losses which the Koreans had sustained were terrifying, but nothing like as terrifying as the loss of civilian life as a result of murder and pillage by the Communist invading forces.

On 15th September, forces under the United Nations landed at Inchon and in accordance with the resolution of 7th October by the United Nations General Assembly, began their sweep northwards towards the 38th Parallel. The arrival of these reinforcements was sufficient to defeat the North Korean Communist forces and push them back to the 38th Parallel. General McArthur had discussed the war with Rhee and it appears that the Koreans were to be allowed to advance over the 38th Parallel but that the Americans could not cross it until such time as a United Nations decision had been reached. Rhee realised that the enemy were on the run and that an immediate strike into North Korea before the enemy had time to recover from the initial blow would result in his forces defeating the North Korean army in North Korea. As soon as South Korean forces moved into North Korea, trouble with the United Nations began. The United Nations maintained that South Korea's sphere of authority should be restricted to that part of the country south of the 38th Parallel and indicated that as soon as law and order had been established in the North new elections would take place under their (United Nations) auspices. Rhee argued that the United Nations had never until that moment questioned the fact that the Republic of Korea's authority extended throughout the entire country. In any case, if the Americans had to undertake the duty of occupation of North Korea it would appear to the villages that this was an American attempt at colonisation and might well be resisted, not only by Communists but also by non-Communist Koreans who would fight what appeared to them to be a new attempt at colonisation.

Suddenly the whole campaign took on a new aspect: the Chinese Red Army crossed the Yalu river to assist the North Korean army. At this point President Truman took fright. MacArthur wanted to bomb the bridges on the Yalu river and so halt the Communist advance, but President Truman announced that the war would not be extended into China. General MacArthur was being asked to do the impossible, to fight a superior force without being allowed to use the only tactics which could have worked, namely the bombing of the bridges of the Yalu river. This single operation would have slowed down the Chinese advance into Korea, enabled reinforcements to reach forward battle lines and last, but not least, given the world time to realise that this was no longer a war between the two halves of Korea, but a major campaign in which the Chinese Communists were active participants. The Red Chinese menace, linked arm in arm with North Korean Communist forces, moved steadily forward. United Nations forces had still not been given proper instructions as to what exactly their task and commitment was to be.

In December of that year the casualties on both sides were enormous, but even worse were the atrocities committed by the Communist forces which were slowly advancing southward. Refugees, wherever they could, tried to keep just ahead of the invading armies across country which was frozen hard and under conditions of biting cold. Hundreds of thousands perished with their families from exposure to the cold, from lack of food or from sheer exhaustion. In the middle of it all came the sad death of General Walker, and his replacement by Ridgway.

The second phase in the war was entirely different to the first campaign when the advancing forces consisted entirely of North Koreans. In the first phase reinforcements brought in by the Western Powers had been sufficient to turn the tide almost as soon as they had arrived in the country. But this second phase was quite different. The combined strengths of the Chinese and North Korean armies represented a force vastly superior in numbers to anything which the Free World could muster.

Once the Free World forces had been able to establish themselves on the 38th Parallel the war took on a more static character and in the years that followed the two sides opposed one another along a line which varied little.

During this long ordeal Rhee's determination and personal bravery were an example not only to his R.O.K. forces but to the Allied armies fighting in Korea. Suffering great personal discomfort, and travelling under difficult conditions, Rhee made a point of visiting the troops in the forward line and in so doing had many narrow shaves. His views on the future had proved to be correct but the United States and the United Nations retained the 38th Parallel as a dividing line between Communism and Freedom. Rhee's view had always been that unless the Western world could force the Communists across the Yalu river, their object had not been achieved. Neither was there any possibility of Korea being united. A United Nations General Assembly resolution on the 7th October 1950, had agreed to the Allied advance over the 38th Parallel and it was only after they had been beaten back by the combined Communist China and North Korean armies that the 38th Parallel was chosen once again as the dividing line.

The war in Korea had been looked at far too much as a separate campaign, whereas it should have been regarded as part and parcel of Communist advance in South East Asia.

Even before the Korean truce in 1953 arms and ammunition were transhipped from this theatre of operations to Viet Nam. The end of the war in Korea gave the Communists the opportunity for full scale intervention in Viet Nam.

In the eyes of the Koreans the victory in their country was only partial, since it left them a divided nation. Even under the Chinese and the Japanese there had never been a division, artificial or real. Had MacArthur had his way and the bridges of the Yalu river been destroyed, the Second Korean War, or phase in the war, would never have occurred. MacArthur was not alone in believing that the proper way of dealing with the Chinese attack on Korea was to use atomic warfare against the source of trouble and so destroy the possibility of China attacking other South East Asian countries. It must have been clear in his mind that Korea was just one of the spheres of activity in South East Asia which would become a constant source of trouble and represent a waste of lives in South East Asia.

The Red Chinese had only just succeeded in pushing Chiang Kai-shek's armies from the mainland, and had they concentrated their attacks on Taiwan they would almost certainly have defeated Chiang Kai-shek unless the United States had intervened immediately. The Red Chinese had made the wrong decision, and should have concentrated their efforts in 1950 on Chiang Kai-shek. If Taiwan had been occupied by Communist forces then, it is almost certain that an exiled Government headed by Chiang Kai-shek would not have been able to retain its place on the Security Council of the United Nations—a position which it holds today because it is a state of twelve million people with a Government which is recognised by many other nations. Chiang Kai-shek's survival was bought at the price of Korean and Allied soldiers killed in years of fighting in Korea.

If the Americans had used atomic bombs against the Chinese in 1950, would the Red Chinese have been in a position to extend their influence in Tibet, Viet Nam, and other South East Asian countries? An atomic attack on China would have caused havoc, but with a population of six hundred million and so many large cities the lasting effects of an atomic attack are questionable. It would certainly have put them back, probably ten to twenty years, and might even have enabled Chiang Kai-shek to re-establish his authority on the mainland.

President Truman's decision to refrain from bombing the bridges on the Yalu river and from the employment of nuclear weapons was based on a fear that these actions could have precipitated a third World War. It did not take into account the fact that Communist China was not properly organised, nor had she had time to assert herself as a great power. At the moment when actual Chinese troops crossed the Yalu river, Red China became involved in a war with the United States, and the United Nations and America had every right if she (U.S.A.) so desired, to pursue the attack across the Yalu river and strike at the origin of the invasion. This would have saved the lives of countless Americans and international troops who perished in the second phase of this horrible Korean War.

In Viet Nam the position is entirely different. Here the Chinese are backing the North Vietnamese with materials and money, but up until now there has never been a Chinese soldier captured in South Viet Nam, so that America could certainly not be regarded as being at war with China and there is no legal justification for America to bomb targets in China.

The present situation in Korea is unsatisfactory with North Korea and South Korea facing one another along a frontier of 151 miles, only prevented from open war by the existence of an armed truce which was signed on 27th July 1953. This Korean Armistice Agreement remains in force, as it has never been replaced by a proper peace treaty.

The United States, Great Britain, the Soviet Union and the Republic of China at the Cairo Conference and in the Potsdam Declaration had undertaken to "create" an independent Korea. At the end of the Second World War it had been decided that the Japanese occupation forces of Korea, north of the 38th Parallel, should surrender to Russia and that south of this line the U.S. forces should accept responsibility for Japanese surrender. The Soviet Government deliberately frustrated the spirit of the Cairo Conference and the Potsdam Declaration by creating an artificial barrier along the 38th Parallel.

The Soviet Government's refusal to permit free elections by denying the United Nations entry to North Korea resulted in the establishment of the Republic of Korea and its recognition by the United Nations as the only lawful Government in Korea; but, of course, this Government had no representation from that part of Korea which lay north of the 38th Parallel.

From then on hopes of re-unification were shattered and the Soviet Union, by setting up a rival Government in North Korea, known as the Democratic People's Republic of Korea, rendered any further chance of a united Korea impossible.

The invasion on 25th June 1950 by Soviet-trained Korean forces across the 38th Parallel began the Korean War. The response by 53 free nations resulted in the formation of combat forces by 16 member-countries of the United Nations.*

The North Korean forces were driven back to the frontiers of China along the line of the Yalu River and it was at this moment (25th November 1950) that the Chinese Communist "Volunteer Army" entered the war. They crossed from China into Korea and inflicted a crushing defeat on United Nations forces. The United Nations forces were never again to reach the Yalu River and it was not until June 1951 that they managed to push the mixed force consisting of North Korean and Chinese "Volunteer" Armies back to the 38th Parrallel.

On 23rd June 1951 the Russian delegate to the U.N. proposed a Korean cease-fire; Armistice negotiations began at Kaesong on 10th July 1951, but broke down and were later resumed near Panmunjom. Two years after the beginning of the negotiations the Korean Armistice Agreement was signed at Panmunjom (27th July 1953). There had been 255 meetings spread over two years and seventeen days and when it came to the final agreement the chief negotiators took only ten minutes to sign the eighteen official copies. Communist and U.N.

*The 16 nations which furnished combat forces were: Australia, Belgium, Canada, Colombia, Ethiopia, France, Greece, Luxembourg, Netherlands, New Zealand, Philippines, Thailand, Turkey, Union of South Africa, United Kingdom and the United States.

representatives rose from the table without shaking hands and left by separate exits. Several hours later General Mark Clark as Commander of the United Nations Command, Kimil Sung of the North Korean People's Army, and Peng Teh-huai on behalf of the Chinese People's Volunteers, put their signatures to the document at their own individual headquarters behind the fighting lines. Searchlights on the frontier went out and the firing stopped dramatically.

The Agreement which was signed is only binding upon the military forces of North Korea, the Communist Chinese "Volunteers", and those sixteen United Nations members who had furnished combat forces. The most remarkable part of the Agreement was that it was never signed by the Republic of Korea Government, who had only participated in the armistice talks as observers. The Government of the Republic of Korea not only observes the terms but supports the Agreement.

The Korean Armistice Agreement is in essence an agreement between the participating combatants, but it does contain a recommendation for the holding of a conference for the unification of Korea. Such a conference was in fact held, in Geneva in 1954, but agreement with the Communists was not possible; the present situation in Korea is determined by the Korean Armistice Agreement, the main provisions of which are:

1. Suspension of open hostilities
2. Withdrawal of all military forces and equipment from a zone (4,000 metres wide) separating the two sides (the demilitarised Zone)
3. Allow a one-for-one replacement of personnel and an item-for-item, type-for-type combat material in order to maintain the military status quo
4. Arrange the release and repatriation of prisoners-of-war and displaced civilians
5. Establish the Military Armistice Commission to negotiate any violation and to assure adherence to the Truce terms.

From the Han river estuary in the west to a point just below the 39th Parallel on the east coast the de-militarised zone stretches across 151 miles of the Korean peninsula. The military demarcation line runs down the centre of a 4,000 metre-wide strip and is marked by 1,292 markers printed in Korean and English on the side facing south, and Korean and Chinese on the side facing north. This was the line of contact between the opposing armies at the time of the cease-fire. This new frontier gives South Korea a better and more defensible line than the original iron curtain boundary which followed the 38th Parallel strictly in accordance with its geographic line.

The Armistice Agreement created the de-militarised zone (D.M.Z.) as a buffer zone, and all military equipment and forces were withdrawn from it. Each side, however, is allowed 1,000 civil police in its particular half of the zone at any one time. On the Allied side this force is made up of 700 Republic of Korea military personnel and 300 Americans. Patrols occasionally encounter and capture North Korean Communists who are attempting to infiltrate by the land route into South Korea.

Under the Korean Armistice Agreement a Military Armistice Commission was set up to supervise the effective implementation of the Agreement. The composition of the the United Nations command is clearly laid down; the presence of one member from each side represents a quorum for the purpose of a meeting, but the senior members are the only ones who are permitted to speak at such meetings on behalf of the delegations which they represent and the senior member of the side calling the meeting speaks first; there is no chairman or agenda. The United Nations Command Advisory Group represents most of the 16 United Nations members who provided military forces and such representatives are qualified to attend the meetings. At such meetings the individual representative speaks in his own language which is subsequently translated. Each side appoints a secretary who is responsible for the keeping of records and for such administrative services as are required to conduct the meetings; and some matters such as minor violations can be discussed at this level.

INTERESTED PARTIES

The Armistice terms made provision for the establishment of five joint-observer teams whose job it is to investigate serious violations which may occur in the de-militarised zone. These teams consist of three field officers from each side together with their administrative assistants. In practice, however, neither side exercises its authority since each side has reserved its right to prohibit entry into its own half of the zone, thus nullifying the role which the teams should have played.

The Agreement also set up a Neutral Nations Supervisory Commission quite separate from the joint-observer teams, and although their duty is to report to the Military Armistice Commission they are in no way under its command. The Communists selected Poland and Czechoslovakia, and the United Nations Command chose Sweden and Switzerland to be their representatives. The definition of Neutral Nations in this case was any nation other than those whose combat forces had participated in the Korean War. The role of the Commission was to investigate and inspect in order to ensure that the provisions of the Armistice Agreement were adhered to and in particular to see that the military status quo which existed at the time of the cease-fire was not altered. The Agreement specifically designated five ports in the North and five ports in the South which were to be the only authorised points of entry for the "one-for-one" replacement of men and equipment.

From the outset the Korean People's Army and the Chinese People's Volunteers set out to frustrate the work of the Commission, whilst in the South the Commission's representatives were given every facility to carry out their duty. The Communists deliberately by-passed the official ports in the North so that they could introduce as much military equipment as they required, unseen by the inspection teams. This deliberate violation of the Armistice compelled the United Nations Command to announce to the Armistice Commission in 1956 that they would withdraw facilities for inspection in South Korea until such time as the other side agreed to honour the Armistice terms. Though its activities have been reduced as a result of these events, the Neutral Nations Supervisory Commission continues to meet each week in accordance with the provisions of the Armistice Agreement. These meetings take place in the Joint Security area.

The Joint Security area is situated near Panmunjom and is roughly circular and about 800 metres wide. The military demarcation line runs straight through it; in fact the line bisects the centre of the conference table at which the two parties sit for their meetings. Thus the Communist side of the table is in North Korea, and the United Nations in the Republic of Korea. The Military Armistice Commission personnel and visitors accompanying them are permitted to move freely in the Joint Security area, but from courtesy neither side enters the other's buildings. When I visited the area it was possible, therefore, to actually go into North Korea and from this position one could see the Bridge of No Return and the flags demarcating the de-militarised zone. The Commission head-quarters are not in the conference area, and in the case of the United Nations Command are located in the capital of the Republic of Korea, Seoul; whilst the Communists have their headquarters at Kaesong. The commanders of the opposing forces are represented in their areas by joint duty officers who meet daily for the exchange of routine reports and to report to their respective commanders. Each side is allowed no more than 35 security police to patrol the area daily and may not exceed the stated number.

With all these organisations and the backing of the United Nations it might be thought that the provisions of the Armistice could be carried out effectively. In fact the Communist record is a long tale of flagrant breaches of the Armistice terms.

By the beginning of 1964 United Nations Command had recorded nearly 3,000 separate violations of the agreement, only two of which, both occurring in the first months after the signature of the truce, have been admitted by the Communists. United Nations Command, on their side, have made a very careful examination of every report made by the Communists which contains an alleged breach of the agreement. Only about 2 per cent of these were found to have any justification.

The most serious aspect of the situation has been the constant build-up of military strength north of the 38th Parallel. How,

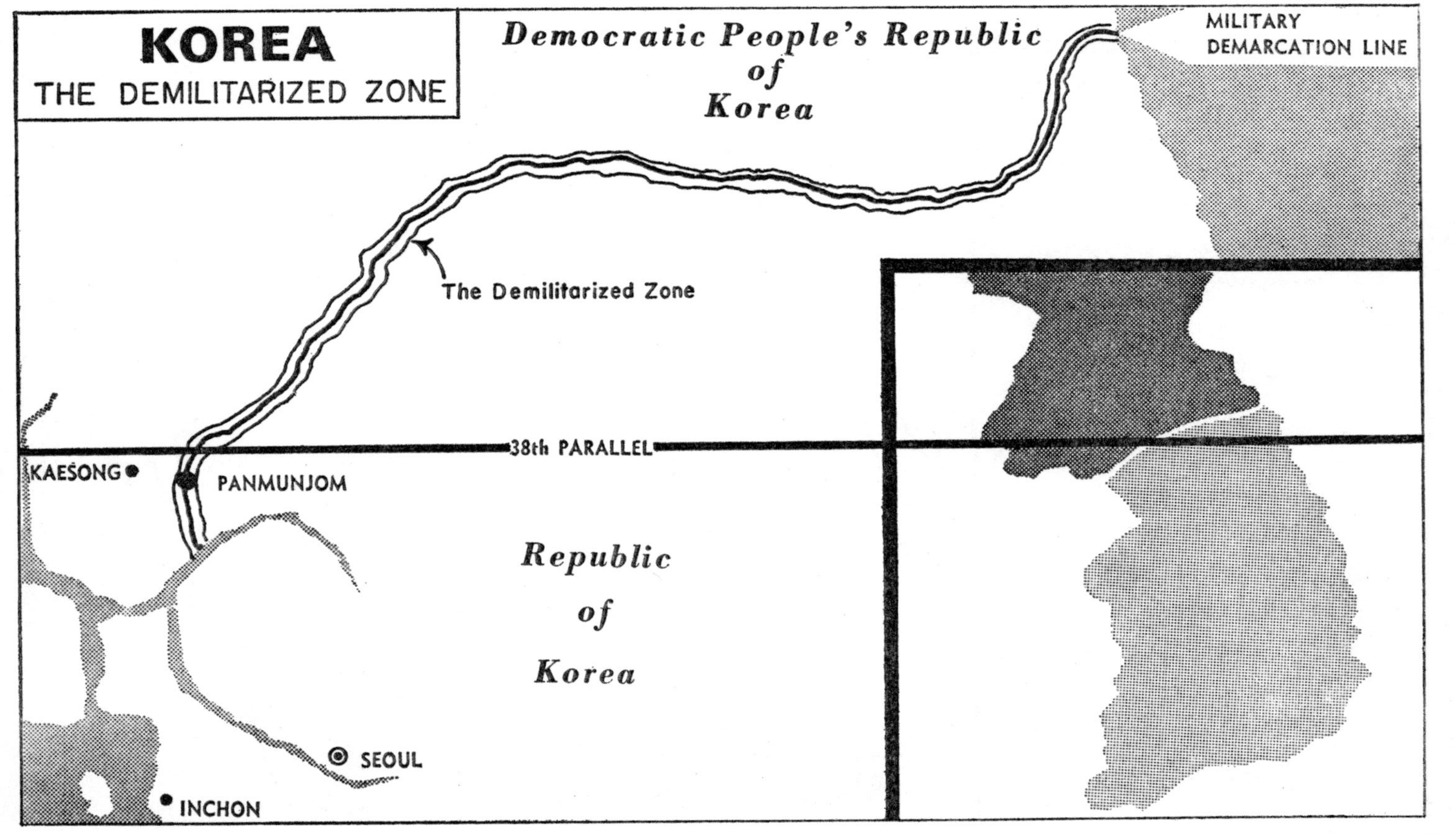

KOREA
THE DEMILITARIZED ZONE
Democratic People's Republic
of
Korea
MILITARY
DEMARCATION LINE
The Demilitarized Zone
38th PARALLEL
KAESONG
PANMUNJOM
Republic
of
Korea
SEOUL
INCHON

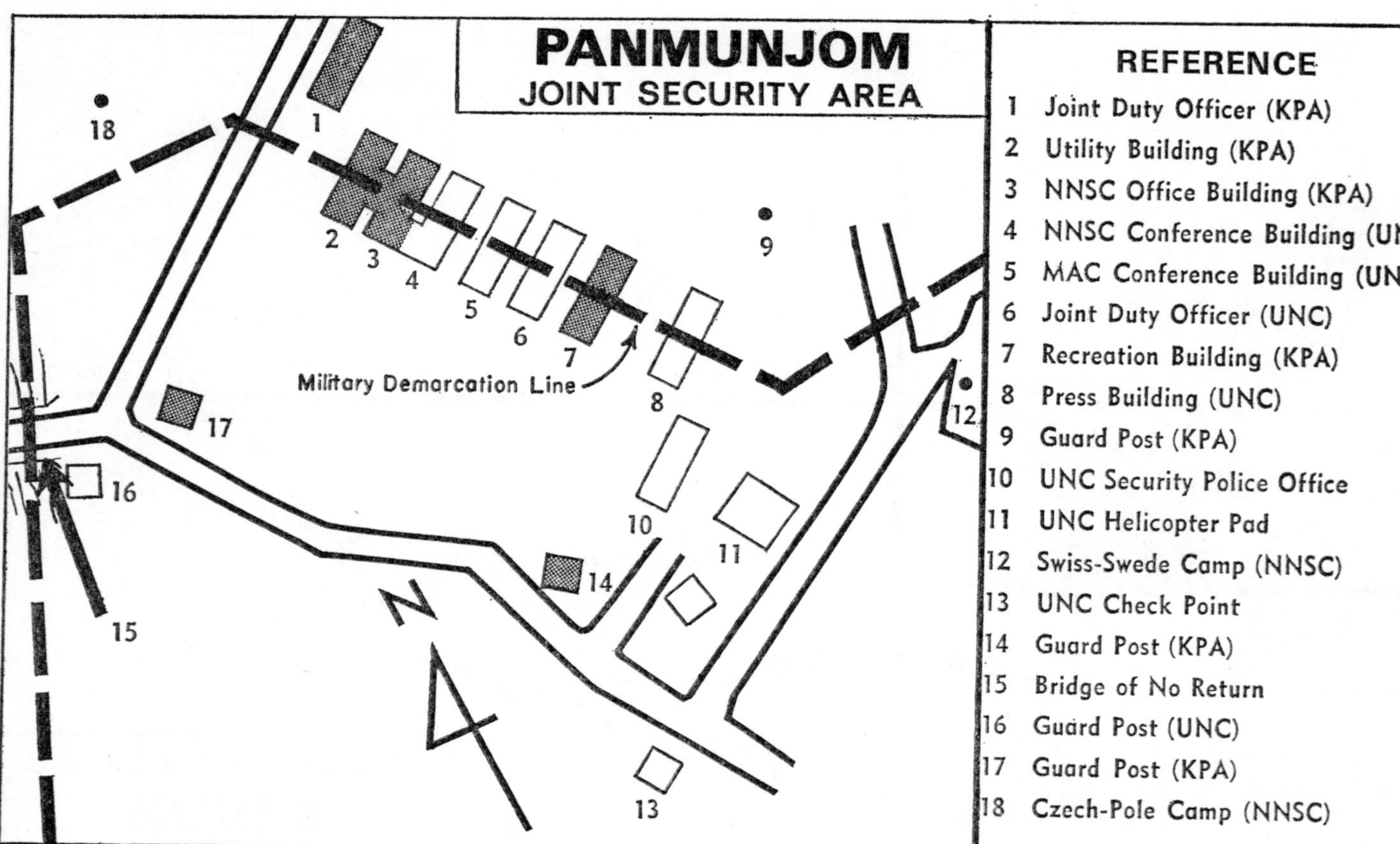

PANMUNJOM
JOINT SECURITY AREA
REFERENCE
1 Joint Duty Officer (KPA)
2 Utility Building (KPA)
3 NNSC Office Building (KPA)
4 NNSC Conference Building (UNC)
5 MAC Conference Building (UNC)
6 Joint Duty Officer (UNC)
7 Recreation Building (KPA)
8 Press Building (UNC)
9 Guard Post (KPA)
10 UNC Security Police Office
11 UNC Helicopter Pad
12 Swiss-Swede Camp (NNSC)
13 UNC Check Point
14 Guard Post (KPA)
15 Bridge of No Return
16 Guard Post (UNC)
17 Guard Post (KPA)
18 Czech-Pole Camp (NNSC)
Military Demarcation Line
N

it may be asked, could this take place and not be noticed by the Neutral Nations' inspection teams? The answer to this is twofold. In the first place a railway has been constructed between Manchuria and North Korea and used for the illegal shipment of war materials. In the second place the Communists have by-passed the authorised ports and sent their war material through other channels.

Communist breaches of the Treaty are illustrated by two facts. When the cease-fire took place the Communist side had no air force stationed in North Korea. This meant that they had no right to introduce any aircraft into this area, since the Armistice terms clearly laid down that weapons were to be brought in only on a one-for-one replacement basis. The Communists are known to have something in the region of 500 jet aircraft, and have made no attempt to conceal the presence of these planes. But in every official meeting of the Military Armistice Commission they have steadfastly denied their existence. They have also refuted any suggestions that the build-up in arms in North Korea has taken place. The second and perhaps more damning piece of evidence has been provided by a tape-recording from an official North Korean radio broadcast of a speech made by the Chief of the General Staff of the Korean People's Army in which he stated: "The North Korean Army's combat capabilities have been strengthened in a proportion incomparable to the time of the past war." When this part of the speech was played by United Nations Command at a Military Armistice Commission meeting it was met by a statement on the part of the Communists that they had never violated the military status quo. Even the existence of fortifications which they have erected in their part of the de-militarised zone, which are clearly visible from the United Nations Command, has been denied. The whole attitude of the Communists had made the provisions of the Treaty a complete farce, and the United Nations Command expressed the view that the provisions would be suspended until such time as the Communists agreed to comply with the terms. This statement was made at the 75th Military Armistice Meeting on 21st June 1957. The Communists continued to use the meetings of the

Military Armistice Commission as a platform on which the puppet régime in North Korea could put out its political propaganda. The use to which they put these meetings is understandable, since their régime is not recognised by the nations of the Free World.

The Communists in the North and the South Koreans still face one another along the 151-mile frontier. All the time, military potential is being steadily built up north of the 38th Parallel in breach of the Armistice Agreement. If the Communists decide to cross the 38th Parallel, will the nations of the Free World rally once again to give adequate military support to the United Nations Command? An equally dangerous threat exists in the persistent infiltration by North Korean Communists into South Korea in an attempt to subvert the Government of the Republic of Korea. The United Nations Command has virtually no control over this illegal entry, nor has it any means by which it can combat the danger.

It cannot be too strongly emphasised that the only hope for survival of the Republic of Korea lies in a rise in the people's standard of living. The Government of Korea has tackled the agricultural problem and been able to increase the supply of electric power by use of both thermal and hydro-electric plants. It has succeeded in building new railroads and raising the overall standard of living in the country. South Korea is now in a position to export textiles, garments, plywood, steel plate, rubber products including motor tyres, silk, iron ore and metal ores including tungsten.

The Government has completed its first five-year economic development plan and is now beginning its second. Its aim is to become economically self-supporting by 1981, by which time it hopes to have been able to build up a country of moderate affluence. Reading through their development plan it is clear that considerable thought and work have been put into the plan, but it is questionable whether the Government will be able to attract sufficient capital from other countries to carry it out. Interest rates on borrowed capital are still enormously high, but private investors from outside tend to be put off by the fear that the country may not have sufficient foreign exchange to enable them to remit their profits to the country of origin. Few investors are prepared to leave their investments and profits in a country which is still threatened by Communism; even the exceptionally high rates of interest are inadequate inducements.

The Korean people and their Government are making a brave attempt to help themselves; they deserve all the assistance which can be given to them, either in the form of private investment or of U.S. aid.

If Communism is to be defeated in South Korea it is essential that there should be a rapid and perceptible rise in the standard of living to form a sharp contrast with conditions existing in that part of Korea north of the 38th Parallel which is Communist-controlled.

Japan

Historically, Japan's whole policy of expansion was dictated by her population explosion which began to manifest itself towards the end of last century. This gave rise to a colonial policy designed not only to solve this population explosion but also to fit in with her military plans. By the end of last century Japan had a first class Navy and a well-equipped and efficient army, and as she looked across from her Island shores she could see the Chinese mainland as a field for expansion. Under the Manchurian dynasty the Chinese Empire was disintegrating; for centuries they had been one of the largest empires in the world, but had been completely self-contained and refused to look outside their boundaries and to appreciate that other nations and groups of nations were arising and becoming powerful.

The Japanese first target was the Island of Formosa, which she occupied after her war with China 1894-95. As a result of the Russo-Japanese War, 1904-05, she occupied Port Arthur and the southern part of Sakhalin Island (the northern part of the Island, she occupied between 1919-24). In 1910 Korea fell under her wing: Japan was now established on the Chinese mainland. After the First World War she was given the mandate of the ex-German Pacific Islands. In 1931 the Japanese invaded Manchuria; this was the beginning of a 14-year power struggle, an attempt by the Japanese to dominate China. The war itself was formalised on 7th July, 1937, when some Japanese troops engaged in drill manoeuvres South East of Peiping were (it is alleged) fired on by Chinese. This is known as the Marco Polo Bridge Incident, and it was followed by a full attack launched against China. The war only finished in 1945, when the Japanese were defeated by the Allies. The previous year Chiang Kai-shek had been kidnapped by some of his Generals in an attempt to persuade him to concentrate his efforts against the Japanese rather than continue his civil war against the Reds.

During this period the Japanese managed to occupy a large part of China itself, which was disorganised by warlords fighting among themselves, Chiang Kai-shek endeavouring to rally his people against the Japanese and at the same time having to fight Communism from within. Pearl Harbour was a signal for Japan's war against the Allies, and her army swept through South East Asia. The British Armies were defeated, Hong Kong and Singapore were occupied.

The fall of Singapore was a classic illustration of the errors of the British defence policy. The defences of Singapore were designed to beat off an attack from the sea, and when the Japanese advanced by land through Malaya on bicycles and any other form of transport they could get, practically the whole of the British force was captured. In Burma part of the British army managed to escape, and the enemy was halted and prevented from actually over-running India. During all these occupations, the Japanese treatment of the people was quite appalling. Age or sex of prisoners made no difference.

A Japanese member of the Royal family asked me what the British feeling was towards Japan, and I told him two instances stuck like stakes into the minds of a generation of British people who fought in the Second World War. They remember the appalling instance in the 'thirties when Japanese stripped women in Shanghai, and the unspeakable way in which the Japanese army tortured and murdered fighting soldiers and civilians who were captured in the Second World War. The rising generation will have forgotten Japanese behaviour in the Second World War, and will judge Japan on her behaviour since VJ day in 1945. But can defeat change the character of a nation and remove that thick band of cruelty from the Japanese character? It still remains for the Japanese to show that they are capable of behaving in a civilised manner. As a result of this mass invasion, and the ill treatment of South East Asians, it is hardly surprising that the latter view with suspicion Japanese intentions. It is this feeling which may make any form of alliance between the other free countries in South East Asia and Japan a difficult operation.

Japan ended the war with her armies defeated, with two of her cities, Hiroshima and Nagasaki, destroyed by atom bombs, and, what is often forgotten, Tokyo, although bombed by conventional weapons, was almost burnt to the ground, for most of her buildings were constructed of wood. The cost in human life was enormous, but the inevitable result was that her cities could be completely re-built with modern sky-scrapers. Aerial attack had carried out the greatest slum clearance in the history of the modern world.

Japanese industry combined with an inventive mind enabled her to create a modern state and to develop her industry so that she was able to export to the rest of the world, electrical, photographic and electronic equipment.

Politically, perhaps, the most important step which was taken was to compel the Japanese to write into their constitution a clause which prevented them from having an army any larger than was necessary for internal defence. It was General MacArthur and the Allies who insisted on this as a precaution against the Japanese military power, and the possibility of aggression in the future. From an economic point of view this was a great help to Japan as she was able to shelter under the protection of the United States and was not required to keep up vast armies; all she was required to do was to pay the various reparations to the nations affected by her occupation. With the exception of the Philippines practically all these liabilities have been discharged.

As to whether Japan should have been made to pay a higher price for the misery for which she was responsible, that is questionable. The Allies imposed on her what they believed to be a burden she could quite easily afford and which would not cripple her economically, or pave the way for Communism. Just as in the Franco-Prussian War the Germans set too low a figure, so possibly the Allies made a similar mistake and erred on the generous side.

The Americans have accepted the role of defenders of Japan, and have throughout the country large numbers of bases and installations, hospitals and convalescent homes for their wounded soldiers. Japan's economy is still razor-edged and her budget dependent upon America. The supplying of her bases, and the money she spends on them in Japan has to be added to the orders which America has placed in Japan for equipment for her troops in Viet Nam and other parts of South East Asia. No sensible Japanese Government could afford to disregard the foreign exchange and earnings which America has put, directly or indirectly, into the Japanese Treasury. In spite of this, there is a feeling in Japan that they would like to rid themselves of American influence and equip themselves with sufficient armed forces to be able to provide their own means of defence.

If Japan became so strong economically, these forces within Japan might exert their influence and endeavour, successfully or unsuccessfully, to get rid of the American presence in that country. From the point of view of world peace this could be very dangerous.

In a country where abortion is legal and methods of birth control on the increase, a second population explosion could be averted. The younger generation of Japanese favour the mini skirt rather than the kimono. But does the leopard change its spots? The simple choice which America and the other nations of the Free World have to make in the near future is whether to incorporate Japan in a multilateral defence treaty as a passive partner, or whether to allow her to take a more active part, and run the risk of Japanese Imperialism raising its head again.

What is the Role of Taiwan and Chiang Kai-shek?

Chiang Kai-shek is now nearly 80 years of age and has spent most of his life fighting for the unification of China. To many of us in the West his name is associated with the help which he gave us in the Second World War when, as head of the Chinese Government, he was an equal partner with Churchill, Roosevelt and Stalin; and he is now the only one of that great team alive

During the war, there was a feeling that perhaps he was storing up the military supplies which were being given to him from the Allies and was more pre-occupied with strengthening his Army so that he would have a strong force to combat Communism after the war. This may or may not be true, but if it is true, it should be interpreted as just one of the ways in which Chiang Kai-shek was looking forward to the events which would occur after the war.

He had first of all fought the war-lords in the 'twenties and then, on the second front, he had to contend with the Japanese invasion of Manchuria. Simultaneously, the Communist threat in his own country was developing to such an extent that he could see that it would be a greater danger in the future than the war-lords or even the Japanese. Time alone was to show that his diagnosis of the situation was correct and that it was Roosevelt who failed to appreciate the steady rise of Communism in South East Asia which today represents the greatest of all dangers to civilisation. It was this same failure to understand the spread of Communism that was, to some extent, responsible for Chiang Kai-shek's defeat and his evacuation to the Island of Formosa.

Had the Americans weighed in at this time, they might well

have tilted the scales and enabled Chiang Kai-shek, in the years which followed the war, to have consolidated his position and eventually to have united China under a democratic Government.

Chiang Kai-shek occupies an extraordinary position in that he is not an exile from the mainland of China, but is the President of the Republic of China. His Government occupies a province of China known as Taiwan (the modern name for Formosa), which has a population of 13 million. He regards the mainland of China as a part of his country which has been the subject of Communist aggression and is under their domination.

The last free elections were held on the mainland of China in 1948. All of the provinces voted, including Mongolia. They elected members to the National Assembly and members to the various Yuans, that is to say, the executive, legislative, judicial, examination and control Yuans.

When Chiang Kai-shek had to leave the mainland, most of these elected members of the Yuans left with him. Those who are alive in Taiwan and were elected in 1948 form the Chinese National Government, with Chiang Kai-shek at its head. There can of course be no further elections on the Chinese mainland, because it is Communist-occupied. Taiwan is regarded as a province of Nationalist China. It has its own local elections and a provincial Government.

What the United States in fact recognise is not this one province in China but Chiang Kai-shek as head of the Chinese Nationalist Government, whose territory has been reduced by Communist aggression to one province of Taiwan with 13 million inhabitants.

To some people it seems ridiculous that Chiang Kai-shek's should be the only Government recognised by the United States and other nations as the legal Government of China, when in fact they only control 13 million out of a total population of some 600 or 700 million. These same people have suggested that the Chinese National Government in Taiwan and the Red Chinese Government should both be recognised. On the face of it, this is quite an attractive proposition and would form some kind of compromise. But on closer examination one finds it is not a practical possibility. Neither the Communists nor the Nationalists would accept it. Neither country is prepared to be accredited to a Government which recognises the other régime.

The Americans have always been firm and they realise that Chiang Kai-shek is a reliable ally. The recently proclaimed desire of Mao to spread Communism throughout South East Asia has hardened their attitude. Chiang Kai-shek represents a reliable and strong ally, whereas to them Red China is the real danger with whom no compromise can be made.

Until recently, most people regarded Chiang Kai-shek's country as a backwater of exiles but they have failed to take into account the strategic importance of the island and the strength of Chiang's army.

In South East Asia, all those people who fear the insidious process of Communism regard Chiang Kai-shek as an ally who should be encouraged and not shed.

From a military point of view, Nationalist China has about 650,000 troops which could be used in South East Asia and in any case are dedicated anti-Communists.

Geographically, Taiwan can be seen on the map to be a vital link in the chain of free nations which stretch from Japan through South Korea, Taiwan, the Philippines, South Viet Nam and Thailand. Chiang Kai-shek has always believed his destiny to be the final re-unification of China but, in recent years, he has had the sense to appreciate that, however efficient his army might be, he could not achieve victory by military action alone. He realises that unless there is a political change within China itself, any form of intervention could only result in a military disaster.

During the time that Chiang Kai-shek has been in charge of Taiwan the country has developed socially and economically, and its 13 million inhabitants are now one of the most prosperous nations in South East Asia. Admittedly, until recently, American capital has been used to develop the country, but the money which has been spent out of the American tax-payer's pocket has been well utilised. Land reform has been carried out; strips of land have been amalgamated so that the holdings are economic. Even now, laws are being considered which would stop the fragmentation of holdings so as to render them uneconomic.

When Chiang Kai-shek first came to the island practically all the large-sized industry had been nationalised, but gradually the Government is moving over to a policy directed at increasing the amount of private enterprise and decreasing control by the State in the larger industries. Some have been transferred entirely to private enterprise. The object is to encourage private enterprise and initiative and create a partnership between private and nationalised industry. From an agricultural point of view, the land has been used to the maximum possible capacity so that, at the end of the fourth 4-Year Plan, the country is self-supporting and has also provided the industrial sector with an increasing supply of raw materials.

The Republic of China in Taiwan has provided an example of how a country with a democratic society can thrive by the judicious use of its own resources and the proper apportionment of U.S. aid.

United States economic aid to the Republic of China began on the mainland in 1948 with an agreement whereby U.S. $275 million were given to help her international payments and to assist in agricultural and industrial development. Only a fraction of this money was in fact received, because the programme was interrupted by the Communist take-over of the mainland.

Events in Korea made the United States realise the strategic importance and value of an independent Nationalist Government based on Formosa, and decide that there should be a resumption of economic assistance. Side by side with the resumption of aid, the Chinese Nationalist Government was able to stabilise its economy within a few years. By 1953 this process had almost been completed and both agricultural and industrial production had surpassed pre-war records.

With the economy stabilised, the Chinese in Taiwan were able to get under way with their first 4-Year Plan, which started in 1953. The second plan ran from 1957 to 1960, so that by 1958 the economy had become stabilised to such an extent that United States monetary grants began their run-down, and virtually ceased in 1961. Loans were advanced but they were repayable, both as regards principal and interest in American dollars. The actual aid itself had been cut by 1962 to an annual sum of 100,000 million dollars. By 1965 it was cut off completely. No reliable figures are available for the amount of military assistance being received at the moment, by the Taiwan Government.

Thus, a Government which left the mainland to occupy a small island where conditions and standard of living were low as a result of Japanese occupation and vicissitudes through which the island had passed, has developed it into a thriving economic community. They have done more than this: having stabilised their economy, they have moved from a receiving state to a giving state, and are helping countries such as Viet Nam at this very moment. But it would be as well to remember that, in spite of all this, Taiwan still has a foreign exchange problem and has to be careful.

It is striking to try and compare what has been done under a democratic society to the total chaos and almost famine conditions prevailing on the Communist mainland.

Chiang Kai-shek's Government could not survive militarily against an all-out attack from the Communist mainland. It is true that the Communist attacks so far have been beaten off, but none of them represents an all-out effort, supported by jet bomber attacks or the resources which China has had at her disposal, nor would it be reasonable to suggest that the repulsion of these attacks was entirely due to the efficiency of Chiang Kai-shek's army. Tribute should be paid to the "umbrella" which the American military forces give to their allies and I think that the Nationalist Chinese would be the first to pay tribute, not only to the economic aid which they have received but to the military supplies and, above all, the "umbrella" of security which the American's presence in the Far East has given to them. Chiang Kai-shek has succeeded in converting a backward island which had been dominated by a ruthless

Japanese master, into a modern economic state which is an example to the rest of South East Asia.

But what of his military aspirations and potentialities? In the first place, his very presence on the Island of Taiwan with its outpost at Quemoy, one of the most fortified islands in the world, presents a threat to Red China. Chiang Kai-shek's son, who is Minister of Defence, admitted that according to his Intelligence Reports the Chinese Nationalists were holding down no less than one million soldiers of the Red Army who were being kept in position along the shores of mainland China opposite Taiwan as a protection against a possible invasion by Chinese Nationalist forces. This is a considerable contribution to the defence of South East Asia, but is it enough? What else could they do? Immediately, assistance to South Viet Nam comes to mind. They could certainly step up their assistance programmes to the South Vietnamese. It is perfectly true that this would only amount to a fraction of American Aid, but it would be a further illustration of Taiwan's determination to stand by her friends in South East Asia. The problem of giving military aid to South Viet Nam is harder to answer.

After centuries of domination by the Chinese, the Vietnamese might not welcome military intervention by Chinese soldiers. But they certainly would not object to a further, and larger, contribution of supplies and food. But the last, and most important, way in which Taiwan, like other nations, could fortify the other free nations, would be to enter into a multimilitary pact which would include the other free nations of South East Asia.

The question which is exercising the minds of many people in South East Asia, and even in Europe, is whether Chiang Kai-shek will ever be able to go back to the mainland. The treaty between his nation and America is not precise. It could be interpreted as giving an understanding between the two nations that Nationalist China should not engage in active operations on the mainland other than in partnership or by express agreement with the Government of the United States.

The position would be different if the United States should

find itself in a position where it is involved in military operations directed against Red China. In a situation of this nature, clearly the United States would be more than willing to enlist the help of Chiang Kai-shek's Government and it would probably give them a free hand in mainland China. In order to do this, Chiang Kai-shek would require United States transport and air cover.

But what of Chiang Kai-shek's army and its loyalties? Probably 20 per cent of his army comes from mainland China; approximately 30 per cent are aborigines from the hills of Taiwan; and the remainder are either from the mainland or are descendants of people from the mainland provinces.

Would they be interested in landing on the mainland? No honest appreciation of this can be made but what is clear is that this army is certainly prepared to defend what they have built up in Taiwan and if this was threatened by Communist aggression, then their attitude towards attacking the mainland as a means of defending themselves, would probably be sympathetic.

Chiang Kai-shek's Government has been taking a realistic approach to the whole problem. In the years immediately following their evacuation to Taiwan they built up an army, both for their own protection and with the object of defeating the Communists on the mainland. But now they realise that their only hope is a split in the ranks of Red China, and perhaps, for example, backing anti-Mao forces. Any landing on the mainland would require a direct invitation from a powerful political force there, with whom they would have to operate in close liaison.

For anyone to believe that a crash military victory by Chiang Kai-shek is possible when taking the mainland, is merely a pipe dream, for how could such an army conquer millions of square miles unless it were able to enlist the support of the mainland Chinese?

Invasions of this nature have frequently taken place, often with unsatisfactory results. On a number of occasions in history the reason has been that the invaders were crueller tyrants than the existing rulers whom they attempted to replace.

Thus, when the Germans invaded the Ukraine in the Second World War, the people were sympathetically disposed towards them at the outset. The Germans, however, set up a cruel and more unpleasant Government, if that was possible, than the Soviets, and even went to the length of bringing back a few of the landlords who had been exiled after the Russian Revolution. The cumulative effect was to turn the welcome given to the German invaders into a resistance, both physical and moral, to them. Had the Germans handled the position differently, the Ukrainian peasants would have been glad to have freed themselves from the Soviet yoke, provided the process was accompanied by the granting to them of some self-determination and not giving them a puppet Government under the thumb of the new masters.

Chiang Kai-shek's Government have prepared a blue-print, but what sort of blue-print, may we ask? It is a blue-print which is based on the ideas which have been put into force in Taiwan. It recognises the desires and aspirations of the average Chinese and appreciates that the ancient system of land tenure, with great landlords, is as unpopular as Mao's communalism of the Chinese people's land. What the blue-print sets out is the system of land reform which has been put into operation so successfully in Taiwan. It explains the need for nationalisation of industries where there is insufficient private or foreign capital to develop them. But Taiwan, itself, has moved on from the necessity of nationalised industries that were created during the period when the Chinese Government had to set itself up in Taiwan. The shortest answer to the blue-print is that the type of Government, and the relationship between Government and people, will be similar to those established by Chiang Kai-shek on the Island of Taiwan.

This is a positive attitude and would eventually represent, to the Chinese people, a better way of living than the one offered by Mao and his associates. But to believe that this blue-print can be sold overnight, like a piece of property to a speculator, would be foolish. The establishment of any alternative form of Government, with or without the support of the Chinese army, would be a speculative adventure with so many unknown factors that the outcome could never be predicted.

Setting aside all these aspirations by Chiang Kai-shek for a united China, we are still left with one clear fact. The Americans have equipped themselves with an ally dedicated to the destruction of Communism. Even in his present role, the Minister of Defence, Chiang Kai-shek's son, admitted that he was holding down well over a million Chinese Communist troops on the mainland, which is no mean achievement.

Diplomatic representation in countries abroad is divided. No country can have an Ambassador from Communist China and Taiwan at the same time. What might appear to be an exception is Taiwan itself. Here, Great Britain has no Ambassador, but we have got a Consul and Vice-Consul who occupy themselves almost entirely with the issue of visas to British territories and, in particular, Hong Kong. This representation is a technicality in that our Consul is legally accredited not to the Taiwan Government but to the Governor of Taiwan. He is, in fact, Consul to one of the provinces of China and that province is the one controlled by Chiang Kai-shek's Government. Elsewhere in the world, neither Communist China nor the Nationalist Government will allow their Ambassadors to remain if the other Government is recognised.

In the Appendix to this subsection I give a list of those members of the United Nations who have diplomatic relations with the Republic of China (Chiang Kai-shek's Government), those which have relations with Communist China, and those which have relations with neither Government. There is also a list of non-United Nations members, showing what relations they have with Communist and Nationalist China.

In Washington, the Chinese Nationalists have a full-scale embassy. In those countries where they have an embassy they enjoy diplomatic privileges.

Where nations do not recognise the Chinese Nationalists, as in England, the Nationalist Government has some form of agency.

In South East Asia, most of the non-Communist countries recognise Chiang Kai-shek's Government. Australia, until recently, allowed Chiang Kai-shek's Ambassador to remain as an Ambassador to their country, but did not reciprocate. Now, they have appointed a new Ambassador, Ambassador Cooper, to Taiwan, and it was no accident that his accreditation followed shortly after their troops became engaged in South Viet Nam. On the surface it would seem that the important embassies are those in the great countries of the West and in South East Asia. This may be so for purposes of prestige.

The tentacles of Chinese Communism, as everyone knows, extend not only through Asia, but their fingernails, as long as those of the old mandarins, are cutting into the flesh of Black Africa and even pushing upwards through North Africa. But the sophistication of Algeria, Morocco and Tunisia has defeated their aims. These countries may allow Trade Missions, but they know how and where to stop.

It is not so in the black African countries. Here the Communist Chinese, by over-staffing their embassies and diplomatic posts, are able to use their diplomatic privileges to work a system of espionage and to ensure that aid to these countries is attached by strings. It is Mao Tse-tung who is pulling those strings, from the security of his position in Red China.

Some African countries, such as Malawi, have become aware of the ultimate aim of Chinese Ambassadors in their country and have changed their allegiance—they now recognise Chiang Kai-shek's Nationalist Government. Chinese representatives have been given instructions to get on with the business of giving aid without strings attached.

To be realistic we must strip Taiwan of any aspirations towards unifying China by controlling the Chinese mainland. We must judge her not for what she might be, but for what she is now: strong, determined, and capable of playing a decisive role in the defence of South East Asia in its struggle to prevent the area from becoming engulfed by Chinese Communism.

APPENDIX

A.   U.N. MEMBERS

Having Relations with Republic of China (58):

Argentina	Guatamala	Nicaragua
Australia	Haiti	Niger
Belgium	Honduras	Panama
Bolivia	Iran	Paraguay
Brazil	Italy	Peru
Cameroun	Ivory Coast	Philippines
Canada	Jamaica	Portugal
Chad	Japan	Rwanda
Chile	Jordan	Saudi Arabia
Colombia	Kuwait	Sierra Leone
Congo, Democratic	Lebanon	South Africa
Republic of	Lesotho	Spain
Costa Rica	Liberia	Thailand
Cyprus	Libya	Togo
Dahomey	Luxembourg	Turkey
Dominican Republic	Madagascar	U.S.A.
Ecuador	Malawi	Upper Volta
El Salvador	Maldive Islands	Uruguay
Gabon	Mexico	Venezuela
Greece	New Zealand	

Having Relations with Peiping Régime (47):

Afghanistan	Congo (Brazzaville)	Hungary
Albania	Cuba	India
Algeria	Czechoslovakia	Indonesia
Bulgaria	Denmark	Iraq
Burma	Finland	Israel
Byelorussian SSR	France	Kenya
Cambodia	Ghana	Laos
Ceylon	Guinea	Mali

Having relations with Peiping régime (47)—*Contd.*

Mauritania
Mongolia
Morocco
Nepal
Netherlands
Norway
Pakistan
Poland

Rumania
Somalia
Sudan
Sweden
Syria
Tanzania
Tunisia
Uganda

Ukrainian SSR
U.S.S.R.
U.A.R.
United Kingdom
Yemen
Yugoslavia
Zambia

Having Relations with Neither (15):

Austria
Botswana
Burundi
Central African
  Republic

Ethiopia
Gambia
Guyana
Iceland
Ireland

Malaysia
Malta
Nigeria
Senegal
Singapore
Trinidad and
  Tobago.

B. NON–U.N. MEMBERS

Having Relations with Republic of China (3):

Holy See

Republic of Korea

Republic of Viet
  Nam.

Having Relations with the Peiping Régime (4):

East Germany

North Korea
North Viet Nam

Switzerland

Having Relations with Neither (7):

Andorra
Bhutan

German Federal
  Republic
Liechtenstein

Monaco
San Marino
Western Samoa

VI

WHO WILL HALT COMMUNISM IN SOUTH EAST ASIA?

SEATO

COMMONWEALTH

SINKIANG

CONCLUSION

SEATO

AFTER the Second World War, civil war raged in China. In spite of its agreement with Chiang Kai-shek, Soviet Russia, which had entered the war against Japan only eight days before Japan's final surrender, allowed a large quantity of arms and military supplies, which had been taken over from the Japanese in the Northern Province, to be turned over to the Chinese Communists. It was this action which tipped the scales against the Nationalists who were compelled to retreat south, first to Nanking and Shanghai and later to Canton and Chungking. Overt Russian assistance had supplied just that amount of extra equipment which the Chinese Communists required, and was responsible for the withdrawal of Chiang Kai-shek's army to the Island of Taiwan.

Britain and her European partners were far more concerned with events that were happening in Europe, and sat back to await the final results. The Labour Government in Great Britain recognised the Communist régime in China and probably believed that China would now content herself by consolidating her Government and settling as a peaceful nation in South East Asia. How wrong they were! Immediately after Great Britain had recognised Communist China the world was awakened from this pipe dream by the Korean War, which demonstrated that the Chinese dragon had woken from its temporary slumbers and was breathing the fire of Communist expansion once again.

A cry went up among the weaker nations of South East Asia and they decided to group themselves together in a collective security pact, and on 8th September 1954, the South East Asia Collective Defence Treaty was signed at Manila, and was later ratified on 19th February 1955. The signatories to this Treaty were Australia, France, New Zealand, Pakistan, Philippines, Thailand, Great Britain and the United States.

The Treaty itself is a loose organisation and unlike NATO has no force under its direct command. It is a skeleton, a peace time frame upon which a full-scale military organisation could be built if the necessity arose. Its members subscribe towards what is essentially an Insurance Policy against any one of its members being threatened by attack from Communism.

"The purpose of the Treaty is clearly set down in Article II, which states that 'the parties, by means of continuous and effective self-help and mutual aid will maintain and develop their individual and collective capacity to resist armed attack and to prevent and counter subversive activities directed from without against their territorial integrity and political stability'. Again, in Article III, they undertake 'to strengthen their free institutions, and to co-operate with one another in the further development of economic measures, including technical assistance, designed both to promote economic progress and social well-being, and to further the individual and collective efforts of Governments towards these ends'.

"Under the first of these pledges, the member nations have created through SEATO a powerful deterrent to aggression in the area covered by its protection, and have strengthened their capacity to counter subversive activities. Each member, through co-operation and the sharing of experience, has increased its defensive strength. The combined power of the alliance together with the mature self-restraint in its actions, are recognised as a stabilising factor in South-East Asia.

"The confidence inspired by collective security is a stimulus to national development, and the fulfilment by SEATO members of the pledges to co-operate in the economic and social fields has made its distinctive contribution to their progress.

"SEATO is a flexible alliance which has responded to the changing needs of the situation in South-East Asia, and has provided full scope for national freedom of action. One of the most important developments in its history was a declaration by the United States Secretary of State in a joint statement with the Minister of Foreign Affairs of Thailand on 6th March 1962. He reaffirmed that the Treaty obligation of the United States 'does not depend upon the prior agreement of all other parties to the Treaty, since this Treaty obligation is individual as well as collective'. A majority of members have agreed to this view.

"In a world threatened by Communism, SEATO is a necessary bulwark of security, and an instrument of peaceful progress".*

SEATO has entered into many economic, social, cultural and medical research programmes and its Council meets regularly, as indeed do its various planning and military divisions. But France and Pakistan's interest in the Treaty has decreased and France's influence, of course, is reduced, since de Gaulle's recognition of Communist China.

Although military exercises are carried out under its auspices, and involve combined operations between its member nations, its principal defect is its lack of a permanent military force. It is an organisation without teeth. Perhaps it was the strongest form of organisation to which its member nations were prepared to subscribe. It should not be disregarded, nor should its capabilities be over-estimated.

Since its inception, the Communist threat has increased. Tibet has been annexed by Communist China and a military attack made against India (who is not a member of SEATO).

Subversion has manifested itself not only in South Viet Nam but also in Laos. South Viet Nam is probably the area in which the Communist threat can best be seen.

Should we scrap SEATO, replace it, or add to it? To scrap it would be to remove one powerful obstacle which stands in the way of Communist aggression. To replace it might well be difficult; the present signatories might not be willing to increase their liability to active participation, and help towards members who were threatened, either militarily or by sub-version, nor might they be willing to include other nations in South East Asia who are not members of SEATO.

The answer might well be to leave SEATO as it is and form an entirely new defence organisation which would be com-

*Extract from "Story of Seato" published by the South-East Asia Treaty Organisation, Public Information Office, SEATO Headquarters, P.O. Box 517, Bangkok, Thailand.

plementary to it. The new organisation, a Multilateral Defence Pact, could include all those existing members of SEATO who were willing to participate together with other nations such as Korea, Taiwan, South Viet Nam and possibly Japan. Other nations in South East Asia like Burma and India (though this might be difficult because Pakistan is a member of SEATO), might well be willing to join if they considered it represented a real protection from Communist China and had economic advantages.

Laos and Cambodia are now regarded, as a result of the various Conferences held at Geneva, as neutrals, and it may be asked how they can possibly be brought into a multilateral defence treaty.

If the majority of the countries of South East Asia were prepared to club together in this new form of security pact then Laos and Cambodia might agree to sit under the umbrella of security which the rest of the nations are offering to hold over them. This would require the agreement of the co-Chairmen of the Geneva Agreement, as it would involve the Control Commission. Unless Russia could be persuaded to co-operate it would mean that these two countries would have to opt out of the Geneva Agreement and the only circumstances under which they would be likely to take this action would be if the conditions of a multilateral defence pact appeared to be more beneficial and brought with them increased American Aid.

Viet Nam represents only a fraction of the problem of Communism in South East Asia, and its importance lies in the fact that it is a theatre in which the Americans and other nations are actively fighting a war against an enemy backed by Russia, China and the satellite countries. The skirmishes which are taking place in Hong Kong between Communist mainland forces or civilians prompted by the Communists against British territory are similar to the exchanges which took place in Viet Nam ten years ago. Until then the British public were under the impression that Hong Kong sovereignty would not be disputed seriously unless there was a major confrontation between China and Great Britain. Malaya in its time was treated as a septic finger because in the public mind it was never associated to any great extent with Peking's grand design for the conquest of South East Asia. Hong Kong is serious enough to bring to the forefront of British politics the problems which have been facing the United States ever since she entered active hostilities in Viet Nam.

The great difference between Viet Nam to the Americans and Hong Kong to the British is that America is deriving no economic benefit and probably will not get any advantage from her military actions and her civilian A.I.D. programme in that country. The United Kingdom and the other Commonwealth countries derive economic benefit from Hong Kong as a trading centre which brings to the Treasury considerable foreign exchange and provides our exporters with an outlet for their products which would be much harder to find if trade had to be carried on direct with Communist countries rather than through Hong Kong acting as honest broker.

The present Socialist Government is unable to understand that Great Britain and the Commonwealth have lasting and worthwhile trading interests lying east of Suez. When I discussed the position with Premier Ky, Mr. Henry Cabot Lodge and General Westmoreland, it was possible to argue that Great Britain ought not to be involved in the Viet Nam War as she was co-Chairman of the Geneva Conference and that any active participation in the war would preclude her in the future from acting as a negotiator and intermediary in a peace settlement of the Viet Nam question. I also drew their attention to the fact that we had fulfilled our commitments by our campaigns in Malaysia and that we still had a large number of troops tied up in that geographical area. Our very presence in Singapore and Hong Kong was a clear indication that Britain and the Commonwealth, though not actively participating in the war, were acting in consort with their other SEATO colleagues.

Policies pursued by the present Socialist Government can only result in an increase of tension in the Far East. Their complete abnegation of responsibility in this theatre must mean that America becomes the dominant power and that in the future she will probably control the commercial markets.

Australia and New Zealand and other Commonwealth countries realised the predicament into which Great Britain was placed as a result of her position as co-Chairman of the Geneva Conference and were prepared to accept the limited role which she was capable of performing in South East Asia, but present Labour policy of phased withdrawal will make it more difficult for Commonwealth friends who helped us so much in two World Wars to understand why we should leave them to rely almost exclusively on the United States as a military ally.

No nation such as Great Britain can expect the United States to continue to hold the umbrella of protection over them unless they are prepared to make their contribution to defence. In the case of the smaller nations of the world it is not unreasonable to expect that their contribution should be small since their defence contributions are limited by the size of their economies.

Since the balance of power has shifted from the Western theatre of operations to the East it would not be unreasonable for Great Britain to cut her European defence commitments and in exchange step up her far Eastern contribution. But this is not the present Labour Government's policy. They want it both ways: having set an unrealistic ceiling of £2,000 million for defence they have not only cut down the European forces at the disposal of NATO but they wish to reduce our force in the Far East.

What rejoicing must have taken place not only in the Arab capitals but throughout the Communist bloc when the debate on Aden took place in the House of Commons! Great Britain should be thinking of ways in which her prestige can be restored and increased throughout the capitals of the world. Mr. Gordon Walker's visit to the Far East in 1965, laudable as his intentions were, carried no weight whatsoever. Arguments and attempts to influence other nations will only be effective when the British Government has announced its intention to continue its role as a great power and shown practical reasons why it should be regarded as such.

The SEATO Treaty was the best that could be obtained at

the time but its weakness has been demonstrated in two ways: first, the enthusiasm of some of its members has dwindled: France and Pakistan are lukewarm in the support which they are prepared to give. The answer to this is not to forget and bury it but to augment it by a new treaty. Looking around the Far East there are many countries which could be persuaded that a multilateral treaty of defence would be of interest to them, but a new Treaty must contain provisions for positive military action similar to those of the NATO Treaty should one of their members be attacked, or experience aggression at the hands of Communism, whether that aggression were in the shape of a direct military attack or, as in the case of Thailand, infiltration by Communist agitators.

Neutralism is one method of protection from aggression but it can last only so long as the country's neutralist policy suits other nations. The moment that its use has departed its whole existence is placed in jeopardy. The attempt by the great nations of the world to create a neutral state in Laos has failed completely and resulted in years of struggle on the part of the Royal Laotian Government to combat Communism in the form of the Pathet Lao.

There is no place today for neutralism. Nations in South East Asia must decide for themselves whether they wish to throw in their lot with the Communist powers or to be part of the Free Nations of the world. There is no third way of neutralism and the sooner these countries realise it the better. One of the difficulties which prevent this realisation is that some of them are still in receipt of marginal aid from the Communist bloc or are able to carry on trading with Communist states, some of whom give such favourable terms as to amount to the equivalent of subsidies. In the long run they have to be persuaded that the resources of the United States are still far greater than anything which can be commanded by China or Russia or indeed a combination of these two. Aid provided by the United States has the great merit that there are few strings attached whereas in the case of the Communist bloc there is always an ulterior motive behind the money or material which the donor nation advances.

When the State Department canvassed the South East Asian capitals with a view to increasing the number of combatant troops provided by third nations in the middle of 1967 the response was almost negative. The United States could find herself in the unenviable position of supplying vast sums in the form of civilian A.I.D., as indeed she is in the case of Thailand, but when she asks for some practical demonstration of that country's willingness to assist her in the anti-Communist struggle in Viet Nam she receives a qualified reply. What can she do? Does she cut down or refuse aid, thereby increasing the danger of Communism, or does she just swallow the reply and send more of Uncle Sam's sons to their death in Viet Nam? This is largely a question of the United States' whole approach to the defence of South East Asia. In the case of Thailand she rushed in with excavators and earth-moving machines and pumped in aid to the Thai coffers without asking anything in exchange. If anti-Communism is to have any meaning whatsoever in South East Asia it must have the backing of the people of the nations concerned. The mere pouring of money into these countries is useless unless their Governments are prepared to shoulder their responsibility, modernise themselves and be in a position to defend their security with their own soldiers and at the same time be able to participate in a multilateral treaty of defence which demands that they should supply to the allied cause that number of military personnel commensurate with their economic strength.

The generosity of the American taxpayers is beginning to become exhausted, and sooner or later they will require tangible benefit for the vast sums which they are being called upon to produce in the defence of South East Asia against Communism.

The Multilateral Treaty of Defence between all these nations interested in saving themselves from Communist domination should include an international armed force capable of fighting in any particular country in South East Asia, and should by its very international composition display to the world that the struggle against Communism is not just a form of American colonialism but something in which the free nations of Asia have faith.

The present Labour Government's policy with regard to SEATO has not been finalised but it looks as if they want to reduce their commitments even to SEATO, so it would be unlikely that they would be prepared to participate in any other treaty organisation in this part of the world. This would mean that the United States would have to go it alone and would undoubtedly become the real power in South East Asia.

Commonwealth

I asked many Australians and New Zealanders whether they thought that the war in which they were participating affected their countries. Their answers were not stereotyped and in most cases the soldiers thought for a minute or two before they replied. All those to whom I talked gave their answers in their own way. A typical conversation with an Australian ran as follows:—

"Digger, what do you think you are fighting here for, surely you do not think that Red China has the power to invade your Continent in the near future?"

"No, sir, not now, but in the next quarter of a century this could happen, and personally I would rather stem the tide of Communism here in Viet Nam than let the battle be raged on the shores of Australia, and leave it to my children to have to fight in Australia against Communist forces, and don't forget that we Australians, whether we be enlisted men or regulars, are given the opportunity, if we wish, to opt out of service in Viet Nam, and to date, I can tell you there have been very few who have taken this course."

The Australians have realised the danger of South Viet Nam being overrun by the Communists, and over four years ago they sent an advisory team there. It was not until May 1965 that a force of 1,500 men of the First Battalion Royal Australian

Regiment together with ancillary troops was actually sent as a fighting force to South Viet Nam. In June 1966 it was replaced by the First Australian Task Force, which now consists of 4,500 troops.

New Zealand has a very small force, which provides part of the artillery support for the Australian Army, but their very presence in Viet Nam indicates that New Zealand herself is also concerned with the Communist threat. Individual soldiers fighting in Viet Nam have the same attitude as the Australians. It is the first time that these Commonwealth countries have fought without the support of Great Britain, but they realise the very delicate position which Great Britain occupies in this area because of Hong Kong and also that we have played an important role in the Far East by our efforts in Malaya, and make contribution to European defences within the NATO framework.

The British taxpayer is footing an enormous defence bill and the present Government have put a ceiling on expenditure. By doing this they have stripped our forces to such an extent that it is questionable whether we shall be able to maintain our presence in the Far East, other than with a token force in Singapore and Hong Kong. It could be argued that now the confrontation of Malaya is finished, the 30,000 troops in that theatre could be redeployed and this would enable us to provide some troops in South Viet Nam.

Is this the best use of our forces in South East Asia, and could we really afford to enter the ring as a fighting force in South Viet Nam? Or should our entire defence policy in this theatre be reconsidered? Let us look at our present bases.

Britain's principal bases are now Singapore and Hong Kong. No base is of any use unless it is capable of being defended and is not located in an area where local feeling is against its presence. Singapore is, at the moment, benefiting economically from our presence, but how long we will be welcome guests depends entirely on political events within Singapore and Malaya.

An agreement was reached in China whereby Hong Kong should be ceded. The agreement was never, in fact, ratified, but the Island was occupied on 26th January 1841. Lord Palmerston, Foreign Secretary, was dissatisfied and insisted that it should be ratified by the Chinese Emperor in Peking. The Treaty of Nanking was officially signed on 28th August 1842, and apart from Hong Kong, this gave Britain other rights in China.

Stonecutters Island and the Kowloon Peninsula were ceded by China under the Treaty of Peking in 1860. Still the British were uneasy about their Colony, and during the Spanish American war they made an agreement with China whereby in 1898 the New Territories were leased for a period of 99 years (the lease runs out in 1997). Today a considerable proportion of Hong Kong's industry is sited in the New Territories.

As a result of the inflow of refugees over the years since 1945, the total population, including the "boat people", amounts to some 3,700,000 but there is very little unemployment on the Island.

Great criticism has been levelled at the form of Government extant in Hong Kong, on the grounds that it does not have an elected Government. The dangers of having an elected Government are twofold. In the first place it might be used as an excuse by Red China for a takeover on the grounds that the Colony was ceded to England as a Crown Colony, and to make it a self-governing unit would abrogate the treaty.

The other danger might be that an elected Government would have an inbuilt Chinese majority. Most of the Chinese residents of Hong Kong have relatives and friends on the mainland and the Communists could bring pressure to bear on individual Chinese (by threats to relatives, such as they have done in other parts of the world), making a takeover by Red China a possibility.

If Red China wanted to take Hong Kong it could do it quite easily; no British conventional force could possibly stop a Red Chinese invasion through the New Territories. A sea landing might be more difficult, because advance warning of the assembly of naval craft and sampans would be available. British and American naval forces would be an obstacle to invasion. In any case, Great Britain and America would have to make up their minds, either to let the Island go or to engage in a full-scale war with Red China.

Demands for the return of Hong Kong to China have not been serious because it represents to Red China a valuable economic unit out of which they are earning between 170 and 200 million pounds of foreign currency every year. This foreign exchange is useful to them both for the purchase of grain in Canada, and for use in other hard currency countries. Red China has control of some banks in Hong Kong and it is a useful clearing house.

Unless circumstances alter there is an overriding economic necessity which prevents Red China from demanding the return of Hong Kong.

It is not those strands of barbed wire which run between the New Territories and the mainland that stop the Chinese invading Hong Kong, but the economic value of the Island to Red China.

This situation could be altered if China's foreign trade and exchange position altered, or they no longer required their foreign exchange earning in Hong Kong. In contrast, China has been putting pressure on Macão which is Portugal's enclave in China because it has virtually no economic value to Red China.

The other factor which could alter the status quo would be if we were involved in active military operations in South Viet Nam and the war escalated so that it became a direct confrontation between Red China and the Free World.

It could be argued that a similar situation has already arisen once, at the time of the Korean war, but here Red China was much weaker, and both sides wanted to contain the war in the local theatre of Korea.

Our bases in Singapore and Hong Kong cannot be regarded as secure, and this must determine our defence policy in South East Asia. These two bases must be regarded as forward tactical areas, but we ought not to allow our main force in the Far East to be wasted on them. Our policy ought to consist of a main base on the friendly territory of Australia, and we could

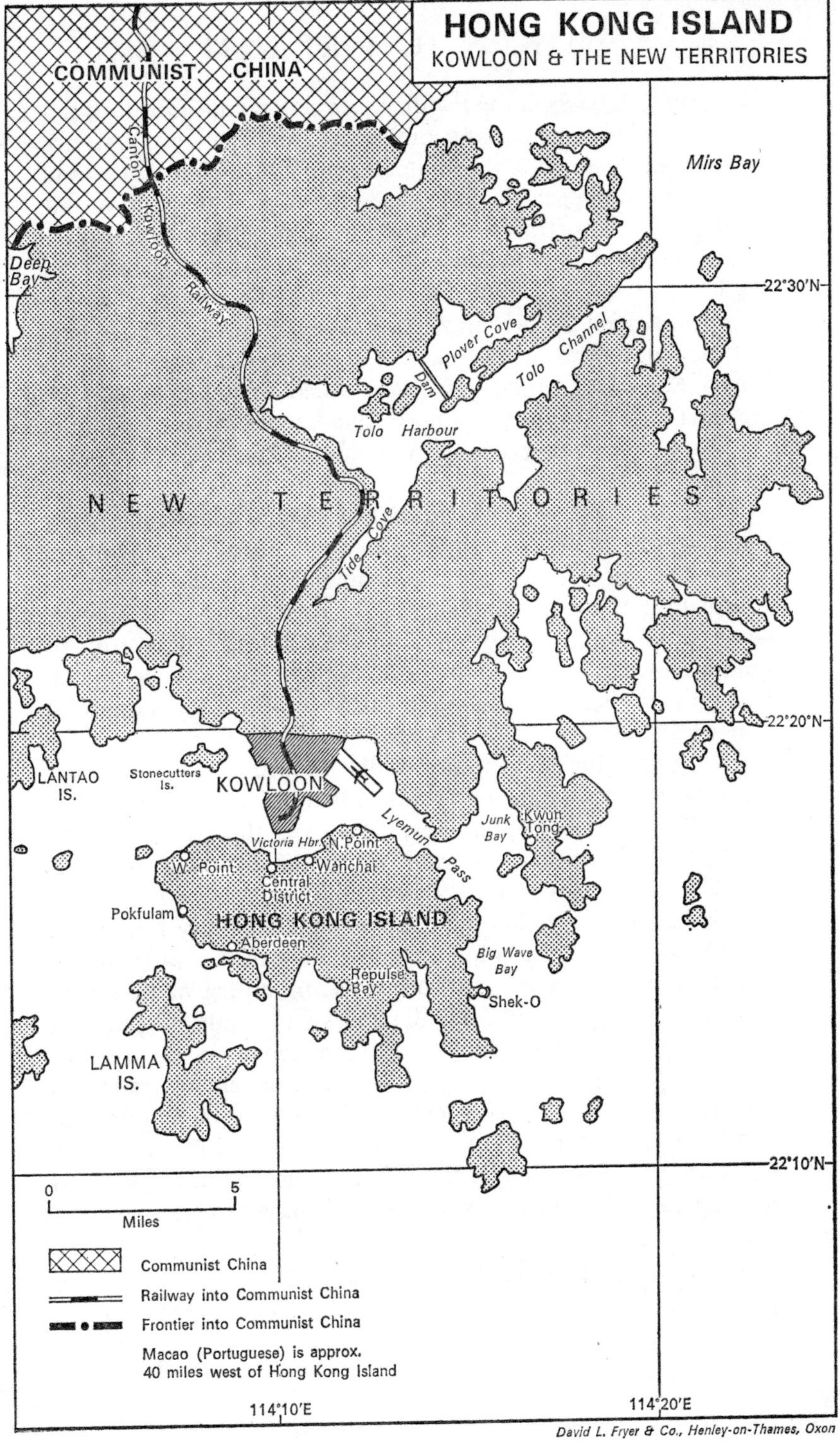

HONG KONG ISLAND
KOWLOON & THE NEW TERRITORIES
COMMUNIST CHINA
Mirs Bay
Deep Bay
Canton
Kowloon Railway
22°30'N
Plover Cove
Tolo Channel
Dam
Tolo Harbour
N E W   T E R R I T O R I E S
Tide Cove
22°20'N
LANTAO IS.
Stonecutters Is.
KOWLOON
Junk Bay
Kwun Tong
Lyemun Pass
Victoria Hbr.
N. Point
W. Point
Wanchai
Central District
Pokfulam
HONG KONG ISLAND
Aberdeen
Big Wave Bay
Repulse Bay
Shek-O
LAMMA IS.
22°10'N
0   5
Miles
Communist China
Railway into Communist China
Frontier into Communist China
Macao (Portuguese) is approx.
40 miles west of Hong Kong Island
114°10'E
114°20'E
David L. Fryer & Co., Henley-on-Thames, Oxon

use American bases in the Pacific as staging points. Our forward position in Hong Kong and Singapore, and our very presence there, combined with our membership with SEATO, would have a stabilising effect, and the knowledge that we have our principal bases further back would do a great deal to illustrate to the world that we were allied with America and the Free Nations in our determination to combat the spread of Communism. British participation in the Viet Nam is undesirable.*

If we could also be members of a new multilateral treaty in South East Asia, then, of course, allied solidarity would be considerably enhanced, as both the United States and ourselves would participate in SEATO and in the new multilateral treaty.

At the moment, all the Communists have to do in Hong Kong is to cut off the water supplies which come from the mainland to supply the colony. The Government is in the process of completing the famous Plover Cove Reservoir,** the storage capacity of which will be over 30,000 million gallons (this in addition to the Island's present storage capacity of 15,000 million gallons). But even when this is completed it is doubtful if it could provide all the water required for a colony whose standard of living is rising so rapidly. It would probably mean some rationing, a state of events which with the residents of Hong Kong are not unfamiliar. Of course, there is always the possibility of utilising sea water for baths and washing, etc., but the cost of this would be astronomical, as it would entail the laying of a complete new set of pipes to every residential and factory unit in the colony. A sudden cut in the water supply which comes to the colony from the Communist mainland (a contract for 15,000 million gallons a year) would, to put it at its lowest, cause considerable inconvenience to the colony. The Hong Kong Government have other schemes in mind in an attempt to make themselves independent of Communist water supplies, but for many years to come this source will continue to be of value to the colony, whose consumption (at present 120 million gallons a day) is rising steadily.

* See page 277.
** Shown on the Hong Kong map on page 285

Sinkiang

Sinkiang is a Western province of Communist China, nestled comfortably on the Soviet border. It is Chinese in name only, for racially it is a mixture of all tribes and colours: Tatars, Mongols, Kazaks, Kurds, a multi-racial society, neither Russian nor Chinese. General Wang is in command of the Sinkiang area, with General Tao-tzeyoh commanding an army of three divisions with a total strength of 200,000. An out-of-the-way province, why should it be of any interest? Yet a change of loyalties of this province could alter the course of world history.

The Chinese for some reason have decided that they would carry out their nuclear experiments in this province. Already a number have been performed, the third of which proved that they could manufacture an intermediate range missile, and the fourth was a nuclear explosion *in situ*. The only thing that is lacking now is the means of linking the third and fourth experiments, so that they can produce a method of firing the nuclear warhead. It is said that the intermediate range missile had a range of 600 miles.

The possible reason that Sinkiang was chosen for these experiments was that it had deposits of uranium. It certainly could not have been chosen for political reasons, although target distance from Sinkiang to Russian cities could have been a consideration. General Tao-tzeyoh was one of Chiang Kai-shek's generals, who defected to the Communist cause about the time that Chiang Kai-shek left the mainland. These powerful generals have now got a lethal weapon under their control. If they were to handle the situation wisely they could assure their own independence from Mao Tse-tung, but whether they could remain neutral is quite another matter. Economically, and for development of the atomic missile, they may be dependent on either China or Russia. If these two generals decided to seek Russian "protection", Russia would be in the position of having the Chinese nuclear deterrent under her control. Russian policy could alter entirely and they might well decide that it would be opportune for them to crush China before China could build a new atomic weapon system.

Whoever wins the internal power struggle in China will have at his command in the near future the means not only to explode, but also to deliver, a nuclear attack. Russian cities would immediately be within the orbit of such a threat and so also would Chiang Kai-shek's stronghold in Taiwan. Chinese domination of the Far East would be complete. Only the American defence "umbrella", and possible Russian intervention, would prevent it. Given that China retains her nuclear deterrent, then there would be four great nuclear powers in the world: America, Great Britain, Russia and China, with France a possible fifth.

China has immense manpower, and with a population of 600 to 700 million could produce the largest single army in the world, which would compare in strength with an army which could be raised jointly by America, Russia and the British Commonwealth. But if she were deprived of her nuclear power then certainly her prospects of Asian domination would be delayed.

The Chinese Communists have 37 armies at their disposal. This corresponds to 2,450,000 regular troops to which must be added 500,000 militia. One million of these troops are being held down along the coast opposite Taiwan, strategically placed so that they could combat an attack from Chiang Kai-shek's army of 650,000. Chiang Kai-shek, therefore, represents not only a possible, but an actual threat to Red China by pinning down this considerable force.

A nuclear weapon would have a devastating effect upon cities but if all the cities in China were destroyed, her civilisation would not come to an end because those cities are widely placed and her rural communities would be left intact. All of this represents speculation. What is quite certain is that eventually Red China will become an atomic power, but if her atomic weapons fell into the hands of the Russians, then the power struggle would take on an entirely new aspect.

CONCLUSION

American post-war policy has had a sharp anti-colonial flavour about it. The United States' attitude towards France's and Holland's recolonising their possessions in the Far East made it virtually impossible for these countries to re-establish themselves after Japan's defeat. The United States failed to realise that the evacuation of these European nations from Asia would leave a vacuum into which Communism would be drawn.

If the United States, both during the war and in the immediate post-war years, had taken a longer term view of the situation, then, in exchange for various aid-programmes to France, she might have been able to influence the French to grant independence to her Indo-Chinese possessions over a period of time and thus enabled these countries to form their own internal Governments and remain part of the French (Colonial) Empire, but acquiring independence status like the countries of the British Commonwealth.

Today the American taxpayer is paying a heavy price for the omissions of previous United States Governments. If the danger had been perceived earlier, it is probable that Viet Nam would have survived as a united country and, if wise counsel had prevailed, the circumstances which set off the present war might never have arisen.

Mao's intention to spread his brand of Communism throughout the Far East became apparent at the end of the Second World War. First we saw the deal made by the Soviets with Mao, whereby much of the Japanese war material was handed over to Mao to enable him to drive Chiang Kai-shek from the mainland and take refuge on the Island of Formosa. Mao then took a few years to recover and consolidate his position and made the strategic mistake of failing to attack Chiang Kai-shek and defeat his army in Formosa; but turned to what he thought was an easier prize, Korea. America's mistakes and mis-apprehensions suddenly became apparent and Uncle Sam woke up with a hang-over. Aid was rushed to Korea, a defence pact given to Chiang Kai-shek, assistance allowed even to the French colonialism in Viet Nam: but American aid in Viet Nam came too late to save the disaster of Dien Bien Phu. Viet Nam, freed from French colonial rule, found itself worse off, divided in two with the North a fully Communist state attempting to defeat the South Vietnamese Government and replace it with a Communist régime.

Britain faced Malaysian confrontation, Indonesia supported Sukarno's Communist Government. Thailand rubbed her hands, thinking that everything had passed over her head. The ugly day came. The mantle was removed, revealing Communist infiltration into three of her eastern provinces, and the South.

Australia and New Zealand, aware of the potential danger and the future devastation which Communism could represent, have decided that it is better to halt the disease now, than allow it to eat into the lives and happiness of the next generation of Australians and New Zealanders.

In the Hitler period, prior to the Second World War, and indeed for the first years of hostilities, there were nations who thought they could remain free from the menace of Hitler if they preserved their neutrality and walked carefully without offending the great master. Had these nations banded firmly together and been backed by Great Britain and the United States from the outset, then Hitler would never have dared to attack one of them because an attack on one would have been an attack on all of them.

Surely the world has learned its bitter lesson from history, for it has only to look back less than 30 years to see that the dangers which were present in the 'thirties are still with us today. In the 'thirties they were in Europe; in the 'seventies they are in Asia.

Tears were shed, sentiments outraged, when Tibet, the land of the Lamas, fell under the Communist heel. The smell of human bodies burning permeated the villages of Tibet, but not the drawing-rooms of Washington and London, and

CONCLUSION

certainly not the United Nations Headquarters in Geneva. Each country in the Far East has a different problem and China represents to them a different type of threat.

In Thailand, it is the insidious encroachment of Communism through infiltration. In Viet Nam that threat is backed by military force. The Koreans are not without fear that one day the 38th Parallel might be violated and their country once again ravaged and ransomed as it was in 1950.

The Communist menace in the Far East seems a long way away to the average American, and the United States Government has difficulty in persuading the electorate why the war in Viet Nam is one of the actions which America must take if she is to halt the advance of Communism in South East Asia.

At each stage in the struggle in Viet Nam the United States can be seen to have underestimated the strength of Viet Cong resistance; it has always fallen into the same trap of committing too few troops and resources too late.

American Presidents in turn have had to use phrases such as "in the light of the circumstances the United States will not hesitate to employ sufficient force". Lyndon Johnson has been obliged to increase personal taxation in the United States in order to maintain a minimum threshold on which the War can be maintained. But even so, the 45,000 additional troops which have been allocated to General Westmoreland's command are still insufficient to make a major impact on Viet Cong military strongholds. A minimum of one million American troops would be required to achieve a reasonably rapid victory over these forces. At last the White House has come down on the side of bombing some of the vital targets in North Viet Nam. In my section "To Bomb or not to Bomb"* I pointed out that pussy-footing on the part of the White House had allowed the North Vietnamese to develop a system of defence which is capable of doing an untold amount of damage to American bombers on their raids over North Viet Nam. Still the United States has not included the Port of Haiphong through which vital supplies are entering North Viet Nam, though it has

* See page 166

yielded to the demands of the Hawks and allowed bombing of the marshalling yards and the railway line which runs from China into Viet Nam. The effect of this massive bombing will be to slow down industrial production in the North, but so long as supplies can be brought by ships belonging to nations allied to the Communist bloc the damage by bombing will be off-set by the supplies reaching the country by sea or by rail.

Only an estimate can be made as to the exact amount of aid which North Viet Nam is receiving from Russia, China and the satellites, because the country is not subjected to any regular international economic surveys. Even the amount of material arriving by sea through the Port of Haiphong cannot be calculated, although no doubt the United States Fleet is capable of estimating, to some extent, the gross tonnage arriving. The actual breakdown of its contents is not made known, nor indeed would it even be certain that the entire cargo load of a ship had been discharged in North Viet Nam.

One of the great advantages of the continuation of the war as far as Ho Chi Minh is concerned is that he is being given a great deal of aid in order to sustain the war effort in South Viet Nam.

The price of this campaign is very small for Ho Chi Minh, and is represented by the deaths of perhaps 3,500 Viet Nam soldiers a month, material which in Communist eyes is expendable. The arms and equipment which they carry with them are supplied from Communist sources. On the credit side, Ho Chi Minh is receiving aid far in excess of what he is being compelled to employ in the war effort and the whole of his economy is dependent on these gifts.

The logical question with which Ho Chi Minh must be faced is whether it is really worth while making peace with South Viet Nam. The moment that this happens his allies in the Communist camp might well feel that he no longer requires all the aid which he is receiving from them. This would mean that the whole of his planning for the next five or ten years would have to be re-geared. Information at the disposal of the West shows that progress in the North is slow enough, and no doubt would

CONCLUSION

be slower and could even come to a complete standstill if Ho were shorn of international Communist aid.

Why should Ho Chi Minh under these circumstances want any sort of peace settlement with the West? If the Americans leave South Viet Nam he could Communise the entire country within a very short space of time and thereby have achieved one of his objects—a united Communist-controlled country. But would he not be better advised to let the struggle continue until such time as he has a stronger economic base in the North from which he could work?

This presupposes that it is Ho Chi Minh who holds the reins of power in the Viet Nam War, but this is not entirely correct. Circumstances could arise in which his principal backers, Russia and Communist China, might wish to utilise their aid programmes to advance Communism in other parts of South East Asia. It would only be under these circumstances that Ho Chi Minh might be prepared to be more amenable to the United States' plans for a settlement in Viet Nam.

From the point of view of South Viet Nam's future as a stable state united against the Communist bloc, time to develop her democratic institutions is essential. If America were to withdraw her forces there is no doubt that the South Viet Nam Government would collapse even if the Americans were to continue their A.I.D. programme. The country has had insufficient time to prepare the rudiments of democratic Government, and, what is far more important, too little time so far to prove to the people of South Viet Nam that the way of life offered to them by their own Government is better than that offered by the Communists.

America and Viet Nam can win the war, but this is not enough; they must win the peace and make the country an example to other nations in South East Asia of what peace and prosperity can mean to the people of Viet Nam.

American policy in the Far East ought to be backed by Great Britain and the Commonwealth, for, having assumed a role which Great Britain appears to be neither willing nor prepared to pay for, the American nation has the industrial power and wealth to be able to continue as the enforcer of peace in the Far East.

Eventually the United States will have to make up its mind how far it is prepared to go to stop Communism in the Far East. So long as she maintains atomic superiority, Communist China is unlikely to make any move which could precipitate a major war between herself and the United States.

Although the American nation is aware that Communism is on the march in Asia, it is doubtful whether they have appreciated the rapidity with which Mao's Programme of Asiatic Communisation could be carried out.

Supposing Mao were to place his nation in direct confrontation with the United States—would the President and Government of the United States be able to threaten Communist China with atomic reprisals? How far would America follow this policy, especially when one considers that such a step would cause a sharp reaction in all nations of the world?

In the Far East today, two organisations exist to prevent the spread of Communism. The first is the South East Asia Treaty Organisation, and the second is the presence of the United States Armed Forces and the U.S. Seventh Fleet operation in that area. The South East Asia Treaty Organisation's most Eastern mainland member is Thailand so there is no organisation which covers Viet Nam, Korea and Taiwan. There is only the American presence, and individual defence treaties.

What is required is a firm link and a non-aggression pact, represented by a mutual defence agreement built around the United States in the form of a multilateral defence treaty.

The United States would be in the SEATO treaty and also in the multilateral defence treaty. They would form the link between these two, and such a pact would impress all free people in South East Asia. The United States, being a member of both pacts, would form a link in the chain which would extend like a belt from Pakistan to Tokyo.

Militarily this could be a formidable alignment, giving confidence to the weaker nations and representing a united front against Communism.

But this struggle in the hearts and minds of the Asiatic people will not, and cannot, be won on the battlefield, nor by

CONCLUSION

the existence of defence pacts. It is true that security must come first, and freedom from outright attack, but the really important thing is to be able to prove to the Communist world that life in a capitalist society gives people, in addition to freedom, more of the things which they want in life.

Thus land reform, that hunger of people to possess the means for production of the soil, must be combined with a full aid programme by the United States, which can make the land more fertile and productive and give the villager a higher standard of living. In taking on the mantle which Great Britain has shed, the people of the United States have assumed an immense responsibility. If they fulfil this, history will accord to them a place which will make them a nation that has been instrumental in making the lives of millions of people in Asia happier, and removed the possibility of a third World War, the results of which could have been the destruction of the human race.

APPENDICES

Speech made by Dr Alan Glyn on Friday, 20th October
—Foreign Affairs Debate, Brighton Conservative Party
Conference, 1967.

I oppose this Motion because it talks about our limited
commitments overseas. This is the point with which I disagree.
Great Britain is still a powerful nation which has world-wide
responsibilities and has a great role to play in the preservation
of world peace in the future.

Also, we have to face the fact that the balance of power in
the world is changing. We all support Tory Foreign policy.
Labour policy has achieved nothing except to reduce the image
of this country throughout the world. Councillor Rodney Smith
asked us to contribute to the greater unity of Europe. None of
us would disagree about that, but it is sometimes forgotten not
only in France but throughout the world, what a great contribution we have already made to the unity of Europe. Do people
realise—and I hope that our leaders will press this in forth-
coming negotiations—that ever since the end of the last war
you people in this hall and throughout the country have been
contributing through taxation, to defending ourselves and,
incidentally, being one of the most powerful forces in defending
Western Europe.

We ask to go into Europe. Is it fair that we, who are spending
so much in Europe, should be denied the economic privileges
of a Europe where our principal markets will probably lie for
the next fifty years, as some form of compensation for paying
for this very heavy defence bill to which each of us has been
contributing? It would be as well if France and other countries
appreciated that our contribution is great, and that we should
be helped economically by entry into the Common Market,
which would help us pay for our military contribution.

In the years following the war Russia represented the

greatest single danger to world peace. I remember—like the mover of the Motion—ten years ago coming to this rostrum when I had seen Soviet divisions crushing the people of Hungary. I believe it was Great Britain and the United States which together stopped those Russians marching through Europe. They could not have been stopped by conventional forces but they were deterred purely and simply because they knew that they would be destroyed as a result of an atomic attack.

Having just returned from Viet Nam and the Far East I am absolutely convinced that we have to take a new look at the balance of world power. We owe obligations still, as some people want to forget, to our friends in the Far East and in particular to Australia and New Zealand. You only have to look at recent events in Hong Kong to realise that China represents the greatest threat to world peace since the Korean War. However, this change in the balance of power is not due to the hordes of Chinese but to a strange event which is happening in the province of Sinkiang where Red China is already developing her own nuclear deterrent. It could be that the balance of power might well be altered overnight if General Wang hands his power over and allies himself with Russia to form one giant nuclear power. However, that has not yet occurred.

I believe that this shift in power puts increased emphasis on our responsibilities in the Far East.

Whatever you may say about SEATO, and we are members of it, its influence is declining because of France and Pakistan. What should we do? Should we scrap SEATO? Should we augment it with a new treaty or should we forget our Far Eastern obligations and responsibilities altogether? I believe that the correct course here is to continue our membership of SEATO but I should like to see Great Britain and the United States unite together to form a new international agreement between those non-committed nations in the Far East who do not want to be overrun by the Communists and who wish to be backed by a strong force. If we and America can get together to form a multi-lateral treaty to augment SEATO then we could carry out our obligations and we could still be a great power for the preservation of peace in the Far East. We are still a great nation and I hope that Tory policy will go forward and that we shall link with America and once again be a power for the preservation of peace, not only in Europe but throughout the world.

Interview with Dr. Alan Glyn on the subject of Viet Nam, BBC Home Service, Ten O'Clock Programme, March 17, 1967, on his return from the Far East

GEORGE SCOTT: The former Conservative M.P., Dr. Alan Glyn, has just got back from a month in Viet Nam, and he's joined me in the Studio now to discuss some of his impressions. Dr. Glyn, let me start with the biggest question of all, do you believe from your experience there that the great problem of Viet Nam and the future of it can be solved by war?

GLYN: It can't be solved by war alone, this is quite clear. It will have to be solved by a combination of both beating the Viet Cong militarily, but at the same time you've got to produce three essential things for the people of Viet Nam. First of all you've got to give them security from attack by the Viet Cong; secondly you've got to be able to produce a better standard of living than that which is offered by the Communists; and lastly you've got to give them the feeling that they can go about their business, tend their fields, in liberty and freedom, and live a normal family life. Not any different from any other community in the world.

SCOTT: Can we take the first of those, security from the Viet Cong? Do you believe at this moment that the forces fighting there on behalf of the South Vietnamese are achieving that?

GLYN: Only in various areas. At the moment they are achieving in certain areas freedom from the Viet Cong, but the great problem of course is that when those military manoeuvres finish to be able to place sufficient force there to provide the people with protection when the main battle's over.

Scott: Did you see much of the fighting yourself?

Glyn: Yes, quite a considerable amount. I spent time both with the Americans, with the Vietnamese, and also with the Koreans.

Scott: Is it as beastly as it's reported to be?

Glyn: Well, all war is beastly, but this war is particularly beastly in that you don't ever really know where your enemy is; there's no front line.

Scott: What about the morale of particularly the American forces there? We hear a lot at this end about the arguments going on in the United States, as they are here about the advisability of continuing bombing, about—indeed the advisability of continuing the war. Is there any such division of opinion there among the Americans about whether they ought to be fighting at all?

Glyn: Well I think that all the American troops are united in one thing, and that is that they know the reason why they're fighting there, that it is simply to stop the spread of Communism. I think their morale is excellent, and if you're involved in a war, then there's no question about it, that the North Vietnamese are sending troops into South Viet Nam, and the soldiers quite rightly say that this is an all-out war where the Viet Cong are committing atrocities on civilian population, and that bombing of North Viet Nam is necessary and—even though there may be civilian casualties, you've got to look to the other side where the Viet Cong are committing atrocities on Vietnamese in the villages.

Scott: And do you get any view yourself that by stopping the bombing for, at any rate a recognisable period of time, it might be possible to achieve some change in the situation?

Glyn: I don't think that that's at all possible, because the whole point really was shown during the truce, where the Viet Cong used this period to move in troops, and I don't think that there's any feeling among the soldiers, at the moment, that the stopping of the bombing would have any effect at all on peace moves.

Scott: Now of course the war is supposed to be about the future of Viet Nam and the people of Viet Nam. What is the morale, what is the feeling of the people of South Viet Nam at this moment?

Glyn: Well the people of South Viet Nam have had a very long period of hostilities, over twenty years, and I think that again it comes back to what I said earlier, that in those areas where security has been attained, and where the benefits of American aid have been shown, and where the land reform is being carried out, because this is a particularly important thing, where people are beginning to get their land, they're getting security, and they're getting a better standard of living, and as long as there's protection, then I think they're wholly behind some form of continuance of the present Government under Marshal Ky.

Scott: There's also—this is the last question—there's also some feeling there should be a democratic government in South Viet Nam. Do you think that exists or is likely to exist in the near future?

Glyn: Well, the Prime Minister assured me that he not only wanted to have elections, but he had every intention of speeding them up and showing the world that he was going to ensure that this country—his country—was run in a modern way and on democratic lines.

Scott: Thank you very much Dr. Glyn.

TERMS USED

A.I.D. (U.S.)
United States Agency for International Development.

Charlie
Colloquial term for the Viet Cong used by Americans and Australians.

Chieu Hoi
Former members of the Communist Viet Cong who have gone over under the Open Arms Programme to the South Viet Nam Government, either as soldiers or civilians.

China
(*a*) Republic of China. Chiang Kai-shek governed Mainland China until 1948 when he was forced to evacuate to Formosa (Taiwan). His Government in Taiwan is still recognised by the United States as the only legal Government of China and still retains its seat on the Security Council. It is not recognised by Great Britain.

(*b*) People's Republic of China. Under Mao Tse-tung, Communist China governs the Chinese Mainland (except Outer Mongolia). This Government has no seat on the Security Council; it is recognised by Britain but not the United States.

Formosa
Modern name, Taiwan.

I.C.P. (Indo-Chinese Communist Party)
Founded 1930, replaced by Viet Minh 1941.

Korea
Republic of Korea—non-Communist Government of South Korea (South of 38th Parallel).

Democratic People's Republic of Korea — Communist Government of North Korea (North of 38th Parallel).

M.A.C.V. (U.S.)

Military Assistance Command, Viet Nam.

R.O.K. (Forces)

Republic of Korea Forces, operating in South Viet Nam.

Viet Cong

This includes all Communist forces operating in South Viet Nam since 1954 and embodies South Vietnamese Communist guerrilla forces and individual soldiers or formed units of the North Vietnamese army operating in South Viet Nam. Viet Cong is an abbreviation of Viet Cong San, the literal translation of which is "Vietnamese Communist".

Viet Minh

Chiang Kai-shek's generals compelled Ho Chi Minh to dissolve the Indo-Chinese Communist Party. Ho Chi Minh changed its name to Viet Nam Doc Lap Dong Minh Hoi (the literal translation being "the Revolutionary League for the Independence of Viet Nam")—known for short as the Viet Minh.

The term Viet Minh is used in this book to cover the forces employed by Ho Chi Minh against the Japanese and later the French until the French Union Forces were defeated at Dien Bien Phu. After the Geneva Agreement in 1954, the majority of the Viet Minh went to the North under the supervision of the International Control Commission. Those members of the Viet Minh who were left behind formed the nucleus of the Viet Cong in South Viet Nam.

Viet Nam

Republic of Viet Nam—Government of South Viet Nam (South of the 17th Parallel).

Democratic Republic of Viet Nam—Communist Government of North Viet Nam (North of the 17th Parallel) under Ho Chi Minh.

World Assistance to the Republic of Viet Nam

Free World Assistance includes some forty Free World Nations supplying technical, agricultural, medical and educational assistance to the Republic of Viet Nam. Seven nations are providing military assistance; their headquarters is the Free World Headquarters in Saigon, which is a military organisation.

Yuans *vide* (page 260)

Legislative and control yuans were elected: others were nominated.

INDEX

A

Acheson, Secretary of State Dean, 239
Agency for International Development (A.I.D.), 197
Agreement on Cessation of Hostilities in Cambodia, 52 *et seq*
Algeria, 44, 129, 168
Allesandria, 25
Along Bay, 76
American Aid, 65
American Air Cavalry, 129
American Forces, 146 *et seq*
American High Command, 44
American Negroes, 156 *et seq*
American O.S.S., 24, 25, 38
American P.O.W.s, 164
American 7th Fleet, 180, 294
American State Department, 79, 173, 232, 233, 235, 236, 280
An Giang Province, 197, 198
Annam, 18, 27, 47, 101
Army of the Republic of Viet Nam (A.R.V.N.), 139 *et seq*
Arnaux, Louis, 70
Auriol, President, 42, 77, 211
Australia, Australians, 128, 129, 143, 164, 221, 267, 273 *et seq*

B

Bangkok, 225
Bao Dai, Emperor, 19, 27, 29 *et seq*, 72 *et seq*, 181 *et seq*
Bela Kun, 161
Belsen, 163
Ben Suc, 192
Bidault, Georges, 5
Binh Duong, 106
Binh Xuyen, 102
Bollaert High Commissioner, 76
Boun Oum, Prince, 218 *et seq*
British Colonial Administration, 19
British Intelligence, 24
Budapest, 5
Burma, 25, 256, 276
Buu Loc, Prince, 79, 84

C

Cambodia, 8, 18, 42, 50, 51 *et seq*, 103, 120, 156, 169 *et seq*
Cambodia, King of, 210
Camu liberation area, 101
Canada, 52, 54
Canton, 273
Cao Dai, sect of, 102
Cao Van Vien, General, 92
Cap St. Jacques, 85

INDEX

INDEX

INDEX

INDEX

INDEX